Dr Leo Ruickbi g about and
sometimes experi - from Black
Masses to haunted sional career.
He has a PhD from King's College, London, on modern
witchcraft and magic. He is the author of *Witchcraft Out of the
Shadows* and *Faustus: The Life and Times of a Renaissance Magician*, as well as being a frequent contributor to *Paranormal*
magazine. His work has been mentioned in the media from the
Guardian to Radio Jamaica, and his expertise has been sought
from film companies to the International Society for Human
Rights. He is a member of Societas Magica, the European Society for the Study of Western Esotericism, the Society for
Psychical Research and the Ghost Club. Visit him online at
www.witchology.com

'Very well written. Exciting, enjoyable and thought-provoking.
Packed with interesting and intriguing ideas.' Rev. Lionel Fanthorpe, President of the Association for the Scientific Study of
Anomalous Phenomena

'It is a pleasure to read such a well-researched and documented
guide to the major fields of interest in the paranormal. Dr Leo
Ruickbie has created a work of tremendous value to readers and
researchers alike. Rosemary Ellen Guiley, author of *The Encyclopedia of Ghosts and Spirits*

'A first-class piece of work!' Nick Redfern, author of *The Real
Men in Black*

A BRIEF GUIDE TO THE
SUPERNATURAL

LEO RUICKBIE

RUNNING PRESS
PHILADELPHIA · LONDON

Constable & Robinson Ltd
55–56 Russell Square
London WC1B 4HP
www.constablerobinson.com

First published in the UK by Robinson,
an imprint of Constable & Robinson Ltd, 2012

A copy of the British Library Cataloguing in
Publication data is available from the British Library

ISBN: 978-1-84901-675-9

Printed and bound in the UK

1 3 5 7 9 10 8 6 4 2

First published in the United States in 2011 by Running Press Book Publishers,
A Member of the Perseus Books Group

US ISBN 978-0-7624-4438-0
US Library of Congress Control Number: 2011933253

9   8   7   6   5   4   3   2   1
Digit on the right indicates the number of this printing

Running Press Book Publishers
2300 Chestnut Street
Philadelphia, PA 19103-4371

Visit us on the web!
www.runningpress.com

Printed and bound in the UK

MIX
Paper from
responsible sources
FSC
www.fsc.org   FSC® C018072

To Antje and Morgana

CAUTION TO THE READER

Before reading the contents of this book,—

PLEASE NOTE

1. —That the narratives printed in these pages had better not be read by any one of tender years, of morbid excitability, or of excessively nervous temperament.
2. —That the latest students of the subject concur in the solemn warning addressed in the Sacred Writings to those who have dealings with familiar spirits, or who expose themselves to the horrible consequences of possession.
3. —That as the latent possibilities of our complex personality are so imperfectly understood, all experimenting in hypnotism, spiritualism, etc., excepting in the most careful and reverent spirit, by the most level-headed persons, had much better be avoided.

THIS CAUTION is printed here at the suggestion of *Catholics*, *Theosophists*, and *Spiritualists*, who declare themselves to be profoundly convinced of its *necessity*.

An actual notice first printed in W. T. Stead, 'Real Ghost Stories: A Record of Authentic Apparitions', *Review of Reviews*, London, December 1891; here reproduced from the 1897 revised edition, p. xiii.

Contents

Foreword

A little while ago I was interviewed on a radio station and the presenter decided to get right back to basics with his first question: 'What does paranormal mean – what *is* the paranormal?' he asked me.

Since I was then the editor of a magazine called *Paranormal* the interviewer had every reason to expect me to answer that question quickly and concisely but . . . in truth, I had to think about it. When it comes to the paranormal the 'simple' questions can be the hardest to answer.

The word paranormal simply means 'beyond the normal', in the same way the word supernatural means 'beyond the natural'. But how far beyond? That's the nub of it.

For many who say they 'believe in the paranormal' the word presumes the acceptance of a spirit world, a world beyond our own with laws different from our scientific laws. For them the paranormal is merely a foyer that leads to the great halls of religion. This is not true of everyone who accepts the reality of paranormal phenomena, however.

Personally, I believe that a great deal of that which is currently 'beyond the natural' will in time be understood as natural. That is to say, it will one day be brought into the realm of science (provided the scientific establishment ever gets round to taking an interest).

Are poltergeists mischievous spirits or the effects of some energy source not currently known to science? Are ghosts the returning dead or images created by our brains in response to some external stimulus we don't understand? If it is found that extraterrestrials really are visiting us, isn't it likely we will also find they are employing principles of some alien science in order to do so?

I think it likely most of the phenomena discussed by Dr Leo Ruickbie in this fascinating book will one day be understood by science.

The few sound-bites laymen like me pick up of quantum physics research implies that the gap between the supernatural and the natural is narrowing. We hear of particles that can arrive at a destination before leaving their point of origin and of particles which, once connected, remain mysteriously linked to each other even when they are light years apart. Such phenomena sound paranormal to me and yet, if true, they are effects manifesting in the natural world at the most fundamental level.

It should also be borne in mind that even the existence of spirits needn't fall forever outside the precincts of science. The idea of a multi-dimensional universe is an old one: who is to say that 'the spirit world' and any number of 'heavens' might not each represent one of these dimensions and that the barrier between them and our world can be – and is being – routinely broached? Maybe some future science will one day be able to understand and quantify what today we currently think of as firmly beyond, indeed antagonistic, to science.

Nevertheless, I doubt very much that one explanation – such as multiple dimensions or, more prosaically, hallucinations – will ever be found to cover the whole gamut of the 'paranormal'.

Taking all the above into consideration, it's no wonder I found it so hard to answer that radio presenter's deceptively simple question during a live broadcast. I was pleased, however, to have been forced to reconsider that central concept of 'what is paranormal?' once again.

In this book Leo Ruickbie takes on the same challenge – to dissect, examine and ratify the paranormal in a *Brief Guide*. It's no easy task but one he is certainly well equipped to accomplish.

He achieves his goal with insight, scholarship and admirable good humour and readability.

Of course, Dr Ruickbie makes no claim to fully explain the phenomena he examines. What he does do is illuminate tantalizing glimpses as he descends into the paranormal's 'bottomless pit' (as he describes it in his introduction). The real fascination of the paranormal for me is that for now it does remain dark and unknown. Paranormal events challenge our perceptions of the world around us and beg important questions about the universe and our place within it.

It's not just the truth that's out there – to quote an iconic TV series – the paranormal is, too. It really is. In your town. In your street. Maybe in your own home. The weird and inexplicable happens to ordinary people somewhere in the world every single day. Before you go in search of it, though, you will need a guide. How lucky for you that you have this excellent one in your hands.

Richard Holland, Editor, UncannyUK.com
and former editor of *Paranormal* magazine

Introduction

Neither Normal Nor Natural

At the edge of what we know, a dark continent of legend and belief stretches to a distant vanishing point. It is a realm inhabited by strange entities – ghosts, poltergeists, the undead, angels, demons, extraterrestrials – and it is a realm explained by strange ideas from the occult to modern parapsychology involving ancient gods, magical powers, alternative universes and multi-dimensional space. From novels *The Exorcist* to *Twilight*, from films *Poltergeist* to *Underworld*, from television programmes *The X-Files* to *Buffy the Vampire Slayer*, from video games *Doom* to *Resident Evil*, our thoughts and fears are drawn to this dark world of the supernatural. It has never been more popular than now.

Human history is also the history of the non-human and the unreal. Throughout our recorded history – from rock carving to the internet – the human race has made reference to another, radically different order of beings and alternatives to physical reality. In referring to this, the term 'paranormal' has come to replace 'supernatural' in scientific discourse on the subject, but they are, essentially, the same. The 'supernatural' is a dissident subject. It deals with things that mainstream science cannot allow, but in which many believe, yet rarely has the same privileges as religion. However, it is also an essential subject. From our earliest myths to our latest fears, the supernatural has always been with us. To paraphrase William James, to study the supernatural is the best way of understanding the natural; certainly it is bound to be more interesting.

The field of the supernatural is often divided sharply between believers and sceptics. At the extremes there are those who will believe anything and those who will deny everything. To avoid such divisiveness, let us think of the supernatural in a different way. If literature is the willing suspension of disbelief, then science is the willing suspension of belief. But let us go further and suspend both belief and disbelief. Let us look at the evidence, that quirky will-o'-the-wisp that promises proof while leading us into the bog of oblivion. And to help us avoid divisiveness and think about this subject in a new way, let us take a new name for it. We need something fashionable, something popular and obscure at the same time: we need quantum physics. I want us to think of the supernatural as 'quantum normality' – a world where things can suddenly appear and disappear, and be in two places at once, a world where there is still room for the astonishing and unlikely. Let us adopt a 'quantum' position ourselves: what follows might be true or it might not be, and it is both of these things until we peek into the box containing Schrödinger's cat and collapse the probability wave function. Not least as history, the supernatural is an undeniable social fact, whether it is real or not.

The supernatural is a vast subject whose boundaries are unfathomable. It is everything beyond the natural. But what is natural? Is it the paranormal – everything beyond the normal? But again, what is normal? In fact, reports of paranormal occurrences are so frequent that we might be better thinking of them as normal. It is often the case, as American writer Elbert Hubbard once put it, that 'the supernatural is the natural not yet understood'.[1] Science is constantly pushing our understanding of what constitutes the natural order of things.

As history it is impossible to define a beginning. Enigmatic cave drawings may hint at supernatural ideas and beliefs, but it is not certain that they do, and if they do, what do they mean? That is why this book is organized thematically. A rough timeline

---

[1] Hubbard, 'The Open Road: Afoot with the Fra', *The Fra*, 1.2, May 1908, p. 22.

can occasionally be drawn through the chapters, particularly the later ones, but they are written primarily as stand-alone guides to key concepts and fields of study within the broad envelope of 'supernatural'.

As a guide to what should be in a book about the supernatural I have, of course, considered the demands and desires of popular culture, but more particularly I have looked to specialist publications such as *Paranormal* magazine and *Fortean Times*, dedicated encyclopaedias on the subject and the scientific literature, such as that produced by the members of the Society for Psychical Research over the last 130 or so years. Today, the supernatural/paranormal encompasses everything from building your own UFO to reanimating corpses with voodoo.

To reflect and, hopefully, organize that expansive range, the book is divided into two parts. The first deals with what I have called supernatural entities. This mostly covers what are considered to be spirits: spirits of the dead (ghosts and possibly poltergeists), spirits of the dead believed to have reanimated their physical forms ('the undead'), good spirits (angels), and evil spirits (demons). I have also included extraterrestrials and UFOs since they are described by witnesses and believers in ways reminiscent of some of the older categories of spirits, such as angels and demons. The second part deals with ways in which humankind has tried to communicate with and control these supernatural entities and tap into the whole range of powers that are thought to be paranormal in origin and function. I have called these 'approaches to the supernatural', since they cover a broad range of activity from magic to science.

Finally, it must be borne in mind that this book is a guide and a *brief* guide at that. Each subject I cover has volumes, sometimes whole libraries, devoted to it. Thus more might have been included – religious visions of gods, God and saints, the fairies and monsters of folklore and the cryptids of current cryptozoology – but as with every project there has to be a point where one draws the line and this book was never intended to be an encyclopaedia of the subject. Sanity is learning what to overlook. Whilst I have endeavoured to delve deeply into the subjects I do cover, due to the constraints of space and the purpose of this book it has not been possible to touch the bottom of what is, essentially, a bottomless pit – or even several bottom-less pits. It is not intended to be an academic textbook, but it is written in a way that it can be relied upon. To allow the reader to follow up the sources consulted I have included full refer-ences in the notes and as is usual in historical research I have used primary sources wherever possible supplemented by the latest research where necessary. For those new to these subjects I have tried to provide a solid starting-point; for those already familiar with them, hopefully, an enjoyable overview with a few surprises along the way. For everyone, these are simply some of the most astonishing stories that have ever been told.

The Experiments

For most people, most of the time, they find out things from other people. A tells B a ghost story, B writes it down and C reads it, and so on, although especially important is the part where C tells D who then gets B's book out of the library and tracks down A, interviews all those involved, reads all the source material, weighs the evidence and writes a book like this one. Here I want to give you the opportunity to find out something for yourself by actually doing it. The reason is that I want to involve you in some of the issues surrounding the investigation of the supernatural. I have devised three simple experiments that you can try right now.

Experiment 1: Mind-Reading
You will need a pen or pencil and a blank sheet of paper. When you have these rounded up, in your mind's eye, I want you to see a simple geometrical shape. Got it? Make it larger, draw it on the paper, then, inside this space I want you to try and get another geometrical shape, and draw that, too. Now you should have two shapes, one inside the other. At the end of the book I will tell you what you have drawn.

Experiment 2: Thought-Transference
From my secret location in central Europe I am now going to mentally project a number between 1 and 50. To make things easier, both digits are odd numbers, but not the same number,

so that it could be 15 but not 11, for example. Open up your mind. Write down the number you receive.

Experiment 3: Psychokinesis

Uri Geller once performed a live paranormal event on television where he told viewers that his psychic powers would reactivate their old, broken clocks and watches. Many people were amazed to find out that it worked. We are going to do the same thing right now. Find an old wind-up watch that no longer works, hold it in your hands for some minutes, concentrating on making it work, as I broadcast my psychic powers to operate on the machinery. You should hold it for at least ten minutes, repeating 'work, mend, work'. It might help if you hold a copy of this book in your other hand.

Part I: Supernatural Entities

Millions of spiritual creatures walk the earth
Unseen, both when we wake and when we sleep.
                    – John Milton, *Paradise Lost*, 1667

Sir, to leave things out of a book, merely because people
tell you they will not be believed, is meanness.
                    – Samuel Johnson, 21 March 1772
              (James Boswell's *The Life of Samuel Johnson*)

1. Ghosts

'Tales of Headless Coachmen and a Lonely Nun': it was early summer, 1929, when news reached the *Daily Mirror* from a forgotten hamlet in a remote corner of Essex. Unusual events were disrupting the lives of the local rector and his household. The rector had written requesting the name of a reputable society involved in psychical research that could help him put an end to the disturbances. The paper dispatched one of its most experienced reporters, V. C. Wall, to investigate. The name of the village was Borley.[2]

Even when it was full of life, the rectory had an air of foreboding. A charmless red brick mansion built in the early 1860s by the Revd Henry Bull to accommodate his vast family of fourteen children, it stood, it was said, on the site of a medieval monastery. In 1928, the rectory, after being turned down by twelve other clergymen, had become the home of Revd Guy Eric Smith and his wife Mabel, despite the warnings. 'It had a sinister reputation,' said Sidney Glanville, one of the later investigators, 'and the huge, melancholy house could not have been very inviting.' Wall told his readers that the strange events the Smiths related to him had all the makings of 'a first-class ghost story'.[3]

---

[2] Sidney Glanville, 'The Strange Happenings at Borley Rectory', *Fate*, October 1951, p. 95.

[3] V. C. Wall, 'Ghost Visits to a Rectory', *Daily Mirror,* 10 June 1929; Glanville, p. 91; Eric J. Dingwall, et al., 'The Haunting of Borley Rectory', *Proceedings of the Society for Psychical Research*, 51.186, January 1956, p. 28. The journalist V. C. Wall did not put his byline to the stories, but he is named by Harry Price,

When the Smiths arrived from India, they found that the rectory had fallen into severe disrepair. There was no mains water, the cisterns were filthy, and fresh water had to be pumped from a well in the courtyard – when it worked. The roof leaked. There was no gas or electricity. It was cold and difficult to heat, and only part of the twenty-three-room mansion was habitable. Unmanaged trees had grown up tall and nigh encircling, almost hiding the house from the sun. The Smiths were about to embark on what they would later describe as 'the darkest years of their life'.[4]

For the Smiths, it began with the sound of footsteps: slow, dragging footsteps echoing from an unoccupied room. The reverend stayed up one night, hockey stick at the ready, waiting for the footsteps to cross the room's floor. They did not disappoint. Although he saw nothing, the sound of feet wearing what he took for slippers began to drag themselves over the bare floorboards. The reverend swung his hockey stick, whistling through the air, at the spot where he thought the footsteps were. But the invisible feet kept their pace across the room.[5]

On another occasion, Mrs Smith was in the library, apparently investigating the nooks and crannies of the house. A large Victorian bookcase stretched the length of one wall with the top half glass fronted and the bottom given over to cupboards. Inside one of the cupboards Mrs Smith found a football-sized parcel. There was no label or indication as to what was inside and so, like Pandora in the Greek myth, she started to unwrap the layers of paper. Inside was a human skull. Revd Smith interred it in the nearby graveyard after a short service, but soon after, mysterious taps started to sound from the mirror on Mrs Smith's dressing table whenever she approached it. According to a certain Mr Hardy, a workman at Borley, the strange phenomena became so intense after the burial that it was decided to restore the skull to its previous place.[6]

The End of Borley Rectory, Harrap & Co., 1946, p. 178.

[4] Glanville, pp. 90, 94; Dingwall, et al., 1956, pp. 28–9.

[5] Wall, 'Ghost Visits to a Rectory'.

[6] Glanville, p. 95. Glanville interviewed the Smiths on 6 October 1937 and

Mystery lights were seen in unoccupied parts of the building. In the library, the heavy wooden shutters to the French windows would slam shut. Doors would be locked and unlocked. Keys would mysteriously vanish. Bells would ring for the servants from empty rooms. The reverend heard whispering voices in the passage outside his bedroom. At one point, someone or something shouted 'Don't, Carlos'.[7]

A servant girl brought all the way from London gave her notice after only two days. She had, she said, seen the ghost of a nun walking in the woods at the back of the house and at another time leaning over a gate near the house. Another servant girl claimed to have seen an 'old-fashioned coach' on the lawn. The previous rector, already dead, had himself told the story of how, when walking along the road outside the rectory one night, he had seen a coach drive by, driven by two headless coachmen. Wall related that 'the villagers dread the neighbourhood of the rectory after dark, and will not pass it'.[8]

Wall's explanation was that, according to local legend, a groom at the monastery and a nun from a nearby convent had fallen in love 'several hundred years ago'. They would meet illicitly in the woods, pledging their love for one another and planning their elopement. When the day came for them to escape, another groom brought a coach round to the woods. But the lovers quarrelled and in a fit of rage, the groom strangled the nun. He was caught and both grooms were beheaded. According to another version, the monks caught all three red-handed, beheaded the grooms and walled up the nun alive within the monastery. In subsequent versions it was a monk and nun who had fallen in love, with the same grisly ending.[9]

---

heard this story first-hand. Price gives the same details, p. 20, with the addition of Hardy's testimony.

[7] Glanville, pp. 94–6.

[8] Wall, 'Ghost Visits to a Rectory'.

[9] Wall, 'Ghost Visits to a Rectory'; V. C. Wall, 'Mystery Light in Haunted Wood', *Daily Mirror*, 11 June 1929; Peter Underwood, *The A–Z of British Ghosts*, Chancellor Press, 1992, p. 31.

The Smiths' experiences were not the first time that ghosts had been reported at Borley. The stories in the *Daily Mirror* prompted a Mrs E. Myford of Newport to write in about her own encounter with the ghost. She had grown up in the area where 'it was common talk that the rectory was haunted'. 'Many people,' she said, 'declared that they had seen figures walking at the bottom of the garden.' Despite that she became an under-nursemaid there in 1886. Installed in what was, according to the other servants, the 'haunted bedroom', she had to wait two weeks before the ghost made itself known. In the dead of night she was woken by the sound of someone walking down the corridor towards her room. It was a slightly muffled, scuffling sound, as if the approaching person were wearing slippers. She expected that it was the head nurse come to wake her as she did at six every morning, but when no one came into the room her thoughts turned to 'the ghost'. Next morning the other maids all denied having walked down to her room. The young Mrs Myford became so nervous that she handed in her notice and never again ventured down by the house after sunset.[10]

Colchester Grammar School's former headmaster, P. Shaw Jeffrey, MA, told veteran ghost hunter Peter Underwood that he had seen the ghostly nun several times when he had visited the rectory in 1885 or 1886. Ethel Bull, one of the last surviving children of Revd Bull, told how she and two of her sisters had seen the nun gliding along the so-called 'Nun's Walk' in the late afternoon of 28 July 1900 – 28 July being the traditional date of the nun's appearance. Another sister was called from the house and promptly decided that there was nothing strange at all about the nun and approached to enquire whether she wanted anything. That was when the nun vanished. One of their brothers, Harry Bull, went on to become a parson and took over the parish after his father: he, too, claimed to have seen the nun, as well as being awakened, along with the rest of the household, by

---

[10] V. C. Wall, 'Haunted Room in a Rectory', *Daily Mirror*, 12 June 1929.

the loud and unaccountable ringing of bells. He also frequently met the dwarfish figure of an old man on the lawn.[11]

Wall and a photographer decided to spend the night in the woods to try and see the ghosts themselves. Gamely, Revd Smith joined them, professing not to believe in ghosts. After some time, they noticed a mysterious light appear in a disused wing of the building. Neither Wall nor his photographer seemed anxious to investigate, so the reverend volunteered. They saw the reverend light a lamp next to the mysterious light, but when they approached, the mystery light winked out. The intrepid reporters were then badly scared by a maid coming out to ask if they would like coffee. Undeterred, they examined some tree stumps that looked a bit like nuns, before finally calling it a night. That was when they decided to call in Harry Price, Honorary Director of the National Laboratory of Psychic Research.[12]

With Price on site, Wall's till then rather tongue-in-cheek account took on a new note of seriousness. This time he claimed to have actually seen the 'nun' moving in the deep shadows at the edge of the woods. By this time the ghost or ghosts seemed to have learnt a few new tricks. After he had investigated the shadowy figure, a pane of glass from the porch 'hurtled to the ground'. As he went inside, a vase flew past the reporter's head and smashed against the iron stove in the hallway. Waiting on the stairs in darkness to see if anything else would happen, a mothball struck Wall on the head. Then from about 1 a.m. to 4 a.m., Wall, the rector and his wife, as well as Price and his secretary Lucy Kaye, communicated with the spirit as it made a series of raps on the back of a mirror. The spirit told them that he was the late Revd Harry Bull.[13]

The press attention brought sightseers in their 'hundreds' to gawp at the house and 'at night the headlights of their cars may

[11] Underwood, p. 31; Glanville, p. 92.

[12] Wall, 'Mystery Light in Haunted Wood'; Wall, 'Haunted Room in a Rectory'.

[13] V. C. Wall, 'Weird Night in Haunted House', *Daily Mirror*, 14 June 1929; V. C. Wall, 'Shy Ghost of Borley Rectory', *Daily Mirror*, 17 June 1929.

be seen for miles around'. One enterprising company was even
running a bus service to the rectory with the slogan 'come and
see the Borley ghost'. Instances of 'rowdyism' were disrupting
the neighbourhood and the reverend appealed to people to be 'a
little more considerate when they come here'. People were trampling the flower beds and peering through the windows. The
police were called. By 17 June 1929, just a week after Wall's first
story, this ugly old building had become 'the now famous
rectory'. And this was only the beginning.[14]

These experiences, the public interest, the subsequent investigations and reports of further phenomena would award Borley
Rectory the name of 'the most haunted house in England'.
There are, arguably, more haunted places. The Theatre Royal
on Drury Lane, London, claims over 500 ghosts, for example.[15]
However, no other case has become so talked about nor been as
controversial. Borley Rectory is either the best authenticated
case of a haunted house, or one of the most heinous frauds ever
perpetrated.

Defining Ghosts

Nuns, white ladies, green ladies, blue ladies, headless horsemen,
as well as coachmen, drummer-boys, underground pipers,
marching soldiers, fighting armies, phantom coaches, ghost
trains, spectral pets – all these and more are the sorts of spirits
that people believe have come back from the dead or the past to
haunt us. It was once calculated that Warwickshire had a ghost
for every square mile, which, if it were a representative figure,
would mean that the United Kingdom alone must be troubled
by some 94,000 spirits of the dead.[16]

---

[14] Wall, 'Shy Ghost of Borley Rectory'; Glanville, p. 96.
[15] John Spencer and Anne Spencer, *The Ghost Handbook*, Boxtree, 1998, pp.
8, 110, according to tourguide Nina Smirnoff.
[16] William Purcell Witcutt, 'Notes on Warwickshire Folklore', *Folklore* 55,
2 (1944), p. 72; I have widened the estimate made by Owen Davies in *The
Haunted: A Social History of Ghosts*, Palgrave Macmillan, 2009, p. 1, for England to include the whole of the UK.

In every culture, in every age, we find people who have seen ghosts. Many more believe in them. A 2001 Gallup poll found that 38 per cent of Americans believed in ghosts with an unaccountably larger 42 per cent believing in haunted houses. At around the same time in Britain, the Consumer Analysis Group found that 57 per cent believed in ghosts. In 1882 the then newly formed Society for Psychical Research (SPR) surveyed 17,000 people and found that nearly 10 per cent had had a ghostly experience. [17]

The terminology that has grown up around hauntings is almost as varied as the hauntings themselves: ghost, phantom, phantasm, shade, shadow, spectre, spook, apparition, wraith, poltergeist (which we will examine separately). We also find a number of more obscure words, such as *lemures, larvae, umbrae mortuorum, spectra* and so on. Then there are new terms, such as orbs, EVP, shadow people.

No definitive typology has emerged, but many authors have sought to order this jumble of terminology. For Ludwig Lavater writing in the sixteenth century, *lemures* and *larvae* were generic terms for the ghosts of the dead, somewhat like *umbrae mortuorum* – shades of the dead – whilst *spectra* referred to 'a substance without a body' that yet could be heard or seen. *Lemures* were also 'evil and hurtful shapes which appear in the night'. *Visum* (also *Visio, Visiones*) he equated with the Greek *phantasia*, a realistic fantasy occurring in sleep or near sleep, to be differentiated (it is not clear how) from a *phasma*. For King James VI and I, writing in his *Daemonologie* at the end of the sixteenth century, the peculiarly Scottish wraiths were the spirits of the newly dead, or soon to die, and, undoubtedly influenced by Lavater, *lemures* and *spectra* haunted houses in various terrifying appearances and with much noise.[18]

---

[17] Brad Steiger and Sherry Steiger, *Gale Encyclopedia of the Unusual and Unexplained*, Gale, 2003, vol. 3, p. 2; George Stuart, 'What is a Ghost?', *Paranormal*, June 2010, p. 59.

[18] Ludwig (also Lewes) Lavater, *Das Gespensterbuch*, 1569, English trans. published as *Of Ghostes and Spirites Walking by Nyght*, 1572, pp. 1–3; James VI and

It is clear that many of these concepts were taken from Latin sources. The Romans had a name for a class of spirits who protected and guided human beings: *genii*. Lavater noted that we have two: one that encourages good deeds and another that encourages the opposite. The term *genius* was a personification of the creative powers, depicted in Etruscan and Roman art as naked winged males. Under Greek influence this became fused with the concept of *daimon*, but the Romans continued their particular belief in a *genius loci*, spirit of place. Lavater also plumbed the depths of Greek and Roman folklore concerning evil spirits, referring to Mormo and Gilo, as well as the Gorgones, Empusae, Lamiae and others (see the chapter on demons). Among the Romans it was believed that evil spirits of the dead wandered the night. Called *lemures* (*larvae*) these ghost-demons could be appeased at the feast of the Lemuria (9 November and 13 May) with black beans scattered at midnight.[19]

In the earliest literature of the Ancient Near East we find many of the same concerns as today, especially with what happens after death. Confronted with a corpse they wondered, as do we all, where the life force that so recently had energized and characterized that body had gone. And in that mysterious place, what did the dead do? The bizarre complexities of Egyptian funerary customs, from the technical wonders of mummification and the gigantic pyramids, to the range of spells in *The Book of the Dead* to prevent such horrors as having to eat dung in the afterlife, attest to this deepest of concerns. The deceased continued as a multiplicity of spiritual forms called *ka*, *ba* and *ah*. In Coptic the *ah* becomes a demonic aspect, but otherwise the dead are not necessarily considered to be ill-disposed towards the living. The dead could be called upon for help and likewise the living could help the dead. Provisions, tools, money, jewels, weapons, warriors and slaves have all been

---

I, *Daemonologie*, 1597, p. 57; see also Davies, pp. 2–3. Spellings modernized.
[19] Manfred Lurker, *Routledge Dictionary of Gods and Goddesses, Devils and Demons*, Routledge, 2004, pp. 68, 111; Lavater, pp. 3, 5.

buried with the dead at one time or another to assist in the deceased's afterlife existence.[20]

We are familiar with the differential fates of the righteous and the ignominious dead: Valhalla for the valiant Northern warrior, the gloomy halls of Hel for the rest; the Elysian Fields for the Heroic Greek, the Meadows of Asphodel for the indifferent and Tartarus for the wicked; Heaven for the good Christian, Hell for everyone else, with Limbo added later as a compromise. In contrast to the idyllic Field of Offerings (or Reeds) that awaited the Egyptian, the Mesopotamians believed that the dead lived in perpetual darkness eating mud and filth and drinking foul water in 'the land of no return'. Given such an unenviable future, the unwelcome attentions of angry ghosts were greatly feared. Reflecting funerary taboos, it was believed by the Babylonians that the spirit of an uninterred corpse remained on the earth as a potentially harmful ghost.[21]

Similar ideas continued to be influential right up until our own times. The Revd J. C. Atkinson (1814–1900) reported the belief current in his Yorkshire parish that if a body on its way to be buried was not carried up the 'church road', then its ghost would return. An inverted form of this idea can be read in the story of the restless Borley skull.[22]

We see from this it was commonly believed that ghosts behaved in a purposeful manner. As well as protesting against the improper implementation of funerary customs, they also returned to right other wrongs. Ghosts interceded in legal cases, as when the spirit of Sir Walter Long's (c. 1591–1672) first wife allegedly scared the wits out of a clerk who was preparing the legal papers enabling Long's second wife to disinherit her stepson. In 1660 the spirit of Robert Parkin supposedly appeared to

---

[20] K. van der Toorn, Bob Becking and Pieter Willem van der Horst (eds), *Dictionary of Deities and Demons in the Bible* [*DDD*], 2nd ed., Brill/Eerdmans, 1999, pp. 223–5.

[21] *DDD*, pp. 223–31, 309–12.

[22] *Routledge Dict. Gods*, p. 60; John Christopher Atkinson, *Forty Years in a Moorland Parish*, Macmillan, 1891, pp. 219–20.

Robert Hope of Appleby in the parish church, crying out 'I am murdered' over and over, which instigated the local Justice of the Peace to begin a murder enquiry. Borley's ghostly nun was likewise believed to have returned because of her cruel murder. The vengeful ghost had its counterpart in the repentant ghost. Remorseful murderers were also believed to occasionally return to reveal their crimes. Other ghosts appeared to mark the date of their death, especially in the case of suicides, whilst others simply continued to do what they had always done and followed their everyday routine. In very rare, but most interesting cases, spirits of the dead return to warn the living, make prophecies, or even to give evidence of the afterlife.[23]

Fictional ghosts are always purposeful. One need only think of the ghost of Hamlet's father who returns to reveal his murder to his son and incite him to exact revenge in Shakespeare's *Hamlet* (c. 1599–1601), or the ghost of the murdered Banquo returning to haunt his killer in *Macbeth* (c. 1603–7). The spirits in Charles Dickens' *A Christmas Carol* (1843) play a central role in transforming the character of Ebenezer Scrooge with grim and prophetic messages. With such precedents it is no wonder that the purposeful ghost continues to be a theme in popular culture. The Oscar-winning film *Ghost* (1990) had Patrick Swayze trying to warn his fiancée, played by Demi Moore, and bring his killers to justice. In *The Sixth Sense* (1999) spirits of the dead use a young boy who can see and communicate with them to resolve their untimely deaths, which ultimately allows Bruce Willis's character to come to terms with his own death and express his true feelings for his wife. In the 2008 film *Ghost Town* with Ricky Gervais, the spirits of the dead were trapped on the earth because of unfinished business with the living. Of course, this is as much a technical requirement as it is a reflection of popular belief: a ghost without a purpose is not a good plot device.

The main problem for earlier writers was a theological one:

---

[23] Davies, pp. 4–6.

how could a spirit return before the resurrection? For James VI and I, it was entirely possible for the Devil and witches to root up bodies, like swine, to borrow his comparison, and use them for their own ends, especially in the case of unfaithful persons.[24] The crucial point for us is that we see a differentiation between visions or fantasies and the spirits themselves. Earlier writers were well aware that some people saw things that were not there, but did not use this to explain (or explain away) all such incorporeal manifestations.

Writers such as James VI and I remained certain that, if they were not the malicious manipulations of witches and devils, ghosts were spirits of the dead. The problem is that, given the range of apparent phenomena reported, which includes 'ghosts' of the living, 'ghosts' of the future, even 'ghosts' of inanimate objects, and, under certain experimental conditions, artificially created 'ghosts', they cannot all be spirits of the dead.

Ghostology

When the Swedish scientist Carolus Linnaeus proposed his classification of the Earth's life forms in the eighteenth century he looked to the organisms' reproductive systems to differentiate them. If ghosts are the mirror and inverse of the living then we should develop a classification based on their *destructive* systems, that is, the nature of their functional interaction, not with each other, but with the living. However, in some cases ghosts appear to have no functional interaction with the living, leaving us with a classification based largely on appearance. We should also expect that a process of *unnatural* selection has matched the pace of evolution to produce the currently reported range of phenomena.

Even before the ghosts of modern machinery were reported people wondered why ghosts of the dead appeared wearing clothes. One of the earliest to pose the question was the philosopher Thomas Hobbes in 1651 within the wider debate of the

---

[24] James VI and I, p. 36.

problem of the spirit or soul itself. Hobbes surely knows the answer now, as it is said that his ghost can be heard muttering and singing to itself at Hardwick Hall in Derbyshire where he died. Popular culture solutions, like that given in the film *Ghost Town* (2008), is that ghosts wear the clothes (or lack of them) they died in. This seems logical for all those cavaliers, nuns, monks, and so on, but there are cases of ghosts reportedly appearing in different clothes at different times, or wearing apparently new clothes. In 1852, one writer mockingly posed the solution that the clothes were ghosts too, the spirits of 'all the socks that never came home from the wash' and so on. In fact, ghost socks may not be entirely out of the question. In the late 1960s a flock of supernatural headgear – top hats, bonnets, caps – flew through a house in Killakee, Ireland, during a poltergeist outbreak.[25]

What would be the ghost story without the phantom coach replete with ghostly horseteam? The idea of ghostly coaches and carriages is a well-known staple of the ghost story. We have already seen how one featured so prominently in the early period of the Borley Rectory haunting. Others career about the highways and byways of Britain: a headless coachman drives his team of four black horses through Brockley Combe in Somerset; in the 1970s a car driver was alarmed to see an old coach and horses bearing down on him outside Bungay in Suffolk; the ghost of Boudicca, Queen of the Celtic Iceni tribe and thorn in the Romans' side in the first century CE, has been seen driving her chariot along the old Roman road Ermine Street as it passes near Cammeringham in Lincolnshire.[26] But with the development of technology we have also seen an evolution of apparitions to include trains, cars, lorries, ships and aeroplanes.

---

[25] Thomas Hobbes, *Leviathan*, 1651, p. 374; *Saturday Review*, 19 July 1852, p. 268; Anna Claybourne, *Ghosts and Hauntings*, Usborne, 2000, p. 2; Richard Freeman, 'Just Too Weird!', *Paranormal*, 50, August 2010, p. 44. On the question of different/new clothes see the cases given in Elizabeth Nowotny-Keane, *Amazing Encounters: Direct Communication from the Afterlife*, David Lovell, 2009, pp. 21, 92.

[26] Spencer, pp. 185–8.

On 28 December 1879 the evening train on the Edinburgh to Aberdeen line was battling stormy weather to reach Dundee station on time. As North British Locomotive 224 and six carriages pulled out onto the Tay Bridge, severe gales estimated to be Force 10 or 11 on the Beaufort scale lashed what was then, at nearly two miles, the longest rail bridge in the world. As the train steamed onto the highest middle section the structure gave way, sending engine, carriages, passengers and all plummeting 88 feet into the dark waves below. 'And the Demon of the air seem'd to say,' as the poet William McGonagall put it, '"I'll blow down the Bridge of Tay".' All of the estimated sixty to seventy-five passengers were lost. The stumps of the old foundations can still be seen running alongside the new bridge, and on 28 December every year at approximately 7.15 p.m. the ghost of the train can be seen charging headlong into the darkness and its doom, or so it is said. Dundee-based group Paranormal Discovery attempted to investigate the haunting in 2007. As well as noting that ghost stories were still doing the rounds in the local pub, several team members witnessed unexplained lights.[27]

Across Britain the Age of Rail has left its mark. The Southend to Sheffield line has a ghostly ticket inspector who was killed in 1913 whilst saving a child who had fallen onto the tracks. A sleeping car said to have been used as a brothel by the Germans during WWII, which is now in the National Railway Museum, is thought to be haunted; as well as the museum itself. In the 1950s the dilapidated parcels depot, Mayfield Station, was reputedly haunted by the ghost of a workman who had fallen to his death down a deep shaft there. Stockholm's metro is said to be haunted by the *Silverpilen* ('Silver Arrow'), an unpainted aluminium train from the mid 1960s. With more than 250 route miles and over 270 stations, the London Underground also has

[27] Tom Martin, taybridgedisaster.co.uk, accessed 4 September 2010; Paranormal Discovery, http://www.paranormaldiscovery.co.uk/taybridge.htm, accessed 4 September 2010; William McGonagall, 'The Tay Bridge Disaster', 1880, in Chris Hunt (ed.), *William McGonagall: Collected Poems*, Birlinn, 2006.

its share of ghosts: an ancient Egyptian in the disused British Museum station; a man in black at Marble Arch; and the sounds of screaming still heard more than half a century after the wartime Bethnal Green station disaster.[28]

If not actually haunted, the car in which Archduke Franz Ferdinand and his wife were assassinated in Sarajevo on 28 June 1914 certainly had the reputation of being cursed. Successive owners met accident and death until the car was destroyed during an Allied bombing raid on Vienna in WWII. One of the earliest ghost cars is the chauffeur-driven 1920 Daimler Landaulette seen by a driver in 1967 in Devonshire on the Modbury to Garabridge road. The Revd David Warner of Wombwell, Yorkshire, was surprised one day when his car switched itself on and drove off. 'If it acts possessed again,' he said, 'I shall have to exorcise it.' Other incidents involve car lights being seen approaching then mysteriously vanishing, such as those seen outside Moretonhampstead in 1969 and at Penhill Beacon in the late 1990s.[29]

The first 'phantom lorry' appeared in 1930 during the inquest into the death of motorcyclist Charles Ridgway on the A75 between Hyde and Mottram-in-Longdale. According to Ridgway's cousin, Albert Collinson, who had been riding pillion and was seriously injured in the accident, a lorry had backed out of a narrow opening in front of them, causing Ridgway to swerve and lose control of his motorbike. The police found no such opening and no lorry tracks. But the investigation did reveal that the area was a mysterious accident black spot, despite being a straight stretch of well-maintained road. More accidents were to follow. One even involved a pedestrian who was apparently run over by the phantom lorry. One of London's trademark red double-decker buses haunted the junction of St Mark's

[28] Spencer, pp. 196–8; Bengt af Klintberg, *Råttan i pizzan*, Nordstedts Förlag, 1992; David Brandon, 'Spooks on the Tube', *Paranormal*, 55, January 2011, pp. 14–19.
[29] Nigel Blundell and Roger Boar, *The World's Greatest Ghosts*, Octopus, 1983, pp. 117–18, 129; Spencer, pp. 191–3.

Road and Cambridge Gardens in Kensington, causing several accidents before the dangerous bend was remodelled.[30]

Even a stretch of modern road, the A616 bypass around Stocksbridge in South Yorkshire, has acquired a reputation for being haunted. Car accidents are attributed to the phantom monk, seen on several occasions by private security guards, police officers, and many others. The well-known UFO researcher and lecturer in journalism Dr David Clarke covered the stories as a reporter for the *Sheffield Star*, coming up with the memorable headline 'Ghostly Stories of Police 'n' Spectre'.[31]

The seven seas play host to many hauntings, none more famous than the legendary *Flying Dutchman*. One of the most dramatic sightings came from a sixteen-year-old midshipman aboard HMS *Inconstant* as it steamed off the coast of Australia on 11 July 1881: 'At 4 a.m. *The Flying Dutchman* crossed our bows. She emitted a strange phosphorescent light as of a phantom ship all aglow'. The young sailor was Prince George, later King George V of Great Britain. A total of thirteen other men witnessed the apparition that morning and it has been sighted many times since. The schooner *Lady Lovibond* sank with all hands on 13 February 1748 and has reputedly appeared every fifty years to the day off the coast of southern England. A WWII landing craft flying the Cross of Lorraine, the flag of the Free French forces, was sighted in difficult weather off the coast of Devon in 1959, fourteen years after the end of the war.[32]

Ghosts also appear onboard ship. A phantom appeared to Captain Rogers of the *Society* as it made for Virginia, New England, in 1664, whose timely warning saved the vessel from shipwreck. The WWI German submarine UB65 was reputedly haunted by the ghost of its second officer, despite being

---

[30] Spencer, pp. 188–9, 190.

[31] Steve Mera and Kirst D'Raven, 'Taking Stock of Stocksbridge', *Paranormal*, 55, January 2011, pp. 58–63 – the authors were sceptical about the stories and reported that a man calling himself 'Dave from Wakefield' had confessed to staging the 'haunting' himself.

[32] Blundell and Boar, pp. 92–3.

exorcised by a Lutheran pastor, until destroyed by a mysterious explosion in 1918. John Smith, ship's engineer aboard the *Queen Mary* said he heard sounds like rushing water. In 1988 Tony Cornell and William Roll used a sound-activated recorder to capture bangs, rushing water and human cries. During WWII the *Queen Mary* had collided with a British frigate: some 300 men had been lost that day. These were not the only ghosts still onboard. Davy Jones's Locker will no doubt continue to give a momentary lease of freedom upon the surface to all those poor souls lost at sea.[33]

After the Wright Brothers' historic flight in 1903, it could only be a matter of time before the skies were filled with their share of ghosts, too. Bircham Newton aerodrome in Norfolk saw service through both world wars and, if accounts are to be believed, is still doing so despite being disused. A film crew there to shoot a management training video instead caught sounds of aircraft engines, human voices and machinery; in fact, all the noise and bustle of a busy hangar in active use. Other members of the film crew also saw ghostly figures in RAF uniform and enquiries revealed a history of hauntings. A lone Spitfire can sometimes still be heard as it returns from a sortie to the famous Battle of Britain airfield at Biggin Hill in Kent. Some witnesses even claim to have seen it perform a victory roll over the runway. The villagers of Hawkinge near Folkestone have heard the unforgettable drone of a Nazi V1 'flying bomb' flying overhead decades after the event.[34]

Of course phantom objects are not restricted to forms of transport. H. Porten claimed to see the face of his dead father in a worn area of wall in his living room in the 1950s. A haunted concrete floor at Street Real 5, Bélmez de la Moraleda, Spain, has produced mysterious images of faces since 1971. Known as

[33] Dennis Bardens, *Ghosts and Hauntings*, Zeus, 1965, p. 220; Blundell and Boar, pp. 92–3, 97–9; William Roll, Review of Tony Cornell, *Investigating the Paranormal*, Parapsychology Foundation, 2002, *Journal of Parapsychology*, 67, 2003, p. 191.

[34] Blundell and Boar, pp. 121–3.

La Casa de las Caras ('The House of the Faces') the property has drawn thousands to witness the allegedly paranormal phenomena. The German parapsychologist Hans Bender sealed some of the faces under transparent plastic and, when they continued to develop, was convinced that they must be paranormal in origin. The theory was that the phenomena were unconscious 'thoughtography' produced by the house's owner, María Gómez Cámara. However, it has also been suggested that several constituents of paint found in a chemical analysis of the floor, oxidizing substances, or even chemical stain removers were used to artificially manufacture the faces.[35]

Clocks often become paranormal foci, perhaps because of their connection to time and hence mortality. The winged hourglass, symbolizing *tempus fugit*, is a frequent *memento mori* and funerary motif. A haunted grandfather clock terrified Elliott O'Donnell (1872–1965) at a friend's house one Christmas with erratic ticking, violent rocking motions and even, at one point, speaking prior to the death of its owner. It was not the only such oddity O'Donnell had come across. He told of other spirit-infested grandfather clocks: one that whined whenever catastrophe loomed for its owners; one that made a thumping noise to portend death; and one where a hooded face would sometimes peer out instead of the clock face. Keeping up with the times, a letter writer to *Paranormal* magazine claimed to have a haunted clock-radio that patriotically turned itself on for the national anthem on Radio 4 and then off again.[36]

Furniture itself can also acquire a supernatural reputation. An old oak chest, blood-stained and coffin-shaped, reputedly caused paranormal disturbances at Stanbury Manor in West

---

[35] H. Porten, *The Miracle of the Walls: A Revelation of Life After Death*, self-published, 1954; César Tort, 'Bélmez Faces Turned Out to Be Suspiciously Picture-like Images', *Skeptical Inquirer* 19 (2), March/April 1995, p. 4; Luis Ruiz Noguez, 'Are the Faces of Bélmez Permanent Paranormal Objects?', *Journal of the Society for Psychical Research*, 59, 1993, pp. 161–71.

[36] Elliott O'Donnell, *Byways of Ghost-Land*, William Rider and Son, 1911, pp. 34–7; Rachel [no surname], 'Somewhat Alarmed', *Paranormal*, 50, August 2010, p. 77.

Yorkshire, leading then owner Mr T. A. Ley to nickname the entity 'Old George'. Mrs Barbara L. Barnes of Waterside, Barton-on-Humber, got more than she bargained for when she bought an antique chair. She and one of her children reported seeing the apparition of a kindly old man sitting in it on more than one occasion. A haunted wheelchair trundled about on its own in a house on Starnes Avenue, Asheville, North Carolina. Rocking chairs that rock by themselves are, of course, another mainstay of the ghost story, but there are attested cases, such as the rocking chair that belonged to Stella Metchling in Charlotte, North Carolina.[37]

I remember an odd occurrence that happened to me in the summer of 2008. It was the opening day of my first exhibition on witchcraft. The town in France where I lived at the time had graciously lent one of its historic buildings, a restored pigeonier called Le Colombier. The exhibits had all been installed the night before, the doors stood open and we stood waiting as the clock ticked down to our official opening. As we waited, a chair made of bent tubular metal collapsed slowly as if a heavy weight had sat down upon it. There were five of us in the room and all of us watched the chair crumple. I was rather pleased – it was a suitable beginning to an exhibition on witchcraft, after all – but the two town employees who worked there looked at each other nervously. No one had been sitting on the chair prior to its collapse. As far as I know it was relatively new: there were no obvious signs of wear and tear. But the logical explanation is that it must have been metal fatigue. Judging by the scared looks, not everyone else was so sure.[38]

Strange indeed, but not quite as terrifying as Elliott O'Donnell's story of the 'Boggle Chair'. Staying in another grand country house for Christmas, as was his wont, O'Donnell, because of his special interests, was conducted to the haunted

[37] Bardens, pp. 226, 228–31.
[38] 'La Sorcellerie en France', 15–29 June 2008, Bureau du Tourisme, Le Colombier, Place du Colombier, Mouzon, Ardennes.

room to there spend the night. The room was coffin-shaped, darkly panelled, swathed in ominous shadows and 'charged to the very utmost with superphysical impressions'. Filled with vintage wine and good food, O'Donnell bravely managed to fall asleep almost at once. He was soon woken by creaking sounds coming from a black ebony chair. O'Donnell reasonably dismissed the sound as the usual creaking of old wood, but as he listened he became aware of the sound of 'stealthy respiration'. As he looked in the direction of the chair he could see 'two, long, pale, and wholly evil eyes' that held him transfixed. The spell was only broken by the arrival of noisy carollers outside the house. O'Donnell sat up on two subsequent nights to observe the phenomenon. He was not disappointed. On the third night, lying paralysed in bed, he was strangled into unconsciousness by the malevolent entity, or so he said. The chair had been bought in Bruges and it had either been the one in which a wicked monk called Gaboni had died or had stood in the studio of a painter of the grotesque, where, it was suggested, it had absorbed his bizarre thoughtforms.[39]

Reports emerged from Ghana in 2009 of another 'haunted chair'. Apparently, the then Ghanaian Parliament's Minority Leader, Alban Bagbin, was 'very uncomfortable' on his new seat after a 'piece of traditional concoction' was discovered affixed to its underside. This was later described as 'a piece of lead probably laced with juju'. As the new parliament convened on its first day, he 'nearly fell off' the chair, sparking rumours of supernatural involvement. A three-man committee was formed to investigate the matter.[40]

---

[39] O'Donnell, pp. 230–43.

[40] 'Parliament Investigates "Haunted" Chair Saga', ModernGhana.com, 28 January 2009, http://www.modernghana.com/news2/200463/1/parliament-investigates-haunted-chair-saga.html, 3 September 2010; 'Parliament Investigates "Haunted" Chair Saga', ThinkGhana.com, 28 January 2009, http://www.thinkghana.com/tools/printnews/news.php?contentid=26229, accessed 3 September 2010; 'MPs Hunt Juju', ModernGhana.com, 29 January 2010, http://www.modernghana.com/news/200591/1/mps-hunt-juju.html, 3 September 2010.

Certain pictures themselves by their verisimilitude seem closer to magic than art and haunted by the figures depicted in them. In 1965 Dennis Bardens (1911–2004), journalist and creator of BBC TV's *Panorama* programme, recalled having inadvertently given a haunted picture as a present. A friend of the occult artist Austin Osman Spare (1886–1956), Bardens once gave one of the artist's pictures to an unidentified female friend. It was one of Spare's 'Magical Stelle', a mysterious coded invocation to Spare's inner demons. Bardens' friend was soon desperate to return the work, blaming a run of bad luck on it. 'The thing,' said Bardens, 'seemed to have a baleful influence'.[41]

In 2000 Bill Stoneham's 1972 painting *The Hands Resist Him* was put up for auction on eBay. It shows a five-year-old boy standing next to a life-size female doll in front of a glass door. Behind them hands are pressed up against the glass. In the sale's description it was claimed that the figures could come to life: 'One morning our four-and-a-half-year-old daughter claimed that the children in the picture were fighting and coming into the room during the night.' There was even a photograph showing the doll threatening the boy with a gun. Quickly becoming known as 'the haunted eBay painting', thousands of curious visitors were accessing the page, some reporting that it made them violently ill, faint, or feel as though an 'unseen entity' had gripped them, whilst children reportedly screamed on seeing it. Bidding went from an initial $199 to end at $1,050. A lengthy disclaimer sought to absolve the sellers from any legal liability resulting from these claims.[42]

Sports equipment has also been known to exhibit supernatural phenomena. In 2005 a woman in St George, Ontario, Canada, bought a set of antique lawn bowls from a junk shop. That night she was woken by a loud thunk and the sound of one of the balls rolling across the floor. There is even the story of a haunted trampoline in the US. Three children all aged around

[41] Bardens, p. 233.
[42] Gavin Bevis, 'The eBay Haunted Painting', BBC.co.uk, July 2002.

nine years old were lying on a trampoline when they saw a face appear underneath it: an orange face with black hair and black-and-blue eyes. The trampoline then started shaking violently and the face let out a terrifying scream. The children ran inside and watched as a gang of spirits appeared to take over their playground, bouncing on the trampoline, swinging on the swings and bobbing up and down on the see-saw. However, the most unlikely ghost has to be the bag of soot that lurks in a lane in Crowborough, East Sussex, waiting to pounce on unsuspecting passers-by.[43]

The most notable absence in the list of ghostly inanimate objects is buildings. Whilst the 'haunted house' is the basis of so many cases, there is no apparitional house in itself. Why this should be so is not clear. The range of locations is diverse in the extreme, from castles and stately homes to council houses and lampposts. The grander sorts of building probably feature more often in the ghost hunter's guidebooks simply because they have been around the longest, although there is an argument that the types of construction materials themselves could be contributory if not actually causal. The single exception I have uncovered so far is Sir Victor Goddard's sighting of an airfield, complete with hangars, aircraft and personnel, about five years before it was built, and here we must note that this is much more in the nature of a premonition than a classic haunting.[44]

G. W. Lambert categorized a number of cases involving buildings and features of the landscape as 'phantom scenery'. The most famous cases were the vanishing buildings/features of Boscastle, Bradfield St George, Hailsham, Man Sands and Versailles. Members of the Society for Psychical Research managed to track down these alleged phantoms and establish

---

[43] Richard Freeman, 'Just Too Weird!', *Paranormal*, 50, August 2010, pp. 42, 44; 'Strawberry Girl', 'Haunted Bowling Balls', About.com, January 2008, http://paranormal.about.com/library/blstory_january08_05.htm, accessed 2 September 2010; Maddie, 'Haunted Trampoline', About.com, June 2008, http://paranormal.about.com/library/blstory_june08_21.htm, accessed 2 September 2010.

[44] Blundell and Boar, p. 116.

that they were real. The explanation then was simply one of what Lambert called 'mislocation': the percipients looked in the wrong places when searching for the original feature. Only the Georgian house in Hadleigh that apparently appeared and disappeared one day in 1946 remained undiscovered by diligent researchers, at least until the late 1990s. Melvin Harris found the house on maps of a local authority neighbouring those that had already been checked.[45]

Orbs

Who could forget the scene in the film *The Omen* when successive photographs of the priest show a dark, spear-like shape moving towards him? Invisible to the naked eye, it seemed as though the camera that never lies could also capture the supernatural. For many ghost hunters it also seems as if their cameras have recorded an invisible paranormal reality lurking beyond the grasp of our human senses. The internet buzzes with talk of spirit orbs, ghost orbs, even unicorn orbs, as well as plasmoids, 'ectoplasm', vortices and rods. 'In the hundreds of Orb pictures we have examined we have seen the spirits of those who have passed away', argue Diana Cooper and Kathy Crosswell in their 2009 book *Enlightenment Through Orbs*. The International Ghost Hunters Society stated 'we discovered that an orb represented the soul of a departed person'. However, according to Maurice Townsend, writing for the Association for the Scientific Study of Anomalous Phenomena (ASSAP) website, 'there is overwhelming evidence that orbs are out of focus bits of dust and raindrops'.[46]

---

[45] G. W. Lambert, 'Phantom Scenery', *Journal of the Society of Psychical Research*, 42, 1963, pp. 1–6; M. H. Coleman, 'Phantom Scenery', *Journal of the Society of Psychical Research*, 63, 1998–99, pp. 47–8.

[46] Diana Cooper and Kathy Crosswell, *Enlightenment Through Orbs*, Findhorn Press, 2009, p. 55. International Ghost Hunters Society (IGHS) quoted in John Potts, 'Ghost Hunting in the Twenty-First Century', in James Houran

Giant shadows of unseen people across the tunnel wall, running, intent on killing – it is one of the most abiding images of the film *28 Days Later*, but for some it has also become a hideous reality. The earlier shades and shadows – the Greek *skia* (σκιά) and Latin *umbra* of the Classical world – have found a new lease of life, if one can use that term, as 'shadow people'. Often seen as a new phenomenon, the concept is not a new one, but it has become extremely popular. The range of interpretation is drifting, too, from ghosts to extraterrestrials to the undead to demons to angels, although they rarely seem to be benign.

In the early years of the twentieth century, Elliott O'Donnell recounted a time when he met what he described as 'a tall, black figure, its polished ebony skin shining in the moonbeams'. It moved without sound and had no face, only two sinister slit-like eyes. Then there was the haunted oak chest from Limerick, bought by a Mrs McNeill, that acted like a magnet to shadowy entities: 'She actually saw them gliding towards the house, in shoals . . . Shadows of all sorts . . .'[47]

One of the earliest encounters with the new shadow people was reported by the editor of *Paranormal* magazine, Richard Holland. In 1976 during a second phase of poltergeist activity in Holland's childhood, he started to see 'swiftly moving shadows' out of the corner of his eye. Ranging from six to ten inches in length they would 'slither across the floor like slicks of oil'. Maurice Towns recalled how, as a child in 1979, he saw 'a huge dark muscular male shadow materialize in front of me' on Exposition Boulevard, Los Angeles. One dark morning in 2007 he saw what he thought was the same shadow figure again. In 1983 a woman called Dottie was disturbed by her cat's growling one night after going to bed. In the

---

(ed.), *From Shaman to Scientist*, Scarecrow Press, 2004, p. 221. The IGHS claims to have coined the word 'orbs' in 1996. Maurice Townsend, 'Orbs – Are They Paranormal?', Association for the Scientific Study of Anomalous Phenomena, 2007, http://www.assap.org/newsite/articles/Paranormal%20orbs. html, accessed 17 December 2010.

[47] Brad Steiger, 'Who are the Shadow People?', *Paranormal*, 44, February 2010, pp. 54–9; O'Donnell, pp. 36, 41.

dim light she could make out a 'black shadow of a man with a hat on'. He was standing flat against the wall and the percipient thought he was trying to hide from the cat. When she switched on her bedside light the figure disappeared, but the cat went over to investigate the spot and 'sniffed and sniffed'. Dottie concluded, 'I'll never forget it and I know they are real'. Another early experience was recorded in 1999 by someone known only as Tracy G.: 'Often at night, but only when I am driving, I can see these dark shadows dashing across the road as I drive. They first started out to be cats, and on the highways I see people.' In 2000 another shadow cat joined the supernatural menagerie of an invisible bird and a 'black lizard' said to be haunting an American house. A shapeless black form lurks about the 'Devil's Elbow' on the B6105 in Longendale, UK. Possibly the earliest experience reported comes from author Jason Offut, who interviewed a man who said he had seen shadow people as a child in the late 1940s.[48]

As well as visible effects, there are ghostly phenomena of sound, smell and touch, but thankfully not taste. Footsteps and voices are common. The smell of lavender seems a favourite of the otherworld. I frequently get unaccountable wafts of a flowery odour as I sit in my study, seemingly from the corner of the room where I keep a picture of my late grandmother, although I would not go so far as to connect the two. At other times, things brush past people, or even, disturbingly, seem to apply direct physical force such as shoves, kicks, pokes and strangulation. And of

---

[48] Richard Holland, 'The Editor's Experience', *Paranormal*, 44, February 2010, p. 58; Maurice Towns, 'Muscular Shadow Man Stalker', About. com, September 2010, http://paranormal.about.com/od/shadowpeople/a/tales_10_09_19t.htm, accessed 2 September 2010; Dottie, 'Shadow Man with Hat', About.com, September 2010, http://paranormal.about.com/od/shadowpeople/a/tales_10_09_07t.htm, accessed 2 September 2010; Tracy G., 'Dark Shadows', About.com, December 1999, http://paranormal.about.com/library/blstory_december99.htm, accessed 2 September 2010; Kamala, 'Shadow Animals', About.com, January 2000, http://paranormal.about.com/library/blstory_january00.htm, accessed 2 September 2010; Paul Devereux, *Paranormal Review*, 15, 2000, p. 28. The 'shadow people' had, at this stage, not yet made it into popular collections, such as Guiley, *Enc. of Ghosts*. Jason Offut, *Darkness Walks: The Shadow People Among Us*, Anomalist Books, 2009.

course, we also get reports of a 'sixth sense': awareness of presence, of being watched, or of feeling 'spooked'.

Electronic Voice Phenomena (EVP)

In the summer of 1959 the Swedish artist and film-maker Friedrich Jurgenson (1903–87) was recording bird song. When he played the tapes back he was surprised to hear faint voices. Intrigued, he conducted further experiments into what he called 'voices from space'. When he heard the voice of his deceased mother calling him by her pet name for him, he was convinced that he had established 'a radio-link with the dead'. The Latvian scientist Dr Konstantin Raudive (1906–74), then lecturing at the University of Uppsala, heard about Jurgenson's work and after making over 100,000 recordings of his own published his findings as *Breakthrough: An Amazing Experiment in Electronic Communication with the Dead* (1971). This led to the phenomena being called Raudive Voices for a time. Generally, the recordings sound like a word, or a short group of words of few syllables, what Dr Carlo Tajna called the 'psychophonic style'. Other researchers, such as David Ellis and Professor James Alcock, have suggested that such 'voices' could be misinterpreted terrestrial radio signals, static interference effects, or auditory apophenia (also pareidolia) – where the brain finds meaningful patterns in random stimuli. Professor Hans Bender in Germany thought that the effect might be a demonstration of psychokinesis, rather than a spiritual phenomenon. After the early audio experiments, German pensioner Klaus Schreiber became famous for receiving images of his dead relatives on a television set in the 1980s. Using a variation of Schreiber's technique, Martin Wenzel even claimed to have received a picture of Jurgenson. The range of phenomena reported has grown to include telephone, video, television and computers – leading to the new term 'instrumental transcommunication' (ITC).[49]

---

[49] See David Ellis, 'Listening to the "Raudive Voices"', *Journal of the Society of*

Ghost Hunters

> Haunted House. – Responsible persons of leisure and intelli-
> gence, intrepid, critical, and unbiased, are invited to join rota
> of observers in a year's night and day investigation of alleged
> haunted house in Home Counties. Printed instructions
> supplied. Scientific training or ability to operate simple instru-
> ments an advantage. House situated in lonely hamlet, so own
> car is essential.

When Harry Price's advert for ghost hunters appeared in *The
Times* on 25 May 1937, 200 people applied. After careful screen-
ing, he chose forty-eight to help him investigate the infamous
Borley Rectory. Each of his ghost hunters, or 'Official Observers'
as they were called, was required to sign the '"Haunted House" –
Declaration Form', Price's unofficial secrets act, which prevented
any of his observers from acting independently. Price published
two books on the rectory and was writing another when he died in
1948, and it was this work, perhaps more than his other interests,
that has kept his name alive. Dr Paul Tabori called his 1950 biography *Harry Price – The Biography of a Ghost Hunter*.

Price was not, however, the first ghost hunter. An early case
of a 'ghost-detector' was recounted in the first issue of *The
Spiritual Magazine* in January 1860. Events took place twenty
years earlier in 1840 at 'the far-famed house' of Willington
Mill, near Newcastle. A certain Joseph Proctor, described as 'a
plain unimaginative Quaker', complaining of being troubled
by an apparition, attracted the aid of Edward Drury of
Sunderland, 'a valiant and self-confident man' and 'ghost-
detector'. Determined to solve the mystery, Drury and an
accomplice searched the house from cellar to garret to rule out

Psychical Research, 48, 1975, pp. 31–42; Arthur S. Berger, Gerd H. Hovelmann
and Walter von Lucadou, 'Spirit Extras on Video Tape?', *Journal of the Society of Psychical Research*, 58, 1992, pp. 153ff; James Alcock, 'Electronic Voice
Phenomena: Voices of the Dead?', *Skeptical Inquirer*, 21 December 2004.

any 'contrivances being played off upon them'. Drury then stationed himself in the haunted room, armed with pistols, whilst his confederate watched the stairs outside the door. At around midnight, as the candles had burnt low, 'the well-known female figure issued from the closet near Drury, walked or glided slowly past him, and approached his friend on the landing'. The writer notes that this was the moment to seize the phantom or discharge a pistol at it. Some say that he did try and grab the ghost, others that Drury's valiant character failed him. By all accounts, he screamed and collapsed on the floor. Briefly coming round, 'he went out of one fit into another till three o'clock in the morning'. His constant refrain was 'there she is. Keep her off. For God's sake, keep her off'. Proctor and his friend feared he had lost his mind, but he recovered after many weeks' recuperation. Drury's career as a 'ghost-detector' was singularly short and unsuccessful.[50]

William Hope Hodgson entertained the reading public in 1913 with his stories of a paranormal investigator in *Carnacki the Ghost Finder*. However, the first person to use the term 'ghost hunter' of himself was Elliott O'Donnell in the title of his 1916 book *Twenty Years' Experience as a Ghost Hunter*. In 1928 he published *Confessions of a Ghost Hunter*. Price caught on to the term and published his own *Confessions of a Ghost Hunter* in 1936 with chapters on the 'Talking Mongoose' and 'How to Test a Medium'.[51]

In 1937 Harry Price supplied instructions to his observers in the form of an eight-page booklet called 'The Alleged Haunting at B----- Rectory – Instructions for Observers', the colour of its cover lending it the more informal title of the 'Blue Book'. This covered such things as how to write up reports and what to do when dealing with unexplained phenomena. The Society for Psychical Research also sets out some guidelines on its website for today's investigators:[52]

---

[50] 'Modern Sadducism', *Spiritual Magazine*, 1.1, 1860, pp. 15–16; W. T. Stead, *Real Ghost Stories*, Grant Richards, 1897, pp. 261, 264–5.

[51] Davies, p. 95.

[52] Adapted from 'Notes for Investigators', spr.ac.uk, 2009, http://www.spr.ac.uk/main/page/notes-investigators-paranormal, accessed 16 December 2010.

1. Do not go by yourself.
2. Keep your relations with the experients/witnesses as relaxed and friendly as possible.
3. Keep an open mind.
4. Be tactful, or even reticent, in expressing your views.
5. Do not play the amateur psychiatrist.
6. Respect the confidentiality of the case.
7. Take particular care where children are involved.
8. Avoid publicity.
9. Learn from one's mistakes.

Price was involved with the first live broadcast from a haunted house. On 10 March 1936 the BBC rigged up four microphones to record the 'muffled footsteps and tappings, a cellar door which opens suddenly, and cold, uncanny winds' that writer G. B. Harrison said were reputed to haunt Dean Manor near Rochester in Kent. Price revealed his ghost-hunting methodology to listeners. Wax and powdered starch were sprinkled on the floor to detect footprints. Powdered graphite was used to dust for fingerprints. Thermometers were set up to record temperature drops – long associated with ghostly manifestations. The thermometer 'fluctuated inexplicably', said Harrison, but all he and the other listeners heard was 'the usual crackling in their loud-speakers'.[53]

Popular US TV shows *Ghost Hunters* and *Ghost Hunters International* feature the use of high-end equipment ranging from the K2 Deluxe EMF Meter, the Zoom H4N Handy Recorder for portable digital audio recording, to the Phonic Personal Audio Assistant for professional real-time digital audio analysis. Other investigators construct their own custom apparatus. Tony Cornell and Howard Wilkinson built what they called the SPIDER (Spontaneous   Psychophysical   Incident   Data   Electronic

---

[53] George Bagshawe Harrison, *The Day Before Yesterday: Being a Journal of the Year 1936*, Cobden-Sanderson, 1938, p. 65; Davies, p. 95. Also reported in the *Revue Métaphysique*, 1936, p. 157.

Popular Ghost-Hunting Equipment

Air Ion Counter	detects natural and artificial ion levels, either scaled to show negative ions (Negative Ion Detector, or NID) or both negative and positive ions
EMF Meter	measures a varying electromagnetic field (EMF) caused by AC or DC fields, usually calibrated to the frequency of mains electricity 50 Hz (US) and 60 Hz (European)
Gauss Meter	measures the polarity and strength of a static magnetic field in milli-Gauss (mG) or nanoTesla (nT) used to measure the earth's geomagnetic field, also described as a magnetometer
Beam Barrier Alarm	uses a transmitter and receiver unit to create an invisible infra-red beam barrier, triggering an alarm when broken
Motion Detector	uses a passive infra-red field to detect movement within a given area, typically 60 to 110° arc, triggering an alarm or other function
Hygro-Thermometer	measures maximum and minimum ranges of humidity, typically 20–99% relative humidity (RH); some models combine temperature measurement
IR Thermometer	non-contact thermometer using infra-red to measure ranges from -33 to +250°C in some models

Recorder), a complex array of sensors and cameras.[54] While this sort of kit would set the ghost hunter back several thousand pounds, for about a hundred pounds the beginner can assemble the basics of today's gadget-led investigation.

The typical starter kit includes a Gauss meter, beam barrier alarm, IR thermometer and a torch.[55] With these the ghost hunter can measure electromagnetic fields and temperature, set up an infra-red beam alarm to detect intruders (who may or may not be supernatural) and, most importantly, see in the dark. The range of devices available to measure everything from humidity to air ionization and ELF to LUX can be quite bewildering. Aimed at diverse professionals – sound engineers, electricians, health and environmental inspectors, etc. – such equipment requires technical expertise to operate and interpret correctly.

Without the benefit of any of this modern gadgetry, investigators at Borley were still able to come to some conclusions about the haunting. In 1947 the legendary ghost hunter Peter Underwood visited Borley for the first time. The burnt out ruins had already been demolished in 1944, but the paranormal anomalies associated with the site persisted. Underwood spent a night there with a colleague and both of them heard unaccountable footsteps in the dark. Rather than any specific instrumentation readings, he cited the number of years over which paranormal phenomena have been reported, the many witnesses to such phenomena and the diversity of the phenomena themselves as convincing proof of the claims associated with the site. After sixty years researching the haunting, he concluded that 'I do think Borley Rectory justified the term "the most haunted house in England"'. Ubiquitous bungalows now blight the spot, but for many it has become something of a paranormal pilgrimage site.[56]

---

[54] See Tony Cornell, *Investigating the Paranormal*, Helix Press, 2002; and the review in *Journal of Parapsychology*, 67, 2003, p. 190.

[55] Starter kit as advertised in *Paranormal*, March 2010, back cover, priced at £104.99.

[56] John Stoker, 'Memoirs of a Ghost-Hunting Man', *Paranormal*, March 2010, p. 55.

Poltergeists

'Marianne get help' read the writing scrawled on the wall: sharp, angular letters amidst illegible scribbles. Bravely, Marianne replied, writing underneath 'I cannot understand, tell me more'. Some days later more messages appeared: 'lights – Mass and prayers'; and on the opposite wall, 'Marianne please get help'. Marianne Foyster, her husband, Revd Lionel Algernon Foyster, MA, and their adopted daughter Adelaide, then two-and-a-half years old, had moved into Borley Rectory on 16 October 1930, only months after the haunting had driven out the beleaguered Smiths.[57]

'It can be said without fear of contradiction,' wrote Harry Price, 'that the Foyster occupation coincided with the noisiest, most violent, and most dangerous period in the whole recorded history of the Borley manifestations.' What began as a classic haunting, with nuns and headless coachmen, was turning into a much more serious poltergeist infestation. Price recalled a case in Amherst, Nova Scotia, during 1878–9, called 'The Great Amherst Mystery', that centred around a young girl called Esther Cox. She was threatened several times in mysterious written messages, including one on the bedroom wall that read 'Esther Cox you are mine to kill'. Did the Borley poltergeist ask Marianne for help, or was it warning her that she needed it?[58]

The idea that poltergeists were spirits of the dead is a relatively recent one. Up until the nineteenth century poltergeists were generally seen as the result of witchcraft or demonic interference, rather than spirits of the dead. The case now called the Epworth Poltergeist was not known as such by the Wesley family at its centre. Samuel Wesley referred to it as a 'deaf and dumb devil', whilst his daughter Emily called it 'Old Jeffrey' and attributed it to the spells of a witch or

---

[57] Glanville, pp. 97, 99.
[58] Price, pp. 64, 195.

cunningman. Writing in German, the theologian Martin Luther (1483–1546) was the first person to use the word 'poltergeist', meaning 'noisy spirit', in print. For Luther the answer was simple: poltergeists were the work of the Devil and one need only quote something of the Bible for them to go away, although he admitted that in some instances one just had to let the poltergeist get on with it. It would be another 300 years before it entered the English language via Catherine Crowe's book *The Night-Side of Nature* (1848). But it took Harry Price to popularize the term.[59]

---

[59] Davies, pp. 31–2, 74; Martin Luther, 'Ein Sermon auff das Evangelion von dem reychen man und armen Lazaro', first published 1523, in Ernst Ludwig Enders (ed.), *Dr Martin Luther's sämmtliche Werke: Kirchenpostille*, vol. 4, Hender & Zimmer, 1869, p. 17. See also 'Von Poltergeistern' and 'Historia, wie ein Poltergeist einen Pfarrherrn geplagt habe . . .' in Martin Luther, *D. Martin Luther's sämmtliche Schriften, vol. 22: D. Martin Luther's Tischreden oder Colloquia*, vol. 3, Sebauer'sche Buchhandlung, 1846, pp. 34–6.

2. The Undead

The undead – vampires, mummies, zombies, and the rest – represent our collective fears of death (and sometimes life as well). As well they might – one need only think of the cold earth and the burrowing worm to cast a cloud over even the brightest day. Darkness and decay await us all, and heaven is but a compost heap of mouldering bones.

In their traditional aspects vampires embody the fear of the dead's return for revenge; mummies – within their original Egyptian cosmology – are an attempt to transcend death and live in the afterlife; and the Haitian zombies, the slave's fear of servitude after death. But all of them have been transformed in modern culture. Vampires have become a dream of triumph over death and power without conscience. Mummies now represent the revenge of the dead. The zombies we see from George A. Romero onwards are in actuality a fear of modern life, that we are dead to life without realizing it in our modern faceless, consumerist culture, controlled by the black magicians of advertising and government. With the modern zombie, it is ordinary people – our friends and neighbours – who become the enemy, an auto-immune disorder of society. With the modern vampire, it is extraordinary people – strangers and foreigners – who become the object of desire. In their many representations the undead tell us more about ourselves – the living – than they do about the dead. Perhaps that is because they themselves are not dead either. Before Boris Karloff played the mummy and Bela Lugosi Count Dracula, people really did believe that the dead could return from the grave and, what is more, they very often had what they thought was the evidence to prove it.

Vampires

In 1725 Frombald, the Imperial Provisor of the Gradisker District of the Holy Roman Empire, received a deputation of villagers from 'Kisolova', thought to be modern Kisiljevo in what is now the Republic of Serbia. The villagers were in a state of great alarm. One of their neighbours, a man by the name of Peter Plogojoviz, had died ten weeks ago and buried according to local custom. However, Peter had come back.[60]

His wife said that he had knocked on the door and demanded his *opanki*, the traditional peasant footwear of the region. After she fled the village, other people started saying that they had seen Peter, too. But not just seen him. They said Peter visited them in the night and lay upon them with such force that they felt the life being squeezed out of them. In 24 hours they were dead. Within the space of eight days, nine people had died from Peter's nightly visits. The villagers knew exactly what he was: one of the 'Vampyri', as Frombald carefully noted. To make sure, they wanted to exhume the body and look for the tell-tale signs – the body undecomposed, and the hair, beard and nails still growing – and they wanted the Imperial Provisor and a priest to be present. Frombald told them they would have to wait whilst he sent a request to his superiors in Belgrade. The villagers refused to wait, threatening to leave the village *en masse* before the vampire could kill everyone, as had happened, they

---

[60] Frombald, 'Copia eines Schreibens aus dem Gradisker District', *Wiener-isches Diarium*, 58, 21 July 1725, Kayserliche Hof-Buchdruckerey, pp. 11–12. 'Kisolova' is the word used in the original text, but many later accounts use 'Kisilova'. 'Plogojowitz' is often given, as well as 'Plogojovic', but 'Plogojo-viz' is the form as first published in 1725. See also Jutta Nowosadtko, 'Der "Vampyrus Serviensis" und sein Habitat: Impressionen von der österreich-ischen Militärgrenze', *Militär und Gesellschaft in der Frühen Neuzeit*, 8, 2004, 2, pp. 151–67.

said, sometime before. Frombald explained to them the necessity of waiting. Frombald ordered them to wait. Frombald no
doubt shouted at them. But the Kisolovans were adamant.
Frombald must have mulled the situation over carefully. Serbia
had recently been snatched out of the jaws of the Ottoman
Turks and the region remained politically tense. A deserted
village could have repercussions, not least with his superiors. So
it was, that he found himself taking the road to Kisolova with
the priest and an escort of villagers.

As they entered the village, they found, no doubt to their
surprise, that the body had already been dug up. Frombald lost
no time in inspecting it:

> First, from the body and its grave there was not the slightest
> smell of death. The body, except the nose, which was fallen
> in, was very fresh. The hair and beard, also the nails, the old
> ones having fallen away, had grown on him. The old skin,
> which was somewhat whitish, had peeled off and a fresh new
> one had come out under it. The face, hands and also feet, and
> the whole body, were so recreated that they, in his lifetime,
> could not have been more complete. In his mouth, not with-
> out surprise, did I see fresh blood, which, after the general
> opinion, he had sucked from those killed by him. In sum, all
> the indications were presented which these people (as already
> noted above) should themselves have.[61]

As Frombald and the priest observed the scene – the fresh earth
around the grave, the extraordinary condition of the body – the
villagers were already busy sharpening a stake. Forthwith, they
drove it through the heart of the corpse. Frombald was aghast
as fresh blood spurted from the corpse's ears and mouth, and
the priest must have blushed at the 'other wild signs' that
Frombald declined to describe in his report 'out of high respect'.
The body was then burnt to ashes. Frombald was careful to

---

[61] Frombald, my translation.

point out that if any mistake had been made in this matter – the desecration of a grave and the summary execution of someone who may not have been quite dead, come to mind – then all blame should rest squarely on the fear-crazed peasants.

On 26 January 1732 a report was submitted by Johann Flückinger, regimental surgeon to Baron Fürstenbusch's Infantry Regiment, to Army Headquarters Belgrade. Earlier in the month, he and several other officers had investigated a series of suspicious deaths in the village of 'Medwedia' in Serbia. The accused was a local 'Heyduck' named Arnod Paole or Arnond Parle (often written 'Arnold Paule' in modern accounts). The problem for the investigators was that five years earlier Paole had broken his neck in a fall from a haycart before allegedly committing the crimes. Locals told Flückinger that Paole had been plagued by a vampire some years previously near 'Cassova' in Turkish Serbia, but claimed to have cured himself by eating earth from the vampire's grave and smearing himself with its blood. However, twenty or thirty days after his death people started complaining that Paole had returned from the grave to torment them. Four people subsequently died. The local head-man, who had experience of these matters, ordered them to dig up Paole. His body had not decomposed and fresh blood was seen to come out of eyes, nose and ears; his nails and skin had fallen off to be replaced by new growth. According to local custom, they pierced his heart with a stake whereupon he uttered a loud cry. They burnt the remains to ashes and similarly disposed of the bodies of his victims.[62]

---

[62] W.S.G.E., *Acten-mäßige und Umständliche Relation von denen Vampiren oder Menschen-Saugern, Welche sich in diesem und vorigen Jahren, im Königreich Servien herfürgethan*, Augusto Martini, 1732, pp. 9–15; Johann Christoph Harenberg, *Vernünftige und Christliche Gedancken über die Vampirs*, Meißner, 1733, pp. 27–35. A number of variations between the two are to be noted. The date of the inquiry is given as 7 January in W.S.G.E., and both 7 and 17 January in Harenberg. Due to the inconsistent spelling of the period, the regimental surgeon is Flückinger in W.S.G.E., Flickinger in Harenberg; we find Arnod Paole in W.S.G.E., Arnond Parle in Harenberg; and the village is Medwedia in W.S.G.E., Meduegia in Harenberg. See also Klaus Hamberger

However, according to the locals, some of them had eaten the meat of livestock attacked by Paole. Within three months seventeen people died, some without any apparent disease, in the short space of only two or three days. The officers marched down to the cemetery and ordered the graves of the victims to be opened. Flückinger spread out his instruments and conducted a series of thirteen autopsies, which he carefully documented. A sixty-year-old woman called Miliza was found to be fat and healthy looking, more so, said those who had known her, than she had been in life. She had eaten the meat of sheep killed by vampires and was suspected of spreading the contagion further. The twenty-year-old Stanvicka (or Stanioicka), daughter-in-law of the Heyduck Joviza, was still florid and healthy looking with fresh blood coming from her nose. A bruise was found under her ear, one finger long. It was said that, whilst still alive, she had awoken one night with screams and in great anguish, saying that Joviza's dead son Millove (or Milloe) had returned from the grave and tried to strangle her. Within days she was dead. Other bodies were found to be in a state of normal decomposition despite, Flückinger noted, being buried in close proximity to those in the vampiric condition. Local gypsies were given the task of decapitating the bodies, which were then burnt and the ashes scattered in the Morava river. The decomposed bodies were reburied.

Then there was the case of Stephen Hubner. Some time in the year 1567 Hubner returned to the town of Trutnov in what is today the Czech Republic. The problem was that Hubner had died five months previously. Various deaths amongst the townspeople and their livestock were attributed to him. The magistrate ordered his body to be exhumed. Being found in the vampiric condition the body was decapitated and burnt, and the bodies of those buried next to him were burnt as well to prevent any spread of vampirism.[63]

(ed.), *Mortuus non mordet: Kommentierte Dokumentation zum Vampirismus 1689–1791*, Turia und Kant, 1992, pp. 49–54.

[63] Dudley Wright, *Vampires and Vampirism*, W. Rider, 1914, p. 168; Montague Summers, *The Vampire in Europe, His Kith and Kin*, Kegan Paul, Trench,

These incidents sparked off a public debate and a flurry of publications across the Holy Roman Empire and beyond. There had been an earlier discussion in the late seventeenth century, but now there were apparently well-authenticated cases to consider. In Leipzig, Michael Ranft published on the 'chewing dead' in 1728. In Jena, John Christian Stock wrote of the 'bloody cadavers' in 1732. In the same year, *A Curious and Very Wonderful Relation* about the Serbian 'blood-suckers' was published and further discussed by the medical practitioner Gottlob Vogt in his *Vampiren*. The following year, the theologian and Director of the Essen Gymnasium, Joannis Henr. Zopfius, presided over Christianus Fridericus van Dalen's public defence of the argument that 'Vampyres, which come out of the graves in the night-time, rush upon people sleeping in their beds, suck out all their blood, and destroy them'. The Archbishop of Trani, Italy, Giuseppe Davanzati, penned his own dissertation, winning the praise of Pope Benedict XIV for his efforts. The biblical scholar Dom Augustin Calmet noted in 1746 that:[64]

In this present age and for about sixty years past, we have been the hearers and witnesses of a new series of extraordinary incidents and occurrences. Hungary, Moravia, Silesia, Poland, are the principal theatre of these happenings. For here we are told that dead men, men who have been dead for several months, I say, return from the tomb.

Trubner and Co., 1928, p. 159. Wright gives the German name of Trautenau for the village; Summers, p. 159, 'Treautenau'.

[64] Michael Ranft, *De Masticatione Mortuorum in Tumulis*, Augustus Martinus, 1728; Johann Christian Stock, *Dissertatio de Cadaveribus Sanguisugis*, Littertis Hornianis, 1732; W.S.G.E., *Curieuse und sehr wunderbare Relation, von denen sich neuer Dingen in Servien erzeigenden Blut-Saugern oder Vampyrs*, n.p., 1732; Gottlob Heinrich Vogt, *Kurtzes Bedencken Von denen Acten-maeßigen Relationen Wegen derer Vampiren, Oder Menschen- Und Vieh-Aussaugern*, Augustus Martinus, 1732; Joannis Henricus Zopfius, *Dissertatio de Vamypris Serviensibus*, J. Sas, 1733; Giuseppe Davanzati, *Dissertazione sopra I Vampiri*, Fratelli Raimondi, 1744; Augustin Calmet, *Traité sur les Apparitions des Esprits et sur les Vampires*, Debure l'aine, 1751, trans. in Summers, p. 27. See also Hamberger. My thanks to librarian Hanke Immega, Aurich, for clarifying the question of the authorship of Zopfius, *Dissertatio*.

In 'The Travels of Three English Gentlemen', published in 1745, the word vampire first entered the English language. Staying in a town they called Laubach (Laibach, now Ljubljana) in what was then the Duchy of Carniola and now Slovenia, their unnamed landlord told them that:

> Vampyres are supposed to be the Bodies of deceased Persons, animated by evil Spirits, which come out of the Graves, in the Night-time, suck the Blood of many of the Living, and thereby destroy them.[65]

Of course, the vampire did not first stir in the eighteenth century. We might trace the theme of blood-sucking back to the demonesses Lamia and Lilith, and the Empusae, Lamiae and Lilitum (see the chapter on demons). The idea of the dead returning from the grave is likewise ancient. We might think of the Nordic *draugr* who haunted burial howes and barrows, abusing those who ventured too close with harsh words and stone-throwing, or even sallying forth, sometimes with other undead companions, to ravage the land and slay the people. Then there are flesh-eating, blood-drinking fairies known in the folklore of Ireland and Scotland: *glaistigs*, *leanan sidhe* and *baobhan sith* – entities that used an attractive female countenance to seduce and destroy unwary males; as well as the night-walking corpses, the *marbh bheo*; and the blood-sucking *dearg-dul*. The folklore of Greece is haunted by the *strigla*, akin to the Italian *strega* and Roman *strix*, a witch who can assume the shape of a bird and so visit her victims and suck their blood. The genuine vampire in this region is the *vourkolakas* or *vrykolakas*, a term that further north shades into the werewolf as the Polish *vilkolak*.[66]

---

[65] Published in *The Harleian Miscellany*, 4, 1745, p. 358. Summers, p. 26, following the *OED*, stated that this was written in 1734.
[66] For the *draugr* see the story of Hrapp in the Icelandic *Laxdoela Saga* (c. 13th century) and that of Thorolf Halt-foot in the *Eyrbyggia Saga* (14th century). William Scrope told of a vampire encounter in the Scottish Highlands in his *The Art of Deer-Stalking*, A. Spottiswoode, 1838, p. 241. The living belief in the

In 2009 archaeologists excavating a mass grave on the Venetian island of Lazzaretto Nuovo discovered the skeleton of a woman with a brick rammed into her mouth. News quickly spread that they had unearthed a vampire. Matteo Borrini of the University of Florence explained that the brick had been placed there to prevent the corpse from chewing its shroud. He claimed that these remains, buried in 1576 following a plague outbreak, constituted the first vampire to have been forensically examined, although Peer Moore-Jansen of Wichita State University said similar skeletons had previously been found in Poland. Post-mortem practices to prevent the return of the dead have a long history.[67]

Noises, especially grunting 'like the sound of porkers', according to Philipp Rohr in 1679, were frequently heard emanating from graveyards, particularly, it was said, during plague epidemics. When the bodies were inspected many of them were found with torn shrouds and bitten or even partially eaten limbs, leading to the theory that the dead had done it to themselves. These 'chewing dead' were widely blamed for spreading the plague.[68]

Even after all the stakings and burnings, the vampire did not find eternal peace in the eighteenth century. Vampires prowled the area in and around Danzig, according to reports from 1820 and 1855. The occultist Dr Franz Hartmann (1838–1912) claimed to know of a number of vampire cases. A certain couple

---

Baobhan Sith was recorded as late as 1908 on the Island of Bernera, Lewis, in 'Fairy Tales', *The Celtic Review*, 5.18, October 1908, pp. 155–71. Bob Curran, *Vampires: A Field Guide to Creatures that Stalk the Night*, Career Press, 2005, pp. 55–79; Rennell Rodd, *The Customs and Lore of Modern Greece*, David Stott, 1892, p. 187; John Cuthbert Lawson, *Modern Greek Folklore and Ancient Greek Religion*, Cambridge University Press, 1910, pp. 364f.

[67] '"Vampire" Discovered in Mass Grave', *New Scientist*, 2698, 7 March 2009; Owen Davies, *The Haunted: A Social History of Ghosts*, Palgrave Macmillan, 2009, p. 71.

[68] Henerici Kornmanni, *De Miraculis Mortuorum*, I. Wolffii, 1610; Philippus Rohr, *Dissertatio Historico-Philosophica de Masticatione Mortuorum*, Michaelis Vogtii, 1679.

in Vienna in the 1880s had the misfortune to have a vampire for an uncle, who not only metaphorically bled them dry, but also consumed the life energy of the lawyer they had engaged to contest the uncle's sharp practice. Shortly before 1895, a young woman living near Vienna was troubled by the vampiric spirit of a spurned suitor who had committed suicide. Another incident from 1909 described as 'An Authenticated Case of Vampirism' reads like *Dracula* fan fiction. In 1900 Augustus J. C. Hare published his autobiography in which we find the story of Captain Fisher's encounter with the fearful vampire of Croglin Grange in Cumberland.[69]

Before they had faced the ghosts of Borley, Harry Price's National Laboratory of Psychical Research (NLPR) had encountered the vampire. In 1926 the Countess Wassilko-Serecki brought a thirteen-year-old Romanian peasant girl to London. The girl, Eleonore Zügun, was being tormented by an entity she called Dracu, the Devil. Captain Neil Gow of the NLPR began the investigation, noting on Monday, 4 October 1926 at 3.20 p.m., that 'Eleonore cried out. Showed marks on back of left hand like teeth marks'. Drinking tea less than an hour later, she 'suddenly gave a cry [. . .] there was a mark on her right hand similar to that caused by a bite'. The captain recorded that 'Both rows of teeth were indicated'. There are other instances of poltergeist activity causing bite marks, such as the bat-like 'puncture marks' noted in the Indianapolis 'Biting Poltergeist' case.[70]

In 1892 F. S. Krauss said that the Serbians still daubed tar crosses on their doors to ward off vampires. By the 1970s

---

[69] Hartmann, 'A Modern Case of Vampirism', *Lucifer*, 4, May 1889, pp. 241f; Hartmann, *Borderland*, III, 1895, cited in Summers, pp. 163–4 – also Hartmann, 'A Miller of D---', *The Occult Review*, November 1924, pp. 258–9; Augustus Hare, *The Story of My Life*, vol. 4, George Allen, 1900, pp. 203–8; Hartmann, 'An Authenticated Vampire Story', *The Occult Review*, September 1909; Summers, pp. 160–1.

[70] *Proceedings of the National Laboratory of Psychical Research*, 1, 1927, quoted in Summers, pp. 5–6; William George Roll, *The Poltergeist*, Cosimo, 2004, pp. 56ff.

Andrew Mackenzie, former Vice-President of the Society for Psychical Research and a frequent traveller to Eastern Europe in search of the paranormal, was unable to find anyone in Transylvania who believed in vampires. The vampires had moved. Like Bram Stoker's Count Dracula, they had left the romantic castles and forested wildernesses to descend upon the modern urban environment.[71]

When Rosemary Guiley interviewed three dozen or so self-proclaimed vampires for her book *Vampires Among Us* it was a disappointment to find that none of them claimed to have come back from the dead, surely the essential requirement of being a vampire, or to be centuries old. Guiley observed that those who called themselves vampires tended to be introverted and claimed an abusive childhood background. As a reviewer remarked: 'vampirism tended to be confined to wearing black, staying up late, and drinking a little blood every now and again'. [72]

'I tried different things,' said the twenty-something woman calling herself Hirudo. 'I was always thirsty, so I would drink gallons and gallons of water. But the craving didn't go away.' She was somewhat tall, red hair pulled back, swathed in a military greatcoat and talking to a journalist in a pub in Burnt Oak, London. 'It just clicked,' she continued. 'I knew I had this specific craving for blood.' For some that craving would become almost impossible to bear. The journalist in this case lived to tell the tale, but not everyone would be so lucky.[73]

Susan Walsh was an attractive blue-eyed blonde, making a living as a stripper in New York and trying to break into journalism with a story on vampirism. There were wild rumours of

---

[71] Friedrich Salomo Krauss, 'Vampyre im südslavischen Volksglauben', *Globus*, lxi, 1892, p. 326; Eric Farge, 'Obituary: Andrew Mackenzie, 1911–2001', *Journal of the Society of Psychical Research*, 66.2, 2002, p. 128; see Andrew Mackenzie, *Dracula Country: Travels and Folk Beliefs in Romania*, Arthur Baker, 1977.

[72] Rosemary Ellen Guiley, *Vampires Among Us*, Pocket Books, 1992; reviewed by Tom Ruffles in *Paranormal Review*, 1993, p. 49.

[73] Nick Compton, 'In Search of the Urban Vampires', *This is London*, 5 April 2002.

Mafia involvement and a government-vampire conspiracy to rule the world. She had allegedly told friends that she was frightened for her life and her boyfriend at the time said that she had been receiving anything up to fifteen threatening calls a day. One of Walsh's contacts in the vampire scene had warned that 'If you begin to hunt for vampires, the vampires will begin to hunt for you.' Walsh disappeared in 1996.[74]

When police were called to the flat of Aaron Homer and his girlfriend Amanda Williamson in 2010, they found a trail of blood leading up to the front door. Homer said that Williamson had been attacked, but the police found stab victim Robert Maley nearby. They were into 'vampire stuff and paganism' Maley told police, alleging that Homer had stabbed him after he refused to let the couple drink his blood. The homeless Maley had been staying with the couple and had apparently let them drink his blood in the past. He was lucky to escape with his life.[75]

For some it was pure blood lust, for others it was the supernatural attraction of blood as the life-force that drove them to murder. From the infamous Countess Bathory in the early 1600s, to the mysterious Atlas Vampire in the 1930s, to Richard Trenton Chase, the 'Vampire of Sacramento', in the 1970s, the 'Vampire Rapist' John Brennan Crutchley convicted in 1986, to 1990s murderer Roderick Ferrell who claimed to be a 500-year-old vampire called Vesago, there have always been individuals willing to cross the line.

'Pitch-black vampire seeks princess of darkness who hates everything and everyone.' When Manuela read those words in an advert in a heavy metal magazine in 2000 she knew she had

---

[74] Katherine Ramsland, *Piercing the Darkness: Undercover With the Vampires in America Today*, HarperPrism, 1998, pp. 1–4; T. A. Kevlin, *Headless Man in Topless Bar: Studies of 725 Cases of Strip Club Related Criminal Homicides*, Dog Ear Publishing, 2007, pp. 55–6.

[75] Michael Sheridan, 'Blood-Sucking "Vampires" Arrested for Attacking Homeless Man with Knife in Arizona, Police Say', *New York Daily News*, 10 October 2010.

found her soul mate. Daniel Ruda was a car-parts salesman in Bochum, Germany, who shared her love of the dark side. When she first met Daniel, Manuela had already been initiated into the underground vampire scene in London. 'We went out at night, to cemeteries, in ruins and in the woods,' she said. 'We drank blood together from willing donors.' She had even had special fangs fitted. With Daniel she would eventually turn to unwilling donors. Manuela would later deny it was murder, saying that Satan had ordered them to kill thirty-three-year-old Frank Haagen on 6 July 2001. Daniel smashed him on the head with a hammer before Manuela 'heard the command to stab him in the heart'. They then carved a pentagram into his flesh and drank his blood. The couple remained defiant in court as the judge handed down sentences of fifteen years for Daniel and thirteen years for Manuela.[76]

In Australia the high-profile trial of Evangelos Goussis for the shooting of crime boss Lewis Moran took the headlines in 2008, but an informant also implicated him in the murder of a self-confessed vampire. In 2003 the twenty-eight-year-old victim, a male prostitute called Shane Chartres-Abbott, was on trial for the brutal rape of a client. Before the violent assault Chartres-Abbott allegedly told his victim, a thirty-year-old Thai woman, that he was a 200-year-old vampire who drank blood to stay young. The woman was later found unconscious and covered in blood. There were teeth marks on her thigh and part of her tongue had been bitten off. Chartres-Abbott was later shot dead as he made his way to the County Court to give evidence. In 2009 a reward of Aus$ 1 million was offered for information to solve the case of the so-called 'gigolo vampire'.[77]

---

[76] 'Satanists Killed Man "on Devil's Orders"', BBC News, 18 January 2002; Rebecca Jones, 'Judgement Day for German Satanists', BBC News, 30 January 2002; Tony Helm, 'Last Kiss as Satanist Killers are Locked Up', *Daily Telegraph*, 1 February 2002. The *Daily Telegraph* gave the victim's name as Hackerts.

[77] Elissa Hunt, et al., 'Evangelos Goussis Named in Vampire Murder', *Herald Sun*, 30 May 2008; Keith Moor, 'Six Murder Charges Loom in "Vampire" Case', *Herald Sun*, 26 October, 2009 Keith Moor, 'Behind the Vampire Gigolo

Lead bullets are not the traditional way of dealing with super-natural blood-suckers. With instances of the true vampire diminishing, new strains of the monster have appeared. In 1896 Dr Hatmann detailed the 'psychic sponge', mental vampires who 'unconsciously vampirize every sensitive person with whom they come in contact'. He related the case of an old woman who hired young maids expressly for the purpose of absorbing them in this manner. In 1924 Dr Eugene Osty, direc-tor of the Institut Métapsychique Internationale, described the baneful animal magnetism of 'heart-vampires who burn and devour all affection approaching them'. But it would be Dion Fortune in 1930 who would establish the idea of what she called 'psychic parasitism' and what would later be known as psychic vampirism.[78]

'We thirst for life,' explained self-described psychic vampire Michelle Belanger, 'and we feed upon it.' Of course, Fortune offered advice on protecting oneself from psychic vampires. It would take a little longer for would-be psychic vampires to get their own manual. Belanger has written widely on the topic, as well as appearing on television programmes, such as History Channel's *Vampire Secrets* (2006), which also covered the disap-pearance of Susan Walsh. According to Belanger, 'a psychic vampire is a person who needs to take human energy from others in order to maintain their health and well-being'.[79]

Want to 'live beyond the usual human lifespan' and 'get your way with people'? The Temple of the Vampire, a legal entity in the USA since 1989, teaches that the vampire is a living god and offers you the chance to join their ranks for a membership fee

---

Shane Chartres-Abbott Murder', *Herald Sun*, 26 October 2009.

[78] Hartmann cited in Summers, pp. 134–5, as *Borderland*, III.3, July 1896, pp. 353–8; Eugene Osty, *Supernormal Faculties in Man: An Experimental Study*, trans. Stanley de Brath, Methuen & Co., 1923, p. 150; Dion Fortune, *Psychic Self-Defence*, Rider, 1930.

[79] Michelle Belanger, *The Vampire Codex*, self-published, c. 2000; re-released as *The Psychic Vampire Codex*, Weiser, 2004. Eleanor Goodman, 'Go Suck Yourself: Psychic Vampires', *Bizarre*, Hallowe'en 2008, p. 88; http://www.vampiretemple.com/, accessed 16 September 2010.

of $75. The Temple of the Vampire is only one of many organizations that have appeared, like blood stains on Count Dracula's shirt front, to celebrate the vampire lifestyle and network its followers. Others include Belanger's House Kheperu, Sanguinarius.org and the Vampyre Connexion.

Vampires are currently enjoying a vogue not seen since the eighteenth century. From Anne Rice's seminal *Interview With the Vampire* to Stephenie Meyer's *Twilight* saga a vein of popular interest has been tapped and shows no sign of running dry. Despite this, the latest research shows that very few people actually believe in vampires today: only 3 per cent in the UK.[80]

Some have looked to rare medical conditions to account for the origination of vampire beliefs. The disease of porphyria whose symptoms are photosensitivity and anaemia is a particular favourite. Blood drinking as a medical treatment in the case of porphyria is ineffective, however. Whilst a condition like porphyria might resemble folk ideas of vampirism it cannot explain them since these folk beliefs are specifically concerned with the problem of the returning dead, not with human illness.[81]

The condition of Plogojoviz's body seemed abnormal – paranormal – to the villagers, even to the Imperial Provisor and the regimental surgeon, but modern medicine has discovered that many of the traditional signs of vampirism are in fact part of the natural process of decomposition. When Frombald and Flückinger saw that the 'old' skin of the vampires had fallen away and had been replaced by a 'new' one, they were not entirely wrong. They had only incorrectly interpreted what we today know is 'skin slippage', the process by which the epidermis comes away from the dermis. The 'new' nails observed were probably simply the nailbeds themselves. The full and

---

[80] Populus, 'Morals, Ethics and Religion Survey', 8–9 April 2005, http://www.populus.co.uk/the-sun-moral-attitudes-090405.html, accessed 17 September 2010.

[81] Paul Barber, 'Staking Claims: The Vampires of Folklore and Legend', in Kendrick Frazier (ed.), *Encounters with the Paranormal*, Prometheus Books, 1998, pp. 374ff, first published in *Skeptical Inquirer*, 20.2, March–April 1996.

'healthy' appearance was caused by gases released during decomposition which bloat the body, hence the old woman who looked better fed than when alive. The florid or ruddy appearance can result from livor mortis (lividity) as the tissues become saturated with blood. The presence of 'fresh', i.e. liquid, blood is also possible: although blood normally coagulates at death, decomposition can cause it to liquefy again. The presence of blood in and around the mouth, taken as a sign of the vampire having sucked blood from the living, is caused by gas putting pressure on the lungs, so forcing blood from the lungs up into the mouth and nose.[82]

However, for all our medical advances we are still left with some untidy, indeed disturbing anomalies. What of the alleged sightings of the dead? What of the people who supposedly died after being visited by Plogojoviz, Paole and the rest? What of the marks on Stanvicka's neck?

Mummies

They could only work in winter. Even in November the sun was bright and warming. The shadows hid in the folds and wrinkles of the bare hills. It was a broken landscape. Lunar. A parched wadi at the edge of the vast desert, the 'hunting-ground of the tomb robber': the Valley of the Kings. And it was Howard Carter's last chance.[83]

The American lawyer and Egyptologist Theodore M. Davis had already pronounced the Valley to be 'exhausted' in 1912 after uncovering some thirty tombs. Carter knew the odds were against him. For five years, from 1917 to 1922, Carter had been working amongst 'open or half-filled mummy pits, heaps of rubbish, great mounds of rock debris, with, here and there, fragments of coffins and shreds of linen mummy-wrappings protruding from the sand'. The necropolis of Thebes was one

---

[82] Barber, pp. 374ff.
[83] George Edward Carnarvon and Howard Carter, *Five Years' Explorations at Thebes*, Oxford University Press, 1912, p. 1.

huge desecrated grave. Now, his patron, George Edward, 5th Earl of Carnarvon, had finally run out of patience.[84]

The valley echoed to the clatter of tools and voices in Arabic, as it had done on innumerable days past. They were digging near the tomb of Ramses VI, underneath the ancient remains of workmen's huts, when a stone step was discovered. It was the first of sixteen leading downwards into the sand. At the bottom of the steps they found a sealed doorway. There were hiero-glyphs: Anubis over nine foes. The seal of the Royal Necropolis. Carter knew he had found the tomb of someone important; a tomb that was much older than that of Ramses VI above it. 'It was,' he said, 'a thrilling moment.' It had taken days to get this far, but now darkness was again descending and the full moon was already high. Carter had the hole refilled as a safeguard and returned home to cable Lord Carnarvon:[85]

At last have made wonderful discovery in Valley. A magnifi-cent tomb with seals intact. Recovered same for your arrival. Congratulations.

When Carnarvon arrived, he had the sunken staircase cleared. This time they uncovered the whole of the sealed doorway and discovered seals bearing the cartouche of a royal name. It read: 'Living Image of Amun, Ruler of Upper Heliopolis'. They had found the tomb of Tutankhamun.

Breaking through the first wall they entered a tunnel heaped with debris. Laboriously clearing it all away they came to another sealed door again bearing the seals of the Royal Necropolis and Tutankhamun. Carter carefully broke a hole wide enough for them to see the astonishing sights within; the

---

[84] Theodore M. Davis, *The Tombs of Harmhabi and Touatânkhamanou*, Consta-ble & Co., 1912; Carnarvon and Carter, p. 1.
[85] Howard Carter, *Tutankhamun: Anatomy of an Excavation. Howard Carter's Diaries*, pt 1, Griffith Institute, 2004, http://www.griffith.ox.ac.uk/gri/4sea1not. html, accessed 18 September 2010. John Venn and John Archibald Venn, *Alum-ni Cantabrigienses*, Cambridge University Press, 10 vols, 1922–58, pp. 337–8.

lamplight illuminated an Aladdin's cave of treasure guarded by the gilded and monstrous statuary of the funeral chamber.

Now would begin the slow and painstaking excavation of the tomb. It would be 16 February 1923 by the time they were ready to enter the burial chamber itself. But already strange incidents had been reported. A *New York Times* correspondent wired his paper with tales of what the native staff had supposedly said was 'a warning from the spirit of the departed King against further intrusion on the privacy of his tomb'. According to the journalist, Carter had installed a canary 'to relieve his loneliness'. Sitting down to dinner on 'the day the tomb was opened', the party was alarmed by a disturbance on the veranda and rushing out to investigate they 'found that a serpent of similar type to that in the crowns had grabbed the canary. They killed the serpent, but the canary died'.[86]

According to the former Chief Inspector of Antiquities for Upper Egypt, Arthur Weigall, this was a royal cobra: 'rare in Egypt, and seldom seen in winter [. . .] each Pharaoh wore this symbol upon his forehead'. He added:

> Those who believed in omens, therefore, interpreted this incident as meaning that the spirit of the newly-found Pharaoh, in its correct form of royal cobra, had killed the excavator's happiness symbolized by the song-bird.[87]

As he was about to enter the tomb, Carnarvon joked to the others that with all the chairs down there they could give a concert. Standing at the retaining wall of the tomb, Weigall, now a correspondent for the *Daily Mail*, turned to his neighbour: 'If he goes down in that spirit, I give him six weeks to live.' Carnarvon's half-brother, Colonel Aubrey Herbert, had also

---

[86] 'Times Man Views Splendors of Tomb of Tutankhamen', *The New York Times*, 22 December 1922.

[87] Quoted in Boris de Zirkoff, 'The Mystery of Egyptian Mummies', *The Theosophical Path*, 38.2, February 1930, p. 136.

entered the tomb. He is reported to have said, 'Something
dreadful is going to happen to our family.'[88]

The theosophist Boris de Zirkoff, writing in 1930, said that
above the unbroken seals to the tomb was an inscription:

> As for any man who shall enter into this tomb, as his mortu-
> ary possession, I will seize him like a wild fowl; he shall be
> judged for it by the Great God. The hand which dares to spoil
> my form will be annihilated; crushed will be the bones of
> those who desecrate my body, my images and the effigies of
> my *ka*.[89]

Shortly afterwards Carnarvon was bitten by an insect and
developed blood poisoning. Carter rushed from the excavations
to visit his sick bed at the Continental-Savoy Hotel, Cairo.
'Found Ld. C. very ill', he wrote in his diary for 21 March.
Carnarvon's weakened constitution then fell prey to pneumo-
nia. He died at 2 a.m. on 5 April 1923. He was fifty-six. The
rumours quickly started.

The day after Carnarvon died *The New York Times* reported
that 'Occultists advance stories of angered gods'. Back at the
family seat of Highclere Castle, his three-legged dog Susie
apparently howled at the moment of her master's death before
collapsing lifeless herself. It was said that a number of people
cancelled their bookings when they discovered that they would
be sailing on the same ship as Lady Carnarvon and her
husband's remains. In 1928 Mr E. Fothergill came to the conclusion, in his lecture entitled 'The Curse of Tut-Ankh-Amen', that
Carnarvon's death had indeed been the result of supernatural
assassination.[90]

---

[88] Weigall quoted in Julie Hankey, *A Passion for Egypt: Arthur Weigall, Tutankhamun and the 'Curse of the Pharaohs'*, I. B. Tauris, p. 4.; Herbert quoted in
de Zirkoff, p. 137.

[89] De Zirkoff, p. 136.

[90] 'Carnarvon's Death Spreads Theories About Vengeance', *The New York
Times*, 6 April 1923 – the story itself is dated 5 April; 'Carnarvon is Dead of

'Almost simultaneously with Lord Carnarvon's death,' wrote de Zirkoff, 'Howard Carter [. . .] was stricken down. Physicians could not diagnose his case. Death seemed imminent.' He lived, but by September 1923 Colonel Aubrey was dead. Carnarvon's friend George Jay Gould, another visitor to the tomb, died soon after. Other visitors met similar fates. Woolf Joel, heir to the 'Diamond King' Solly Joel, died of 'a strange malady'. In 1924 Sir Archibald Douglas Reid, engaged to X-ray the mummy, retired to bed feeling unwell and died some days later. That same year Professor Laffleur of McGill University died 'in a most mysterious way'. In September of that year H. G. Evelyn-White died by his own hand, saying in his suicide note, 'I knew there was a curse on me'. Professor Paul Casanova of the Collège de France died while at work in the tomb 'of the same mysterious illness'. Prince Ali Fahmy Bey was shot dead by his wife, whilst his secretary Hallah Ben passed away 'and the cause of his death was never ascertained'. In March 1926 Professor George Bénédite, Director of Egyptian Antiquities at the Louvre, 'died suddenly'. Countess Evelyn Waddington-Greeley committed suicide in Chicago. In 1930 the Hon. Richard Bethell 'was found dead at the Bath Club, Mayfair': he had jumped to his death. When the hearse carrying his body accidentally killed a boy, this, too, was attributed to the curse, as was the death of Weigall himself in 1934.[91]

The Director of the Egyptian Section of the Metropolitan

an Insect's Bite at Pharaoh's Tomb', *The New York Times*, 5 April 1923; 'Notes on Periodicals', *Journal of the Society of Psychical Research*, 24, 1928, p. 375; de Zirkoff, p. 137; Robert Hardman, '£12m Curse of King Tut', *Daily Mail*, 6 August 2009.

[91] De Zirkoff, p. 137 – J. C. Madrus had tabulated the curse-stricken victims for *The New York Times*, 28 March 1928; 'Aged Peer Dies in Seven Story Leap in London, Reviving Talk of Tut-ankh-Amen "Curse"', *The New York Times*, 22 February 1930; 'Hearse with Lord Westbury's Body Kills Boy; Museum Death also Laid to "Pharaoh's Curse"', *The New York Times*, 26 February 1930; 'A King's So-Called "Curse"', *The New York Times*, 9 March 1930; 'Death of Mr A. Weigall, Tut-ank-Amen Curse Recalled', *Daily Mail*, 3 January 1934; 'Curse of the Pharaohs Denied by Winlock', *The New York Times*, 26 January 1934; Hankey, p. 3.

Museum of Modern Art, New York, Herbert Winlock, refuted the idea of the curse. Speaking to reporters from *The New York Times* in 1934 he stated that only six of the original twenty-four people present at the opening of the tomb had died. Still, 25 per cent seems like a high mortality rate. Other accounts, such as that given by de Zirkoff, had already found thirteen victims with additional reports bringing the total to as many as fifteen, and more could no doubt be found.

Carter marvelled at how the body of Tutankhamun had escaped the depredations of robbers and miscreants through its millennia of repose and half-wonderingly added 'we may believe, as those ancient Thebans might readily claim, that Tut·ankh·Amen's long security is due to Amen·Re's protection'.[92] Protection for the pharaoh; a curse to everyone else – except in the Middle Ages.

Our word 'mummy' entered the language in the Middle Ages from medieval Latin *mumia* (and Old French *mumie*) as a medicinal ingredient. In a circa 1400 translation of Lanfranc's *Chirurgia Magnia* (1296) we read a recipe: 'take [. . .] mirre, sarcocol, mummie (*v.r.* mumie) [. . .] & leie it on þe nucha'. In 1615 we read its first use in the modern sense in George Sandys' travelogue *A Relation of a Journey*: 'The Mummes (lying in a place where many generations have had their sepultures) not far above Memphis'. The word comes ultimately from Arabic *mūmiyā*, 'embalmed body', derived from the embalming wax *mūm*.[93]

Ground to a powder, mummy was good for everything from abscesses to fractures and as an antidote to poison. It was a stock ingredient on apothecaries' shelves from the twelfth to seventeenth centuries and did not fall out of use until well into the eighteenth century. Indeed, one German pharmaceutical company was still listing 'genuine Egyptian mummy' in its catalogue in 1908. The great sixteenth-century mystico-physician

---

[92] Howard Carter, *The Tomb of Tut-Ankh-Amen*, Cambridge University Press, 2010, p. 38.

[93] Guido Lanfranc of Milan, *Chirurgia Magnia*, 1296; George Sandys, *A Relation of a Journey*, W. Barrett, 1615.

Paracelsus mixed his own 'balsam of mummy' and the even less appetizing 'treacle of mummy'. This popularity derived from the mistaken idea that mummies were preserved using bitumen – resin is used – and the belief among the ancients of bitumen's great therapeutic value. The Roman writer Pliny the Elder (23–79 CE) described all sorts of medicinal uses for bitumen, from eye infections to leprosy. The Greek writer and physician Pedanius Dioscorides (c. 40–90 CE) further cemented belief in its efficacy in his influential *De Materia Medica*.[94]

Over time the idea transferred itself from the supposed bitumen content to the actual cadaver. As well as mummy remedies, Paracelsus prescribed the use of human blood, fat, marrow and even excrement on the homeopathic principle that like cures like, showing how the body itself could be seen as a drug. The high demand for medicinal bodies led Oswald Croll (c.1560–1608), a professor at the University of Marburg in Germany, to posthumously publish a recipe for making one's own mummy, ideally from the 'Carcase of a red Man' who had been executed at the age of twenty-four – the youth and vigour of the living body was thought to be retained by the corpse. Mummy was included in the Royal College of Physicians' *Pharmacopoeia Londinensis* of 1618, which was officially sanctioned by King James VI and I, and in later editions. In 1752, Dr Johnson's friend Dr Robert James described mummy as 'a resinous, hardened, black shining Surface, of a somewhat acrid and bitterish Taste, and of a fragrant Smell'. He noted that there were three different types then available: the best was the 'Arabian', embalmed with 'Aloes, Myrrh and Balsam' and 'obtained in Sepulchres'; next was the 'Egyptian', 'a Liquament of Carcases seasoned with

---

[94] Warren R. Dawson, 'Mummy as a Drug', *Proceedings of the Royal Society of Medicine*, 21, 1927, pp. 34–9; Mark Greener, 'Corpses and Robbers', *Paranormal*, 52, October 2010, p. 27; Pliny, *Natural History*, v, 15; Louise Noble, '"And Make Two Pasties of Your Shameful Heads": Medicinal Cannibalism and Healing the Body Politic in Titus Andronicus', *English Literary History*, 70, 2003, p. 686.

Pissasphaltus'; and least was 'a Carcase torrified under the Sand, by the Heat of the Sun'.[95]

Whilst this horrifying medical cannibalism had turned many a poor patient into a ghoul, it is perhaps in Louis Penicher's *Traité des Embaumemens* of 1699 that we get the first horror story concerning the mummy. According to Penicher, a Polish traveller acquired two mummies in Alexandria, undoubtedly for medicinal uses, and had them shipped out. On board he was apparently tormented by strange dreams of two ghostly figures. Fearing the worst as the seas grew stormy, he ordered the bodies to be thrown over the side, and calm was restored.[96]

The nineteenth century would see such snippets of travellers' tales become fully fledged mummy stories. Perhaps the first mummy to be brought back to life is found in Jane C. Loudon's *The Mummy!* of 1827, which owes much to Mary Shelley's *Frankenstein*. Another hops out of the pages of Theophile Gautier's rather ludicrous romance *The Mummy's Foot* of 1840. Edgar Allen Poe had a group of scientists electrically revive a mummy in his 1845 social satire *Some Words With a Mummy*. We read of 'The dark, parchment-like skin, wrinkled and rough' in the anonymous *The Mummy's Soul* of 1862. Louisa May Alcott, famous for *Little Women*, has been identified as the anonymous author of *Lost in a Pyramid; or the Mummy's Curse* published in 1869. The popularity of the mummy was such that even Sir Arthur Conan Doyle turned his hand to the subject, first in 1890 with *The Ring of Thoth*, then in 1892 with the short story *Lot No. 249*. Here he presented the mummy in what is now a familiar role as the Golem-like automaton controlled by a diabolical, vengeful master. Bram Stoker, the creator of *Dracula*,

[95] Oswald Croll, *Basilica chymica*, n.p., 1609, trans. John Hartman as *Bazilica Chymica & Praxis Chymiatricae. Or Royal and Practical Chymistry*, John Starkey and Thomas Passinger, 1670, p. 156; Royal College of Physicians, *Pharmacopoeia Londinensis*, John Marriot, 1618; Robert James, *Pharmacopœia Universalis, or a New Universal Dispensatory*, 2nd ed., J. Hodges, 1752, p. 340; Noble, pp. 677–708.
[96] Louis Penicher, *Traité des Embaumemens selon les Anciens et les Modernes*, Barthelemy Girin, 1699, pp. 70–4.

published *The Jewel of Seven Stars* in 1903, but forsook the animated corpse for a ghost. The theme was now firmly cemented, embalmed as it were, in the horror genre.[97]

After Carnarvon's death, the media turned to the great writers of the day for their explanations. H. Rider Haggard – whose *She* echoed some of the mummy themes – wisely refused to comment on the curse. Conan Doyle, however, already searching for his dead son in the darkened séance rooms of Spiritualism, was drawn out to remark upon the possibility of 'elementals' within the tomb.[98]

The Curse of Tutankhamun is not the only mummy curse. There is the British Museum's 'unlucky mummy', for example, which was said, incorrectly, to have sunk the *Titanic*. However, it is the Curse of Tutankhamun that has remained the most enduring in the popular imagination. Anything untoward that happens to Lord Carnarvon's descendants is routinely reported as an effect, or possible effect, of the curse.[99] Indeed, anything untoward that happens to anyone remotely connected with the tomb of Tutankhamun is attributed to the curse. When she came into possession of samples taken from the tomb in the 1920s for bacteriological analysis, author Lesley-Ann Jones implicated the curse in a run of bad luck that took her to the brink of death with meningitis, skin cancer and violent robbery.[100]

But what of Howard Carter himself? He had been the one to find the tomb and break its aeons of grimly hallowed taboo. Surely he must have been blasted by the curse? Carter made no

---

[97] Lisa Hopkins, 'Jane C. Loudon's *The Mummy!*', *Cardiff Corvey: Reading the Romantic Text*, 10, June 2003; Jasmine Day, *The Mummy's Curse: Mummymania in the English-Speaking World*, Routledge, 2006, p. 56; Carter Lupton, '"Mummymania" for the Masses', in Sally MacDonald and Michael Rice (eds), *Consuming Ancient Egypt*, Left Coast Press, 2009, pp. 26–30.

[98] Lupton, p. 32.

[99] Richard Kay, 'Tut! Tut! That's One Earl of a Mistake', *Daily Mail*, 17 April 2009.

[100] Lesley-Ann Jones, 'Am I Cursed by King Tut?', *Daily Mail*, 17 October 2007. Despite denying that she believed in the curse, Jones laid out a long list of disasters that she clearly attributed to it.

note of any curse inscription above the entrance to the tomb. Under the headline 'Carter Ignores Curse Idea', *The New York Times* reported that he had 'Never thought of it'.[101] Carter made no note of the alleged death of his canary in his diary. He either thought it of little significance, or it never happened at all. Carter was not 'stricken down' by a mysterious ailment after Carnarvon's death, but, as his diary reveals, carried on working. Carter died at home in Kensington, London, in 1939 at the age of sixty-four, seventeen years after first setting foot inside the tomb of Tutankhamun.

Archaeology as a profession is often a dangerous one. In delving into the earth and digging amongst the dead, archaeologists are exposed to a range of diseases from tetanus to anthrax, as well as accidental injury. Consequently, it has been suggested that the deaths of those who entered the tomb of Tutankhamun were caused by infectious agents, possibly developing histoplasmosis, for example, from exposure to bats. However, research by Mark Nelson at the Department of Epidemiology and Preventive Medicine, Monash University, Australia, found that most of the Westerners likely to have been exposed to the curse at the time of the tomb's opening lived for another twenty years before dying at the average age of seventy. He concluded that 'there was no significant association between exposure to the mummy's curse and survival and thus no evidence to support the existence of a mummy's curse'. Speaking about the curse in 2009, the current Lord Carnarvon, great-grandson of the Egyptologist, said 'Well, I've been into Tutankhamun's tomb and I'm still breathing.'[102]

---

[101] 'Carter Ignores Curse Idea', *The New York Times*, 14 April 1923.

[102] G. Dean, 'The Curse of the Pharaohs', *World Medicine*, 10, 1975, pp. 17–21; H. A. Waldron, 'Occupational Health and the Archaeologist', *British Journal of Industrial Medicine*, 42.12, December 1985, pp. 793–4; Mark R. Nelson, 'The Mummy's Curse: Historical Cohort Study', *British Medical Journal*, 21 December 2002, 325(7378), pp. 1482–4; Carnarvon quoted in Robert Hardman, '£12m Curse of King Tut', *Daily Mail*, 6 August 2009.

Zombies

I am teeming with corpses
Teeming with death rattles
I am a tide of wounds
Of cries of pus of blood clots
I graze on the pastures
Of millions of my dead
I am shepherd of terror.[103]

It was spring 1918. The terrible slaughter in Europe had yet to come to an end. Across the ocean, untouched by heavy artillery and poison gas, yet still a pawn in the Great Game, the Caribbean islands roasted in the sun, steeped in cruelty and indolence, simmering rebellion, and voodoo. To American President Theodore Roosevelt, 'beautiful, venomous, tropical [. . .] a land of savage negroes'.[104] And that spring it was a bumper sugar cane harvest.

The Haitian-American Sugar Company (Hasco) had a modern processing plant outside Port-au-Prince in the cane fields of the Plaine du Cul-de-Sac. They paid low wages, but gave regular work, and this season they were hiring everybody and anybody. They came in droves, whole families, even whole villages, from the plains and the mountains beyond. Amongst them was Ti Joseph from Colombier with his wife Croyance and a nine-strong work gang. There was something strange in the way Joseph's workers shuffled along, clothed in rags and giving no answer when spoken to. Joseph said they were simple people from the isolated mountain country around Morne-au-Diable, the Devil's Peak, on the Dominican border, frightened by the huge factory and its marshalling yards.

Joseph's team kept themselves to themselves. People wondered

---

[103] René Depestre, *Un Arc-en-ciel pour l'occident chrétien*, 1967, quoted in Joan Dayan, *Haiti, History and the Gods*, University of California Press, 1998, p. 38.
[104] Roosevelt in 1906, quoted in Markmann Ellis, *The History of Gothic Fiction*, Edinburgh University Press, 2000, p. 218.

why Croyance kept two pots on the fire and why she and her husband ate from one, whilst the workers ate from the other. From the neighbouring camps they might have seen her add a pinch of salt to the one and not the other. But they worked hard and every Saturday Joseph collected their wages. When the Fête Dieu came round even Hasco granted the workers a long weekend and Joseph set off to Port-au-Prince with the money clinking in his pockets, leaving Croyance to look after the workers. But Croyance got bored looking after the workers at their isolated camp and convincing herself that she might do something to cheer up the dull, expressionless crew, she led them into Croix de Bouquet to see the religious procession. The workers were unmoved by the pageant, so she bought them *tablettes pistaches*, pistachio nut and cane sugar biscuits. Little did she know, the pistachios had been salted. When the workers bit into the biscuits it was as if their consciousness flooded back and with it a terrible realization. Croyance could do nothing as they abandoned her and made their way back to their village, desperate and determined.

As they approached the village, friends and relatives recognized them. Some thought it must be a miracle, but the others knew the truth. Joseph's former work gang stumbled through the collection of huts and out again, taking the path to the graveyard. They were zombies, reanimated by the black magic of Joseph, restored to their senses by the taste of salt. They clawed their way back into their graves, finding peace again at last.

The villagers turned to black magic themselves, hiring a *bokor* to curse Ti Joseph. Impatient to wait for the magic to work, some of them also laid an ambush. Going down to the plain they waited for him to pass and hacked him to pieces with their machetes.

William Buehler Seabrook had heard the story first-hand, or so he said, sitting on a farmer's porch and trading stories of the supernatural – of firehags, demons and vampires – as the full moon rose over the cotton fields. But even here, on what he would later call 'the magic island', Seabrook did not believe the storyteller. So the farmer promised to show him a zombie, several, in fact: 'If you ride with me tomorrow, I will show you dead men working in the cane fields'.[105]

Seabrook had joined Field Section No. 8 of the Franco-American Ambulance Corps and saw action at Verdun in 1916. He came home with a medal and joined the *Augusta Chronicle* in Georgia, but a strange inner drive would take him to the ends of the earth, metaphorically as well as literally. In 1920 he sat up all night drinking a gallon of moonshine corn spirit with the infamous magician Aleister Crowley as they experimented in communicating without human language. He would go on to travel Arabia, publishing his account in 1927, and found himself in Haiti in the late 1920s. In 1929 he would publish his experiences as *The Magic Island* – 'a most interesting and level-headed book', according to a contemporary reviewer for the *Journal of the Society for Psychical Research*. Afterwards he would travel Africa, living with the Guéré cannibals and tasting human flesh. 'It was,' he said, 'like good, fully developed veal.'[106]

In the 1920s Haiti still had most of its original forest cover before its spiralling population cut down all but 2 per cent of it for fuel. Sugar was still its most important cash crop. It was also then occupied by the USA. A rebellion had been crushed by force of arms. The Marine Corps had been installed to run the provinces and the country was under martial law. One marine, Sergeant Faustin Wirkus, would be proclaimed King Faustin II by his loyal subjects of the Haitian island Île de la Gonâve, to the great embarrassment of the republic's president. Seabrook was there to see it.[107]

---

[105] William Seabrook, *The Magic Island*, George C. Harrap & Co., 1929, excerpted in Bill Pronzini (ed.), *Tales of the Dead*, Crown/Bonanza, 1986, pp. 77–88.

[106] William Seabrook, *No Hiding Place: An Autobiography*, J. B. Lippincott Company, 1942, pp. 149, 164, 166; H.D.S., *Diary of Section VIII*, privately published, 1917; *The Rotarian*, 10.1, January 1917, p. 68; William Seabrook, *Witchcraft: Its Power in the World Today*, Harcourt, Brace and Company, 1940, pp. 223–4; *Journal of the Society of Psychical Research*, 25, 1929, p. 96; 'Books: Black & White', *Time*, 6 April 1931.

[107] Richard A. Haggerty, *Haiti: A Country Study*, GPO for the Library of Con-

Seabrook was then living in the high country of La Gonâve in a peasant *lakou*, a communal compound of half a dozen thatched huts typical of the region. He lived like 'an adopted son' to the 'old black priestess' Maman Célie and would sink his soul into the 'living, vital, violent, bloody, flaming Religion' of voodoo. And the farmer, Constant Polynice, would be true to his word.[108]

They rode out together across the Plaine Mapou, through deserted cane fields until, near Picmy, Polynice spotted a group of four workers a hundred yards up on the terraced slope. He recognized the woman as Lamercie and they approached. The three other workers continued hacking at the rough, stony ground with their machetes 'like automatons'. Seabrook thought there was 'something about them unnatural and strange'. Polynice touched one of them and signalled him to rise from his toil. What Seabrook then saw 'came as a rather sickening shock':[109]

> The eyes were the worst. It was not my imagination. They were in truth like the eyes of a dead man, not blind, but staring, unfocused, unseeing. The whole face, for that matter, was bad enough. It was vacant, as if there was nothing behind it.[110]

Zombie Origins

Seabrook was probably the first person to describe the full horror of the Haitian reanimated corpse, although earlier references to the word can be found. The French were early aware of the word and its meaning. Pierre-Corneille Blesseboise (1646– c. 1700) wrote a novel on the theme in 1697 called *Le Zombi du Grand-Pérou* – the zombi being, as his later editor the poet

gress, 1989. Seabrook wrote about Wirkus in *The Magic Island* as well as contributing the introduction to Faustin Wirkus and Taney Dudley, *The White King of La Gonave*, Doubleday, Doran & Co., 1931.

[108] Seabrook, *No Hiding Place*, pp. 278, 280.
[109] Pronzini, p. 86.
[110] Pronzini, p. 86.

Guillaume Apollinaire pointed out, a spirit, phantom, or sorcerer, and muttered darkly of midnight orgies. It was some years later in 1819 that the poet Robert Southey noted that 'zombi' was used as the title of the chief of the Palmares negroes in Brazil, and thereby introduced the word into the English language. His explanation was that it came from the Angolan word for 'deity', although Southey noted that the Brazilian historian Sebastiao da Rocha Pitta had said that the word meant 'devil'. Southey rejected this meaning, but Maximilian Schele de Vere would later note in 1872 how the word 'zombi' was used for 'a phantom or ghost' and 'not infrequently heard in the Southern States in nurseries and among servants'. This was the understanding the French writer Moreau de Saint-Méry had in 1797 when he said 'zombi' was a Creole word meaning 'spirit, revenant'. Schele de Vere suggested that it was a Creole corruption of the Spanish *sombra*, 'shadow, shade', which could also mean a ghost. However, Southey's was the more accurate etymology. In Angola and other parts of West Africa they speak, amongst many others, the Kongo language and following the deportation of human slave labour from this region the language formed the basis for Creole spoken in the Caribbean. In Kongo we find *nzambi*, 'god, spirit', and *zumbi*, 'fetish', clearly indicating supernatural meanings.[111]

The travel writer and literary critic Lafcadio Hearn (1850–1904) was commissioned by *Harper's Magazine* in 1887 to investigate the folklore and culture of the West Indies. He took a cruise to French Guiana and later spent two years on Martinique where he learnt of the zombie. He described costumed, dancing natives taking part in the carnival in St Pierre in 1887: *ti nègue*

---

[111] Pierre-Corneille Blesseboise, *L'ouvre de Pierre-Corneille Blessebois*, ed. Guillaume Apollinaire, Bibliothéque des curieux, 1921, pp. 219–82; Médéric Louis Élie Moreau de Saint-Méry, *Description Topographique, Physique, Civile, Politique et Historique de la Partie Française de L'Isle Saint-Dominique*, self-published, 1797, pp. 47f; Southey, *History of Brazil*, vol. 3, Longman, Hurst, Rees, Orme and Brown, 1819, p. 24; Sebastiao da Rocha Pitta, *Historia da America Portugueza*, F. A. da Silva, 1880 [1730], p. 536; Maximilian Schele de Vere, *Americanisms:The English of the New World*, C. Scribner & Co., 1872, p. 138.

gouos-sirop, Creole for 'little molasses negro', covered in molasses and soot; the *guiablesse* ('she-devil') dressed in black; the *Bon-Dié* ('Good God'); and the Devil with his *zombis*, a crowd of hundreds of chanting boys. Da Rocha Pitta was not wrong and Hearn's first-hand testimony would concur with Schele de Vere. There was something more here than Southey had realized, or even Seabrook had discovered.[112]

Hearn had heard the word *zombi* in common phrases – *I ni pè zombi mênm gran-jou*, 'he is afraid of ghosts even in broad daylight' – but a doubt remained that they were not exactly like ghosts. He quizzed Adou, the daughter of the woman who rented him his lodgings. 'It is something which "makes disorder at night",' she told him, just like our 'things that go bump in the night'. She was afraid of passing the cemetery at night because the dead folk, *moun-mò*, would keep her there, but the *zombi* was not one of the dead: 'the *moun-mò* are not zombis. The zombis go everywhere: the dead folk remain in the graveyard.' Hearn probed for more: 'It is the zombis who make all those noises at night one cannot understand . . . Or, again, if I were to see a dog that high,' she held her hand five feet above the ground, 'coming into our house at night, I would scream: "*Mi Zombi!*"' The mother stopped her cooking to join in the debate. 'You pass along the high-road at night, and you see a great fire, and the more you walk to get to it the more it moves away: it is the zombi makes that,' she explained. 'Or a horse *with only three legs* passes you: that is a zombi.'[113]

From Ezekiel's vision of the Valley of the Dry Bones (Ezekiel 37) and the resurrection of the dead supposed to occur at the Final Judgement of the Judaeo-Christian imagination to the *draugr*, Wild Hunt and walking dead of Europe, the dead who come back is certainly not an unknown concept in the West. Hearn's fairy-like shape-shifting bogeyman would find himself

---

[112] Lafcadio Hearn, 'La Verette and the Carnival in St. Pierre, Martinique', *Harper's Magazine*, October 1888, pp. 737–48; and Lafcadio Hearn, *Two Years in the French West Indies*, Harper & Brothers, 1890, pp. 181f.

[113] Hearn, *Two Years*, pp. 161–3.

at home in Scotland or Ireland. But Seabrook's Haitian zombie is unique. One finds distant echoes of the homunculus or golem – the artificial magical monsters of the Renaissance – but the slave dead are peculiar to the country and culture that created them.

Zombie Culture

It would not stay that way. Director Victor Halperin's *White Zombie* (1932) stuck to the folklore, portraying zombies as undead slaves. The modern zombie did not start out as a zombie. Richard Matheson's 1954 novel *I Am Legend* described an apocalyptic future in which most of the earth's population have succumbed to a mysterious disease that turns both living and dead into vampires, perhaps drawing on a similar pandemic theme in H. G. Wells' *The Shape of Things to Come* (1933). Vincent Price and Charlton Heston starred in film adaptations – *The Last Man on Earth* (1964) and *The Omega Man* (1971), respectively – that brought Matheson's story to even wider audiences. Often seen as the creator of the modern zombie, George A. Romero's inspiration for his 1968 film *Night of the Living Dead* was Matheson's novel and the 1964 film. Crucially, however, during the film the zombies are referred to as ghouls. This is the key.

The ghoul, from Arabic *ghūl*, 'demon', is a creature of the burial ground and wasteland whose characteristic trait is an appetite for human flesh. Like Seabrook, the ghoul has a taste for 'good, fully developed veal'. First mentioned in English in the 1786 translation of William Beckford's novel *Vathek*, it is this creature that Romero has emerge from the graveyard and assault his beleaguered characters. It is this creature that is subsequently and erroneously called a zombie. Romero's subsequent films detailing the 'zombie apocalypse' have cemented the idea of the flesh-eating zombie loosed from its origins in West African and Caribbean culture.

Some people have interpreted all of this as an obsession with race – Matheson's diseased hordes as blacks, Stoker's Dracula as the Jew[114] – but this reflects current concerns, more particularly, current academic concerns. The parasitic, aristocratic Dracula was more obviously a class critique, if anything; and Matheson's hordes were the reverse, the great unwashed, although, it has to be said, there were incidental and understated signs that this was a demonologist's version of *The Planet of the Apes*. Instead, today we find people identifying with the zombie as a form of social protest and aspiring to be vampires/vampirized as an expression of teenage sexual awakening.

Some philosophers and cognitive scientists have involved themselves in arguments over the 'philosophical zombie', a postulated functional human being that is otherwise devoid of conscious experience. Some have suggested that we are already 'zombies'. Professor Daniel Dennett, co-director of the Center for Cognitive Studies, Tufts University, USA, argued that the self is 'no more than a fiction which serves as a reference point for the narratives which the brain constructs'. Take that with a pinch of salt.[115]

What differentiates Seabrook's Haitian zombie from its near undead relatives, the vampire and the mummy, is the role of the sorcerer in creating it. Some instances of the mummy in literature are governed by this theme, most notably Conan Doyle's *Lot No. 249*. But where the vampire and the mummy are most typically aspects of the vengeful or unplacated dead, the zombie is here the sorcerer's slave in a colonialism of the spirit. Hearn's Martiniquan zombi was something much more like one of the fairies in Celtic folklore: a terrifying supernatural entity that could assume a variety of forms. It is only in later fictional interpretations that the zombie takes on the mantle of the restless dead and

---

[114] Mikhail Lyubansky, 'Are the Fangs Real? Vampires as Racial Metaphor in the Anita Blake and Twilight Novels', *Psychology Today*, 10 April 2010, http://www.psychologytoday.com/blog/between-the-lines/201004/are-the-fangs-real-vampires-racial-metaphor-in-the-anita-blake-and-twi, accessed 24 September 2010.

[115] Daniel C. Dennett, *Consciousness Explained*, Penguin, 1991. This whole subject is a minefield and this not the place to venture into it.

appropriates the function of the ghoul to become the flesh-eating monster of the 'zombie apocalypse'.

Zombie Explanations

As he stared into those lifeless eyes, Seabrook felt all his certainties slipping away. Here he was face to face with the supernatural. But then he remembered something similar he had once seen: a lobotomized dog in a laboratory – alive but devoid of the higher mental processes. More for his own sanity than anything else, Seabrook concluded that the zombies were 'poor ordinary demented human beings, idiots'. Polynice was less convinced. 'How could it be,' he asked, 'that over and over again, people who have stood by and seen their own relatives buried have, sometimes soon, sometimes months or years afterward, found those relatives working as zombies?'[116]

Seabrook got his answer some time later, sitting with a certain Dr Antoine Villiers in his book-lined study. According to Seabrook, after he raised the subject of zombies, Villiers took down an edition of the *Code pénal* from the shelves and read out Article 249: 'Also shall be qualified as attempted murder the employment which may be made against any person of substances which, without causing actual death, produce a lethargic coma more or less prolonged. If, after administering of such substances, the person has been buried, the act shall be considered murder no matter what result follows.' This has been quoted repeatedly ever since. What Article 249 of the *Code pénal* actually stated was that 'homicide committed wilfully is termed murder', nothing more. In the second edition of the *Code* published in 1938 this became 'Murder shall carry the death penalty, when preceded, accompanied or followed by another crime or misdemeanour'. The death penalty has since been amended to penal servitude for life. There was no mention of 'substances' or burial and of Dr Antoine Villiers there is no trace.[117]

---

[116] Seabrook in Pronzini, p. 87.

[117] Seabrook in Pronzini, p. 87; *Code pénal d'Haiti*, L'Imprimerie du

However, Seabrook's substance-induced zombification found support in the work of Zora Neale Hurston (1891–1960) and Wade Davis (1953–). In her 1938 book *Tell My Horse*, Hurston claimed 'I know that there are Zombis in Haiti' after she supposedly met one. With the Maroons in the St Catharine Mountains of Jamaica she had already been party to 'The Nine Night', a riotous funerary rite whose purpose was to prevent the 'duppy', walking dead, from returning. Later in Haiti, she took part in another funerary ritual where the corpse suddenly 'sat up with its staring eyes, bowed its head and fell back again', or so she said. So when she was introduced to a zombie, she was primed to believe that 'people have been called back from the dead' and snapped a photograph of the creature as proof.[118]

Dr Rulx Leon, director-general of the Service d'Hygiene, had told her of Felicia Felix-Mentor, currently lodged in a government hospital. Hurston rushed over to see her, later recalling 'That blank face with the dead eyes. The eyelids were white all around the eyes as if they had been burnt with acid'.[119]

The case was examined by Dr Louis Mars, Professor of Psychiatry at the School of Medicine and of Social Psychology at the Institute of Ethnology, Port-au-Prince, and a public health officer for the government. Mars recounted the alleged zombie's history. On the morning of 24 October 1936, an elderly woman dressed in rags caused 'tumultuous and frenzied consternation' when she was discovered wandering in a confused state in the village of Ennery in the foothills of the Puylboreau mountain

---

Gouvernement, 1826, p. 61; Auguste Albert Héraux, *Code pénal avec les dernières modifications, annoté*, 2nd ed., Aug. A. Héraux, 1938, p. 66. Amended 4 July 1988: *Le Code pénal haitien*, http://www.oas.org/juridico/mla/fr/hti/fr_hti_penal.html and http://www.crijhaiti.com/fr/?page=article_code_penal accessed 27 September 2010. There was an author called Antoine Villiers, apparently a chemist, writing in French at the beginning of the twentieth century, but there is no compelling reason to connect the two, other than name alone.

[118] Paul Witcover, *Zora Neale Hurston*, Holloway House Publishing, 1994, pp. 148–9.

[119] Quoted in Robert E. Hemenway, *Zora Neale Hurston: A Literary Biography*, University of Illinois Press, p. 250.

range. She appeared to be suffering from dementia, as well as some sort of eye disease. Her eyelashes had fallen out and to protect herself from the harsh and painful glare of the sun she had covered her face with some tattered dark-coloured material, adding to her uncanny appearance. The owner of a farm near the village claimed to recognize her, believing the woman to be his sister, Felicia Felix-Mentor, who had died in 1907. Felicia, like his sister, had a limp. Felicia herself was not able to confirm or deny any of this: 'all her answers were unintelligible and irrelevant'. Mars thought her schizophrenic. He had her legs X-rayed and discovered that, unlike the real Felicia who had limped in life after sustaining a fracture, this woman had no such injuries and her limp got better with hospital care. 'I have never met anyone in Haiti,' he said, 'who was able to testify to me that he had seen a Zombi.'[120]

Hurston testified: 'I saw the broken remnant, relic, or refuse of Felicia Felix-Mentor in a hospital yard.' But she did not, or would not, look beyond the explanations of her informants. She considered that zombies could be created either by the sorcerer sucking out the soul of the victim, calling upon one of the violent *Petro loas* (spirits), or secretly administering a special poison. She was convinced that 'if science ever gets to the bottom of Voodoo in Haiti and Africa, it will be found that some important medical secrets, still unknown to medical science, give it its power'.[121]

Wade Davis would claim to have discovered those secrets. In the spring of 1980 a middle-aged man introduced himself to a woman in the village of l'Estère, central Haiti, using the private childhood nickname of her brother. Her brother had died in 1962. He said he was Clairvius Narcisse, zombified by his brother after a dispute over land and forced to work as a slave on a sugar plantation. His family and about 200 other people recognized him. Dr Lamarque Douyon, director of the Centre

---

[120] Hemenway, p. 250; Louis P. Mars, 'The Story of the Zombi in Haiti', *Man: A Record of Anthropological Science*, XLV, 22, March–April 1945, pp. 38–40.

[121] Hemenway, p. 250; Zora Neale Hurston, *Dust Tracks on a Road*, 2nd ed., University of Illinois Press, 1984, p. 205.

de Psychiatrie et Neurologie, Port-au-Prince, examined the case. He discovered that Narcisse had indeed been declared dead in 1962 and concluded that poison must have been used to lower his vital functions to the point where he could be mistaken for dead.[122]

Investigating this lead, Davis travelled to Haiti to collect samples of the so-called *coup poudre*, 'blow' or 'strike powder', a magical preparation said to cause illness or death. All of the samples contained hallucinogenic plants and animals such as tarantulas, snakes and millipedes. Also thrown into the mix was a species of toad, *Bufo marinus*, and two genera of puffer fish, *Diodon hystrix* and *Sphoerides testudineus*, all of which are deadly poisonous in the extreme. The puffer fish contains tetrodotoxin, a nerve toxin so lethal that an amount the size of a pinhead is sufficient to cause death. Because of this the puffer fish has become a macho delicacy in Japan where specially licensed chefs prepare the dish so that it is not lethal, at least most of the time. The symptoms of tetrodotoxin poisoning – paralysis, reduced heartbeat and respiration – can lead to the victim being certified clinically dead when still alive, as sometimes happens in the case of unlucky Japanese diners and, so Davis thought, victims of zombification. At lower doses the victim usually recovers. Terence Hines, a professor of psychology and neurology, pointed out that a paralysed individual who appears to be dead does not a 'zombie' make. Davis argued that a paste containing the poisonous hallucinogenic plants *Datura stramonium* or *Datura metel* is then fed to the 'zombie' to produce what he calls 'an induced state of psychotic delirium'. His critics, however, have cried 'fraud' and 'bad science', claiming that Davis's samples were either devoid of tetrodotoxin or did not contain enough to produce the supposed effects.[123]

---

[122] Wade Davis, *The Serpent and the Rainbow*, Simon & Schuster, 1985, and *Passage of Darkness: The Ethnobiology of the Haitian Zombie*, University of North Carolina Press, 1988; Catherine Caufield, 'The Chemistry of the Living Dead', *New Scientist*, 15 December 1983, p. 796.

[123] Nick Saunders, 'Law and Order in the Land of the Living Dead', *New*

Whatever the zombies are, they are still out there. A German traveller to Jamaica in the late 1980s told friends that he had encountered a zombie in the jungle. Like Seabrook he described the eyes as being the worst. Other recent encounters have been closer to home. It was revealed in 2010 that the police in Wales had received sixteen reports of zombies since 2005. Another zombie sighting hit the headlines in February 2008. A sewage treatment plant at Prince William Parade in Eastbourne, East Sussex, is reputedly the stalking ground of what workers have called a 'zombie'. A Southern Water employee told reporters 'I dread doing the night shift. It's not funny going to work and worrying that a zombie might be around the corner.' Although no one has been torn to pieces and consumed by the undead prowler, à la George A. Romero, workers have reported hearing voices and seeing a shadowy figure.[124]

Scientist, 7 August 1986, p. 47; Davis quoted in Caufield, p. 796; Terence Hines, 'Zombies and Tetrodotoxin', *Skeptical Inquirer*, May–June 2008, pp. 60–2; W. Booth, 'Voodoo Science', *Science*, 240.4850, 15 April 1988, pp. 274–7.
[124] The German traveller's tale was reported to me personally, 10 October 2010; 'Welsh in Fear of Witches and Demons', *Paranormal*, 53, November 2010, p. 10; Alan Murdie, 'Ghostwatch', *Fortean Times*, 267, October 2010, p. 17.

3. Angels

The summer sun that Sunday morning was darkly shrouded in cloud and mist. The church bell was yet quiet and the townspeople slept on. Beyond their dreams and wooden doors, a fine drizzle slowly soaked the men in khaki. Crouching behind makeshift barricades and in hastily dug scrape trenches, they rubbed sleep from their eyes and loaded their rifles. Distant shots and cries had already punctuated the grey dawn and for the soldiers the atmosphere was heavy with expectation. As the old clock tower chimed 9 a.m. the artillery of General Alexander von Kluck's First Army opened fire on the British Expeditionary Force (BEF). It was 23 August 1914. The first battle of World War I between the British and Germans had begun: the Battle of Mons.[125]

The BEF, so famously maligned as 'that contemptible little army', had crossed the English Channel and made its way with great haste to join the French Fifth Army. Only the British now found themselves outnumbered almost three to one and the army they had been sent to support was in full retreat. They had to hold the Germans, or France would fall.

---

[125] David Clarke, *The Angel of Mons: Phantom Soldiers and Ghostly Guardians*, John Wiley & Sons, 2005, p. 43; Herbert Arthur Stewart, *From Mons to Loos*, W. Blackwood, 1916, p. 19; W. Douglas Newton, *The Undying Story*, E. P. Dutton & Co., 1915, p. 12; Sir James E. Edmonds, *Military Operations, France and Belgium, 1914*, Macmillan & Co., 1937, p. 76. Lord Ernest Hamilton gives an incorrect account of the weather in *The First Seven Divisions*, E. P. Dutton & Co., 1916, p. 20.

Consisting of four infantry divisions and one cavalry division, less than 100,000 men in total, the BEF was divided into two main groupings: I Corps and II Corps. The II Corps were stretched along a twenty-mile line north of the Belgian town of Mons with the Eighth and Ninth Infantry Brigades holding an exposed section along the bend in the canal between Nimy and Obourg. It was here that two battalions from the Middlesex and Royal Fusiliers regiments bore the brunt of the bombardment: 'the sky precipitated to steel, and shivered fragments into the British'; and 'as the heat of the day increased, so did the fury of that terrific cannonade.'[126]

Fast on the heels of the shells came advancing infantry columns of the German IX Corps. Here, the shattered line faced an enemy perhaps ten times as strong. As the casualties mounted, the Second Royal Irish were moved up to support. Corporal John Lucy was among them and later recalled his amazement as the rapid rifle fire of the British knocked the Germans down in waves.[127]

Undeterred, the Germans began pushing to the west and east, trying to encircle the exposed salient. Faced with the likelihood of being cut off and wiped out, the British began to pull back. They were between the hammer and the anvil. The future of the war, of Europe, hung in the balance. Only a miracle could save them.

'There is the story of the "Angels of Mons" going strong through the II Corps,' wrote John Charteris in a letter dated 5 September 1914. Later to become Chief Intelligence Officer, the Glaswegian was at the time aide-de-camp to Lieutenant-General Sir Douglas Haig, commander of the I Corps. His letter continued: 'of how the angel of the Lord on the traditional white horse, and clad all in white with flaming sword, faced the advancing Germans at Mons and forbade their further progress'.[128]

---

[126] Quotations from Newton, p. 15; Arthur Machen, 'The Bowmen', *Evening News*, 29 September 1914, in Clarke, p. 247.

[127] John Frederick Lucy, *There's a Devil in the Drum*, Faber & Faber, 1938.

[128] John Charteris, *At GHQ*, Cassell and Co., 1931, pp. 25–6.

Of Sarah Marrable, a clergyman's daughter, it was reported in the press that 'she told me she knew the officers, both of whom had themselves seen the angels who saved the left wing from the Germans when they came right upon them during our retreat from Mons'. Phyllis Campbell, a nineteen-year-old volunteer nurse serving with the French Red Cross, later said that she had spoken to one of the wounded from Mons who told her that 'he saw at a critical moment an angel with outstretched wings – like a luminous cloud between the advancing Germans and themselves. The Germans could not advance to destroy them'.[129]

It seemed like that miracle had happened. The outnumbered and outmanoeuvred BEF had escaped certain destruction. The number of German dead has never been disclosed, but is estimated in the range of 5,000 to 10,000. Against this the British lost 1,600 men. However, over the course of what was called the Great Retirement as the BEF retreated more than 200 miles in 13 days, British losses would rise to 15,000.[130]

The rumour of angelic reinforcements spread quickly, gaining greater conviction and variety in every retelling. Charteris' letter notwithstanding, the writer Arthur Machen argued that he had started it all with his short story 'The Bowmen' published in the *Evening News* on 29 September 1914, but few people wanted to believe him and much apparent evidence to the contrary was quickly forthcoming. Today, the official battlefield guidebook published by the City of Mons Tourist Board states that 'angels descended from heaven dressed as archers stopping the Germans in their tracks' with similar text appearing on the city's official website. It has been described as 'the single most influential paranormal event in British history'. It was certainly the most important angelic encounter in British history. In the

---

[129] For Marrable see *Hereford Times*, 3 April 1915; for Campbell see Alexander Boddy interviewed by the *Sunderland Echo*, 16 August 1915, quoted in Clarke, p. 134.
[130] Alan John Percivale Taylor, *English History, 1914–1945*, Oxford University Press, 1965, p. 9.

slaughter of industrialized warfare, angels had entered the modern world.[131]

The Origin of Angels

The Angels of Mons were not the cute little figures from the top of the Christmas Tree, but warrior spirits straight out of the Old Testament. Marrable herself said she was reminded of the story of the siege of Dothan.[132] Claimed to have been written sometime in the sixth century BCE, the second book of Kings relates a legend concerning the Hebrew prophet Elisha that reputedly took place several hundred years earlier in the ninth century BCE. The Assyrian armies had surrounded the city of Dothan, intent on capturing Elisha. His servant despaired, but Elisha told him 'they that be with us are more than they that be with them' and suddenly the servant saw that 'the mountain was full of horses and chariots of fire round about Elisha' that protected them (2 Kings 6:16–17).

It is appropriate that Marrable should have been reminded of the Old Testament. Our word 'angel' comes from the Greek *aggelos* (ἄγγελος), a masculine noun used by Jewish scribes in Alexandria in the third to second centuries BCE to translate more than 200 occurrences of the Hebrew word *mal'āk*, meaning messenger, found in the *Tanakh* or Hebrew scriptures, which, for Christians, have become the Old Testament. The Hebrew was originally employed to mean a messenger in general, either spiritual or human. Prophets (Haggai 1:13), priests (Malachi 2:7) and kings (1 Samuel 29:9) could all be messengers of God. In the earlier books of the Old Testament human agents are usually meant with a transition to supernatural beings occurring in the later books, increasing from the third century BCE onwards. This

---

[131] Yves Bourdon, *Mons: August 1914: Notes on the Mons Battlefield*, City of Mons Tourist Board, 1987, quoted in Clarke, p. 45; www.mons.be accessed 15 July 2010; Kevin McClure, 'Visions of Comfort and Catastrophe' in Hilary Evans (ed.), *Frontiers of Reality*, Aquarian Press, 1991, p. 170. For a pro position see Ralph Shirley, *The Angel Warriors at Mons*, Newspaper Publicity Co., 1915.

[132] Clarke, p. 123.

development was shaped by the appearance of Jewish apocalyptic literature, the take up of popular belief and by the influence of other pagan religions. It appears likely that the supernatural angel developed as a means of maintaining Jewish monotheism by denying the messenger full godhead, especially as we find such roles paralleled by gods in all of ancient Near Eastern mythology. In other Mesopotamian belief systems the concept of supernatural messengers is well attested. There is even a Mesopotamian (Akkadian) messenger god called Malak.[133]

The earliest appearance of angels in the Old Testament is not with Elisha, but with the mythological character Abraham in Genesis. Traditionally ascribed to the authorship of Moses, the book of Genesis is thought to have been composed by a variety of authors in the sixth century BCE at the earliest.[134] Here we read 'And the Lord appeared unto him [. . .] And he lift up his eyes and looked, and lo, three men stood by him' (Genesis 18:1–2). The three are described as human with no mention of wings or white robes. They are not even sufficiently distinguished from 'the Lord', so that later Christians could interpret the group as a

---

[133] K. van der Toorn, Bob Becking and Pieter Willem van der Horst (eds), *Dictionary of Deities and Demons in the Bible* [*DDD*], 2nd ed., Brill/Eerdmans, 1999, pp. 45–9, 51. Clarke, pp. 17–18 and David Albert Jones, *Angels: A History*, Oxford University Press, 2010, p. 12, argue for a Zoroastrian influence, but the evidence for this is weak and contradictory.

[134] Dating the Bible is both controversial and problematic, if not to say confusing. The oldest surviving biblical manuscripts, the so-called Dead Sea Scrolls, all date from the second century BCE to the first century CE. However, the oldest supposed translation, the Greek Septuagint or LXX, dates from the third to second centuries BCE, although the oldest surviving manuscripts only date from the second century BCE (see Natalio Fernandez Marcos, *Scribes and Translators*, Brill, 1994, p. 7). Origination in this period is generally confirmed by textual analysis of later versions of the Bible that find a Hellenistic historical background to many of these texts. Traditional views ascribing extremely ancient authorship to these texts are not supported by the evidence. Thomas L. Thompson, a biblical scholar academically ostracized by conservative theologians for his views, put it forcefully when he said 'Not only has archaeology not proven a single event of the patriarchal traditions to be historical, it has not shown any of the traditions to be likely' (*The Historicity of the Patriarchal Narratives*, Walter de Gruyter, 1974, p. 328).

symbol of the Trinity, as is often found in Byzantine and medieval Russian art, such as the famous icon known as *The Hospitality of Abraham* or *The Holy Trinity* by Andrei Rublev.[135]

Often appearing singly, especially as the 'angel of Yahweh', they were also grouped as a 'camp' (Genesis 32:2–3) and envisioned travelling between heaven and earth by means of a ladder (Psalms 91:11–12). When not employed in the specific messenger role, they offered blessings and praise to Yahweh (Psalms 103:20, 148:2) and increasingly served in a protective capacity for believers (Daniel 3:28, 6:23; Baruch 6:6 [Epistle Jeremiah 6]) such as Elisha.

Only two angels are mentioned by name in the canonical books of the Old Testament: Michael (Daniel 10:13, 21, 12:1; Revelation 12:7) and Gabriel (Daniel 8:16, 9:21). The infamous 'fallen angel', Satan, only appeared as the legalistic role of 'the accuser' and not as the name of a divine being at this stage. Significantly, both the names Michael and Gabriel end with *-el*, as would later angelic names, and therein lies a tale.

Between the world wars in spring 1928, a peasant was ploughing his strip of rented land south of Minet-el-Beida in Syria when he struck something hard just under the surface. He had occasionally unearthed antiquities before, so it was with a keen interest that he knelt to the ground and swept away the earth with his hand. This time, however, he discovered more than an old broken vase. It was a chambered tomb full of pottery. As he and his friends began systematically looting the site and selling the pieces to local dealers, it accidentally came to the notice of the local governor. He called in the archaeologists (with armed guards) and slowly the ancient Canaanite city of Ugarit (modern Ras Shamra) emerged from the dust. Amongst the ruins they discovered thousands of clay tablets, some complete but most in fragments, dating from 1600–1200 BCE, that have overturned our understanding of the Bible.[136]

---

[135] Jones, p. 2.

[136] Edinburgh Ras Shamra Project, http://www2.div.ed.ac.uk/other/ugarit// home.htm, accessed 19 July 2010; Victor Harold Matthews, *Judges and Ruth*, Oxford University Press, 2004, p. 79.

The noun *'el* occurs more than 200 times in the Old Testament; in Ugarit over 500 references were discovered to a supreme god called El. The *-el* ending of both Michael and Gabriel comes from this Canaanite god El whom the Jews first worshipped as a separate entity before merging with the god Yahweh, so we read of 'El, the god of Israel' (Genesis 33:20) and 'El, the god of your father' (Genesis 46:3). The 'lord' that appears to Abraham with his two angels, the 'lord' that Abraham worships, is El Elyon ('El the Highest One') and 'creator of heaven and earth' (Genesis 14:18–24). Michael means 'like El', or more commonly 'who is like God', whilst the name Gabriel is usually taken to mean 'man of El', but is perhaps more accurately understood as 'El is my hero/warrior'. These two angelic names thus record the very roots of Judaism. Michael himself may also have once been a god in his own right and is tentatively connected with the Canaanite deity Mikal and in Islam this is still the name for him.[137]

Both Michael and Gabriel make their appearances in the book of Daniel. Daniel, 'my judge is El', was already a legendary figure in the time of Ezekiel and ultimately derives from the mythical Canaanite king *Dn'il*, whose ancient (but different) story was discovered amongst the ruins of Urgarit. Traditionally attributed to Daniel in the time of the Babylonian kings Nebuchadnezzar II (reigned 605–562 BCE) and Belshazzar (incorrectly identified as his son), the book is the work of several authors at different periods of history. Michael and Gabriel appear within a distinct group of chapters (7–12) confidently dated to between 168–164 BCE.[138]

The book of Daniel begins with Nebuchadnezzar's siege of Jerusalem in 598 BCE. His army of infantry, chariot and cavalry surrounded the city, deploying the tried siege methodologies of

---

[137] Mark W. Chavalas, *Mesopotamia and the Bible*, Continuum, 2003, p. 258; *DDD*, pp. 338, 912. Manfred Lurker, *Routledge Dictionary of Gods and Goddesses, Devils and Demons*, Routledge, 2004, p. 125. For Michael a derivation from the Persian deity Vohumanô has also been suggested, *DDD*, p. 569.

[138] *DDD*, pp. 219–29; Paul J. Achtemeier and Roger S. Boraas (eds), *HarperCollins Bible Dictionary*, HarperCollins, 1996, pp. 223–4, 743–4.

battering ram, escalade, sapping and starvation. The Jews might have been expecting divine intervention. An earlier siege by the Assyrians in the eighth century BCE had been broken, according to the legend, by the miraculous appearance of the 'angel of Yahweh' who single-handedly slew the 185,000 strong besieging force (2 Kings 18–19).

However, when Nebuchadnezzar himself arrived outside the walls in 597 the Judean king Jehoiachin surrendered the city. The victorious forces took Daniel and several others – 'certain of the children of Israel, and of the king's seed, and of the princes' (Daniel 1:3) – back with them to Babylon. This was the beginning of the Jewish captivity or exile and a large proportion of the Jewish population was taken prisoner, perhaps as many as 10,000 people. Yet Daniel and his companions fared especially well. They were raised in the Babylonian court, taught 'the learning and tongue of the Chaldeans' (Daniel 1:4) and 'God gave them knowledge and skill in all learning and wisdom' (Daniel 1:17). Now known as Belteshazzar among the Babylonians, Daniel in particular 'had understanding in all visions and dreams' (Daniel 1:17) and Nebuchadnezzar thought him 'ten times better than all the magicians and astrologers that were in all his realm' (Daniel 1:20), calling him 'master magician' (Daniel 4:9).[139]

After a successful career interpreting Nebuchadnezzar's dreams as his chief wizard and surviving being thrown into the lion's den after the old king died, Daniel began to have his own prophetic dreams. When he is unable to interpret the second of these concerning a fight between a ram and a billy goat, he 'heard a man's voice [. . .] which called, and said, Gabriel, make this man to understand the vision' (Daniel 8:15). An angel then appeared to him – 'behold, there stood before me as the appearance of a man' (Daniel 8:15) – and, as 'Daniel' explains, 'I was afraid, and fell upon my face' (Daniel 8:16), however, he was still dreaming as he continued 'I was in a deep sleep' (Daniel 8:18).

---

[139] Paul Bently Kern, *Ancient Siege Warfare*, Indiana University Press, 1999, pp. 44–5.

Some time later, after the historically suspect 'Darius the Median' had conquered Babylonia, Daniel became somewhat hysterical over Jeremiah's prophecy that the 'desolation of Jerusalem' (Daniel 9:2) would last seventy years. He donned sackcloth and ashes, fasted and offered a long, emotional prayer to his god asking for forgiveness. In the midst of all this teeth-gnashing 'the man Gabriel, whom I had seen in the vision at the beginning, being caused to fly swiftly, touched me about the time of the evening oblation. And he informed me, and talked with me' (Daniel 9:21–2). The angel explains the prophecy in terms of 'seventy weeks' (Daniel 9:24), usually taken to mean 'seventy weeks of years', i.e., 70 times seven, or 490 years.

The angel Gabriel appeared to Daniel in human shape. There was otherwise nothing remarkable about him. He appeared in dreams or in altered states induced by fasting. His precise function was to interpret dreams and prophecies. Michael, on the other hand, was more dramatically introduced. Daniel was again fasting: 'I ate no pleasant bread, neither came flesh nor wine in my mouth' (Daniel 10:3). After three weeks of this he experienced a vision:

> Then I lifted up mine eyes, and looked, and behold a certain man clothed in linen, whose loins were girded with fine gold of Uphaz. His body also as like beryl, and his face as the appearance of lightning, and his eyes as lamps of fire, and his arms and feet like in colour to polished brass, and the voice of his words like the voice of a multitude. (Daniel 10:5–6)

Daniel passed out – 'then was I in a deep sleep on my face' (Daniel 10:9) – but the vision seemed to pick him up and spoke:

> Fear not, Daniel: for from the first day that thou didst set thine heart to understand, and to chasten thyself before thy God, thy words were heard, and I am come for thy words. But the prince of the kingdom of Persia withstood me one and twenty days: but, lo, Michael, one of the chief princes,

came to help me; and remained there with the kings of Persia.
(Daniel 10:13–14)

This, then, was not Michael, for the being referred to Michael as
having helped him. Neither was it Gabriel, who always appeared as
a man and not so obviously supernatural in origin. Mysteriously,
he is not named at all. He is described as 'the servant of this my
lord' (Daniel 10:17), so is clearly an intermediate divine being; an
angel. Michael is 'one of the chief princes'; for Daniel he is 'Michael
your prince' (Daniel 10:21). Later he is identified as 'the great
prince which standeth for the children of thy people' (Daniel 12:1),
i.e., he is the specific angel of the Jews. Together, the unnamed
angel and Michael defeat the 'prince' of Persia, evidently another
angelic being, showing that it was thought that each kingdom or
people had its own protective spirit and that, like the kingdoms and
people on earth, they came into conflict with one another.

The unnamed angel delivered a thinly disguised version of
Hellenistic history, ending with the persecution of the Jews by
Antiochus Epiphanes. He prophesies the death of Epiphanes,
that Michael will be victorious and that the dead will rise from
the grave to be either rewarded with eternal life or everlasting
damnation. Daniel is told to 'shut up the words, and seal the
book' until the End Times (Daniel 12:4).

Additional orders of supernatural beings from the Old
Testament – the cherubim and seraphim – would come to be
classed as angels. In the book of Ezekiel, the legendary prophet
Ezekiel – traditionally another Babylonian captive – has a series
of visions. In the first, Ezekiel is by the river Chebar, a tributary
canal of the Euphrates river, to the south-east of Babylon:

And I looked, and, behold, a whirlwind came out of the north,
a great cloud, and a fire infolding itself, and a brightness was
about it, and out of the midst thereof as the colour of amber,
out of the midst of the fire. Also out of the midst thereof came
the likeness of four living creatures. And this was their appearance; they had the likeness of a man. (Ezekiel 1:4–5)

However, these were strange-looking men. They had four faces – a man's, a lion's, an ox's and an eagle's – four wings, the soles of their feet were like the soles of calves' feet, and they shone with the colour of burnished brass (Ezekiel 1:6–7, 10). They appeared 'like burning coals of fire' and 'out of the fire went forth lightning' (Ezekiel 1:13). These cherubim then resolved into a psychedelic four-wheeled chariot with strange rings (wheel-rims) full of eyes and above it Ezekiel saw a throne bearing Yahweh (Ezekiel 16–28). Yahweh delivers a series of speeches about Israel and the wicked dying and so on, which we can safely skip over.

In all, the term 'cherubim' occurs ninety-one times in the Hebrew Bible, referring to a variety of supernatural or monstrous beings having the presence of wings in common. The cherubim are, in particular, directly associated with the Hebrew deity as his steed (Psalms 17), his chariot (1 Chronicles 18), or his throne (2 Kings 19:15). In Genesis (3:24), Yahweh sets the cherubim to guard the entrance to the Garden of Eden after expelling Adam and Eve. According to various Bible legends, images of cherubim were used extensively in the ornamentation and furnishings of the Jerusalem temple. Gold figures of cherubim were said to adorn the top of the Ark of the Covenant (Exodus 25:18–21). Cherubim were said to be embroidered on the Veil of the Tabernacle (Exodus 26:31). The exterior and interior panelling of the temple was said to be engraved with cherubim (1 Kings 6, 7). Solomon supposedly had two enormous gold-plated olivewood statues of cherubim made to stand either side of the Ark (1 Kings 6:23; 2 Chronicles 3:11). Cherubim were clearly an important and meaningful motif, quite distinct from the messenger angel.

The origin of the word is disputed, but the most likely theory is that it comes from the Akkadian *k ribu* or *kuribu*, terms denoting genii in Mesopotamian mythology and art. Cherubim are functionally and iconographically prefigured by the Egyptian sphinx, the human-headed winged lion. The sphinx functioned as a throne guardian, becoming artistically integral to the throne itself in a later Syrian development, and a simpler lion-paw throne is known from the city of Ugarit as the throne of El. Additionally, the cherub is almost certainly connected with the Mesopotamian winged half-human, half-animal protective spirits called *lamassu* and *shedu*. We find sphinx-like human-headed winged lions, although the human-headed winged bull is the more well-known representation. These then were the cherubim: fierce sacred beings that would be undoubtedly perturbed by their current representation as overweight children (*putti*), so famously evoked by Raphael in his *Sistine Madonna* (c. 1513–14) and now reproduced on everything from biscuit tins to Christmas cards.[140]

But the cherubim were not alone. In the book of Isaiah, the prophet Isaiah has a vision of strange beings attending God. These are the seraphim (Isaiah 6:1–7) who surround God's throne, singing 'Holy, holy, holy is the Lord of hosts. All the earth is filled with his glory' – the so-called *trishagion*. Seraphim is the plural of *seraph* (*sarap*), 'the burning one'. In Isaiah they are described as having six wings: two to cover their faces, two to cover their 'feet' and two with which to fly. Elsewhere (Numbers 21:6–8; Deuteronomy 8:15) they appear as 'fiery serpents'. In searching for the origin of these beings some have suggested a connection with the seven thunders of Baal; however, iconographic evidence points to the Egyptian uraeus serpent. The uraeus was a cobra – its poison being the 'burning' – sometimes represented with two or four wings and was a motif well known from scarabs and seals in Palestine. In Isaiah (6) they stand above Yahweh just as the uraeus stands on the forehead of Egyptian gods and kings. It is unlikely that an early Israelite would have seen these beings as angels, *mal'akh* (messengers), and it is only in later interpretation that they have become organized into a strict hierarchy of angelic beings.[141]

---

[140] *Harp. Coll. BD*, pp. 175–6; *DDD*, pp. 189–92; *Jewish Encyclopedia*, 12 vols, 1901–06, pp. 13–16.

[141] *DDD*, pp. 742–3; Othmar Keel, *Jahwe-Visionen und Siegelkunst*, Verlag Katholisches Bibelwerk, 1977, pp. 70–124.

Apocryphal Angels and Archangels

> And behold! He cometh with ten thousands of holy ones
> To execute judgement upon all,
> And to destroy the ungodly[142]

The archangels enter with Enoch. Enoch, the mythical seventh patriarch from the time of the creation – more ancient than Moses – who lived 365 years, walked with God and was mysteriously 'taken' by him (Genesis 5:18–24). He seems to have been partly modelled on the seventh king of Sippar in Mesopotamia, the hero-magician Emmeduranki, and partly on a contemporary of Emmeduranki called Utuabzu, the seventh sage who was taken up to heaven. According to tradition, Enoch also composed a book or books: the so-called Ethiopic Apocalypse of Enoch (1 Enoch),[143] the Slavonic Apocalypse of Enoch also known as The Secret Book of Enoch (2 Enoch),[144] and the later Hebrew Book

---

[142] 1 Enoch, 1:9. All quotations are from the English translation by R. H. Charles, *The Book of Enoch*, Society for Promoting Christian Knowledge, 1917.

[143] There were 29 manuscripts of 1 Enoch written in the cryptic Ge'ez or Ethiopic language scattered across Europe and America from various eras, none of them earlier than the sixteenth century. It was only in 1886–7 that a partial Greek version, apparently a translation of a Hebrew or Aramaic text, was discovered during excavations at Akhmîm on the banks of the Nile by the Mission Archéologique Française. This Greek version was dated about the sixth century CE and had been the basis for the later Ethiopic texts. It would take until 1947 and the famous discovery of the Dead Sea Scrolls at Qumran (Cave 4) to produce evidence of the original. The oldest of these discoveries – The Astronomical Book and The Book of the Watchers – were dated to between the end of the third century and the first half of the second century BCE. See J. T. Milik, *The Books of Enoch: Aramaic Fragments from Qumran Cave 4*, Clarendon, 1976, p. 7; John Joseph Collins, *The Apocalyptic Imagination: An Introduction to Jewish Apocalyptic Literature*, Eerdmans, 1998, p. 44.

[144] 2 Enoch was not known outside of Eastern Europe for over 1,000 years. It only came to Western attention when the German *Jahrbücher für Protestantische Theologie* made mention of it in 1892. It is believed to have been written around the first century CE by a Hellenistic Jew or Jews in Egypt, probably Alexandria, and to have had a direct influence on the New Testament. It appears to be a Slavic translation of a now lost Greek text and is only preserved in medieval

of Enoch (3 Enoch).[145] These texts, another biblical mystery in themselves, are classed as apocryphal, which means that they are not an accepted part of the Christian canon. However, their influence on Christianity and later Jewish mysticism is undoubted. Without Enoch there would be no archangels.[146]

From the Greek *arch-* (ἀρχ-), 'to rule', and *aggelos*, as we saw above, the archangels are the officer class of the heavenly host. We have already seen how Michael and Gabriel held an exalted status as specifically named angels, with Michael the 'great prince' (Daniel 12:1),[147] and in Joshua we find a captain of the heavenly army (Joshua 5:13–15), hinting at a hierarchy of Yahweh's supernatural subordinates, but this idea is not fully developed until 1 Enoch. The archangels are at first only four, Michael, Uriel (Greek) or Suryal (Ethiopic), Raphael and Gabriel (1 Enoch 9), being later expanded with the addition of Raguel, Saraqâêl, and Remiel (1 Enoch 20). They are particularly known as 'the holy angels who watch' (1 Enoch 20:1), hence the appellation 'the watchers'. This already gives them a guardian aspect, but their remit is broad and impersonal. Uriel is described as 'over the world and over Tartarus' (1 Enoch 20:2). Raphael is 'over the spirits of men' (1 Enoch 20:3). Raguel 'takes vengeance on the world of the luminaries' (1 Enoch 20:4). Michael 'is set over the best part of mankind [and] over chaos' (1 Enoch 20:5). Saraqâêl is 'over the spirits, who sin in spirit' (1 Enoch 20:6). Gabriel is

and later manuscripts, the oldest being fourteenth century. See Robert Henry Charles and William Richard Morfill, *The Book of the Secrets of Enoch*, Clarendon, 1896, pp. xi–xxvi.

[145] 3 Enoch is also known as The Book of the Palaces, The Book of Rabbi Ishmael the High Priest and The Revelation of the Metatron. 3 Enoch gives its source as the High Priest Rabbi Ishmael (90–135 CE); however, it is generally dated to the first half of the ninth century CE. See Hugo Odeberg, *The Hebrew Book of Enoch*, Cambridge University Press, 1928, p. 27.

[146] *Harp. Coll. BD*, p. 293, 895; *DDD*, p. 80; Gershom G. Scholem, *Major Trends in Jewish Mysticism*, Schocken, 1961, p. 67; Collins, *Apocalyptic*, pp. 45–6.

[147] It has been argued that given the early date of 1 Enoch, the book of Daniel already demonstrates a second phase in the development of Michael, see *DDD*, p. 569.

'over Paradise and the serpents and the Cherubim' (1 Enoch 20:7). Finally, Remiel is 'set over those who rise', i.e., at the Last Judgement (1 Enoch 20:8).

Archangels

1 Enoch	3 Enoch	2 Esdras (4 Ezra)	Testament of Solomon	Gregory the Great*	Pseudo-Dionysus**	Raziel***	Blessed Angels****
Uriel	Mikael	Michael	Mikael	Michael	Michael	Gabriel	Raphael
Raphael	Gabriel	Gabriel	Gabriel	Gabriel	Gabriel	Fanuel	Gabriel
Raguel	Shatqiel	Uriel	Uriel	Raphael	Raphael	Michael	Chamuel
Michael	Baradiel	Raphael	Sabrael	Uriel	Uriel	Uriel	Michael
Saraqâêl	Shachaqiel	Gabuthelon	Arael	Simiel	Chamuel	Raphael	Adabiel
Gabriel	Baraqiel	Beburos	Iaoth	Orifiel	Jophiel	Israel	Haniel
Remiel	Sidriel	Zebuleon	Adonael	Zachariel	Zadkiel	Uzziel	Zaphiel
		Aker					
		Arphugitonos					

*Gregory the Great (540–604 CE), *Moralia in Job*, in M. Adriaen (ed.), *Corpus Christianorum Series Latina*, Turnhout, 1979, iv.xxviii.i.9.

**Pseudo-Dionysius the Areopagite, *De Coelesti Hierarchia* (Celestial Hierarchy), chap. vi-ix.

***The so-called 'throne angels', from 'The Book of the Angel Raziel', thirteenth century. See Steve Savedow (trans.), *Sepher Rezial [sic]: The Book of the Angel Rezial*, Red Wheel/Weiser, 2000.

****Thomas Heywood, *The Hierarchy of the Blessed Angels*, Adam Islip, 1635,

Archangels

Raphael 'was sent to heal' (Tobit 3:17) and describes himself as 'one of the seven holy angels' (Tobit 12:15). He is 'set over all disease and every wound of the children of the people' (1 Enoch 40:9). Raguel is the 'friend of God', although compare Ra'uel, 'the terrifier'. Remiel is doubtless the angel Jeremiel ('El is merciful') found in 2 Esdras ([4 Ezra] 4:36), as we also have a Syriac version that reads Ramael. The names come from the Hebrew root *rûm*, 'to be high, exalted' plus the usual '-el' ending, thus we get Ramiel, Rumiel and Eremiel. In 2 Baruch (55:3) he 'presides over true visions', but confusingly in 1 Enoch (6:7) he is also one of the fallen angels. The name Uriel is known in the Old Testament as a personal name, derived from either 'light' (Hebrew) or 'fire' (Aramaic). As an archangel he is connected with astrology (1 Enoch 72–82), later becoming a revealing angel (2 Esdras [4 Ezra] where his name is sometimes given as Phanuel). Uriel is also sometimes written as Sariel, Suriel and Suryal (Suriyel), linking him with Saraqâêl, who is also sometimes named Sariel, and even Remiel. More variations of these names exist, confusing their roles and identities as separable beings.[148]

As well as the archangels, Enoch describes 'the sleepless ones who guard the throne of his glory' (1 Enoch 71:7). These are the seraphim, cherubim and ophanim. The new group here, the ophanim, takes its name from the Hebrew for 'wheel', leading some to identify these beings with the strange wheels mentioned in Ezekiel (1:15–21) and the 'wheels as burning fire' on the throne of the 'Ancient of Days' in Daniel (7–9). They are later termed 'thrones', although in 1 Enoch they are clearly distinct from the throne of God.

The rank and file angels, the 'host of the heavens' (1 Enoch 61:10), the 'troops of hosts', 'children of heaven' and 'the heavenly household' are designated as 'ministering angels' (*mal'ᵃke ha-ššārēp*) and are organized in 'camps', 'companies' or 'parties'

---

[148] *DDD*, pp. 81, 466–7, 688, 885–6; *Jewish Enc.*; Gustav Davidson, *A Dictionary of Angels*, The Free Press, 1971, pp. 238–9, 258.

(3 Enoch 5:2). In all, 1 Enoch designates seven classes of supernatural beings:

> And He will summon all the host of the heavens, and all the
> holy ones above, and the host of God, the Cherubic, Seraphin
> [*sic*] and Ophannin [*sic*], and all the angels of power, and all
> the angels of principalities, and the Elect One, and the other
> powers on the earth (and) over the water. (1 Enoch 61:10)

In 2 Enoch, the prophet is taken up to heaven by two angels,
Samuil and Ragnil (33:6), rising through seven heavens to
witness:

> A very great light and all the fiery hosts of great archangels,
> and incorporeal powers and lordships, and principalities, and
> powers; cherubim and seraphim, thrones and the watchful-
> ness of many eyes. There were ten troops, a station of
> brightness, and I was afraid and trembled with a great terror.
> (2 Enoch 10:1)

Unlike 1 Enoch, there are now supposed to be ten orders of
spirits here who stand upon ten steps, which only works if we
take the 'very great light' to also be some sort of being.[149] Finally,
in 3 Enoch, the prophet ascends to heaven in a storm chariot
and, after being transformed into fire and lightning, becomes
the angel Metatron.

Angels in the Christian Era

Angels take on a wider range of functions in the New Testament.
When Jesus supposedly tells the story of a poor man who dies
and is 'carried by the angels to Abraham's bosom' (Luke 16:22)
we see that angels now assume the role of psychopompos, guiding or leading the spirit (soul) after death. Mark (12:25) records

---

[149] Rutherford H. Platt solved the problem by simply amending the text to read
'nine regiments' in his *The Lost Books of the Bible*, Alpha House, 1926.

Jesus as having said that the risen will live like angels in heaven. Angels appear on earth (Gabriel in Luke 1–2), in dreams (Matthew 1:20, 2:13, 19), bring messages from God and offer assistance (e.g. Acts 5:19). Raphael helps Tobias (Tobit 5:4–12:22) drive out the demon who killed an earlier husband of his bride Sarah (8:2–3). The most detailed account is given in the Book of Revelation where more than a third of all angel references in the New Testament occur.[150]

The Book of Revelation is traditionally attributed to John the Apostle and appears to have been composed some time in the first or second centuries CE. It only became a canonical book of the New Testament in 397 CE at the Council of Carthage and when Martin Luther came to translate the Bible into German in the sixteenth century he placed it on his list of suspect texts, the Antilegomena. Its position has always been an uncertain one. Like Ezekiel, John sees four 'living creatures' before the throne of God (4:4–11). He witnesses the Lamb of God break the Seven Seals, unleashing the Horsemen of the Apocalypse, natural catastrophe and the Final Judgement. Judgement begins with seven angels sounding seven trumpets to bring further destruction, release Abaddon's army from the bottomless pit and set loose four angels to kill a third of humanity. There is a great battle in heaven between Michael and 'the dragon', also known as 'the Devil, and Satan' (12:7, 9). Both lead armies of angels, but Michael is triumphant and the Devil 'was cast out into the earth, and his angels were cast out with him' (12:9).

Further attempts to establish an intelligible hierarchy of angels continued to be made. The fifth-century writer known as Pseudo-Dionysius the Areopagite no doubt saw the problem with Enoch's arithmetic and described what has become the classic threefold hierarchy of three spheres of three choirs. In the first sphere we find seraphim, cherubim and thrones, in the second, dominions, virtues, powers, and in the third, principalities, archangels and

---

[150] *DDD*, pp. 50–2.

angels.[151] Showing its influence, we find it repeated in the thirteenth century by Thomas Aquinas in his influential *Summa Theologica*. The Christian writers generally agreed on what should come at the top and bottom of the hierarchy, but repeatedly re-ordered and sometimes enlarged the middle ranks.

Keeping Enoch's number ten, the medieval Jewish scholar Moses Maimonides presented an influential schema in the twelfth century of Chajjoth, Ophannim, Arellim, Chashmallim, Seraphim, Mal'achim, Elohim, Bene Elohim, Kerubim, Ishim. The thirteenth-century cabbalist Abraham ben Isaac of Granada had a different list in his *Berit Menuhah* of Arellim, Ishim, Bene Elohim, Mal'achim, Chashmallim, Tarshishim, Shina'nim, Kerubim, Ophannim, Seraphim. Ten had important connotations for the cabbalists as it related to the ten sephiroth (emanations) of the Tree of Life and hence reflected the universal order.[152]

---

[151] Pseudo-Dionysius the Areopagite, *De Coelesti Hierarchia* (Celestial Hierarchy), chap. vi–ix.
[152] Maimonides, *Mishne Thora* S. I.; Jesode Thora C. 2, quoted in Charles and Morfill, p. 25.

Christian Angelic Hierarchies[153]

4th Century St Ambrose	Apostolic Constitutions	5th Century Pseudo-Dionysius	6th Century Gregory the Great	7th-8th Centuries Isidore of Seville	St John Damascene	12th Century Hildegard of Bingen
Seraphim	Seraphim	Seraphim	Seraphim	Seraphim	Seraphim	Seraphim
Cherubim	Cherubim	Cherubim	Cherubim	Cherubim	Cherubim	Cherubim
Dominations	Aeons	Thrones	Thrones	Powers	Thrones	Thrones
Thrones	Hosts	Dominions	Dominations	Principalities	Dominions	Dominations
Principalities	Powers	Virtues	Principalities	Virtues	Powers	Principalities
Potentates (Powers)	Authorities	Powers	Powers	Dominations	Authorities (Virtues)	Powers
Virtues	Principalities	Principalities	Virtues	Thrones	Rulers (Principalities)	Virtues
Archangels	Thrones	Archangels	Archangels	Archangels	Archangels	Archangels
Angels	Archangels	Angels	Angels	Angels	Angels	Angels
	Angels					
	Dominions					

[153] St Ambrose, *Apologia Prophetae David*, 5, fourth century; Clement of Rome (attributed to), *Apostolic Constitutions*, fourth century (purporting to be first century); Gregory the Great, also St Gregory (c. 540–604), *Homiliarum in Ezechielem Prophetam*, sixth century; Isidore of Seville (c. 560–636), *Etymologiae*, Bk 7, seventh century; St John Damascene (c. 676–c. 754–87), *De Fide Orthodoxa*; Hildegard of Bingen, *The Letters of Hildegard of Bingen*, trans. Joseph L. Baird and Radd K. Ehrman, Oxford University Press, 1998, p. 65; and Hildegard of Bingen, *Scivias*, trans. Columba Hart and Jane Bishop, Paulist Press, 1990, Bk 1, 6, composed 1141–51.

As one of the so-called 'religions of the book', Islam shares much of its mythological framework with Judaism and Christianity. According to the Qur'an, when Allah created Adam he ordered the angels to prostrate themselves before him. One of them refused: Azazel. 'Me thou hast created of smoke-less fire, and shall I reverence a creature made of dust?' Allah banished him from heaven to be known henceforth as Iblis (or Eblis), deriving either from the Arabic for 'despair' or a corruption of the Greek *diabolos*, and he became the enemy of humankind – *al-shaytan*, 'the satan'. The other angels remained at their place beside the throne of Allah, arranged in four orders: throne bearers, cherubim, archangels, and the lesser angels. There are four archangels: Jibril (Gabriel), the revealer; Mikal (Michael), the provider; Isra'il (Azrael), the angel of death; and Israfil (Raphael), who puts souls into bodies and is ordered to sound the trumpet announcing *Qiyamah*, the Last Judgement. The angels record the deeds of humans, both good and bad, occasionally interceding with God on their behalf. They reward the good and punish the wicked, and escort the soul at death.[154]

In 610 CE, according to tradition, Allah sent an angel to reveal the Qur'an to Muhammad. After receiving a thorough beating from the angel, Muhammad thought that he might be possessed by evil spirits, djinn, and decided to throw himself from a mountain-top. A voice spoke out as he was about to do so, saying: 'O Muhammad, thou art God's apostle and I am Gabriel.' Reassured, Muhammad was able to go on and continue receiving the Qur'an. There is an interesting range of paranormal phenomena described here: visionary dreams, poltergeist-like activity, possession (or fear of it), and auditory hallucinations, with apparent angelic intervention proving crucial to the story.[155]

---

[154] Oliver Leaman (ed.), *The Qur'an: An Encyclopedia*, Routledge, 2006, pp. 105, 179–81.

[155] Quotation from the Hadith *Sahih al-Bukhari* 1.3; Muhammad ibn Jarir Al-Tabari, *Tarikh al-Rasul Wa al-Muluk (History of the Prophets and Kings)*, Brill, 1879–1901, I, p. 1151; David A. Leeming, Kathryn Madden and Stanton Marlan (eds), *Encyclopedia of Psychology and Religion*, Springer, 2010, p. 37;

Although the term 'angel' develops out of a Judaeo-Christian context, the idea of divine messengers or intermediary spirits between humans and the gods is also found in other cultures. In Chinese and Japanese religion there are a number of beings with roles similar to the angels of the West. Hinduism has its messengers known as angiris. In Buddhism a Bodhisattva functions in a comparable manner. In pagan Europe, Hermes and Iris of the Greeks take the role of divine heralds, in the North, Odin's son Hermod took this part, and swans often appear in Celtic mythology as messengers from the Otherworld.[136]

Guardian Angels

He shall give His angels charge over thee, to keep thee in all thy ways. (Psalms 91:11)

It happened some years ago when I was still a student. It was an ordinary day and I was walking down an ordinary London street. My head was in the clouds and I was paying little attention to the world around me. A sidestreet broke the pavement and as I lifted my foot from the kerb, a voice in my head, so it seemed, shouted 'Car!' I stopped dead as a car shot out from the sidestreet at speed, missing me by inches. As I was to later find out, the experience is not uncommon, with many people attributing such phenomena to the intervention of guardian angels.

Almost every other person thinks they have a guardian angel watching over them. According to a 1993 survey of US adults, 46 per cent believed that they had a guardian angel. As reported in 2010, this figure had risen to 53 per cent. It is a popular idea – that we have a special supernatural bodyguard looking out for us – but where does it come from and did one really save me that fateful day in London?[157]

Leaman, p. 509.

[136] *Enc. Psych. Rel.*, p. 36.

[157] 'Angels Among Us', *Time*, 27 December 1993, p. 56; Christopher Bader, F. Carson Mencken and Joseph Baker, *Paranormal America*, New York University

Again the trail takes us back to Mesopotamia for the origin of current ideas about guardian angels. In the later Assyrian period we find winged creatures guarding temple and palace gates – such as the two colossal statues that once guarded the entrance to Sargon II's throne room in the eighth century BCE, for example. These creatures derive from the female *lama* (Sumerian), or *lamassu* (Akkadian) and the male *shedu*, winged half-human, half-animal hybrids. They also functioned as personal guardians, protecting against evil spirits, and carrying the individual's homage to the gods and bringing back divine blessing. It was a saying that 'he who has no god when he walks in the street wears a headache like a garment' because illnesses, such as headaches, were believed to be caused by demonic forces. Spells were used to invoke their protection, such as this one originally written in cuneiform:[158]

ilušîdu damiḳtu ilu[lamassu damiḳtu] [. . .] *-kiš itti-yà* ('may the favourable [shedu] and favourable lamassu [. . .] [be] with me!')[159]

In both the Old and New Testaments this type of magic is rejected and angels, particularly guardian angels, are only available to the faithful. In the Old Testament, 'the angel of the Lord encampeth round about them that fear him, and delivereth them' (Psalms 34:7) – fearing the Lord is meant in a positive sense in this context. In the New Testament, angels are 'ministering spirits, sent forth to minister for them who shall be heirs of salvation' (Hebrews 1:14). Later Christian writers were less exacting. In the second century CE St Justin the Martyr said 'every man is attended with a guardian angel'. St Jerome (c.

Press, 2010, p. 184, using Baylor Religion Survey data, 2005 and 2007.
[158] *Routledge Dict. Gods*, 2004, pp. 109, 169; Felix Guirand (ed.), *New Larousse Encyclopedia of Mythology*, trans. Richard Aldington and Delano Ames, Crescent Books, 1987, p. 74.
[159] Leonard W. King, *Babylonian Magic and Sorcery*, Weiser, 2000 [1896], pp. 82, 84.

347–420) implied as much when he said 'Great is the dignity of souls, who have from their birth a delegate angel, commissioned from heaven, for their custody'. Thomas Aquinas (1225–74) did not disagree.[160]

In the mythology of Northern Europe we know of Heimdall (Heimdallr), the 'guardian of the gods' who may also have functioned as a boundary figure, or perhaps derived from a household spirit – the lack of surviving sources makes this speculative. The gradual feminization of the Judaic male angels brings them into greater sympathy with the Northern valkyries. Known amongst the Germans in general as *idisi*, amongst the Anglo-Saxons as *waelcryie*, and amongst the Norse as *valkyrja*, the name means 'she who chooses warriors destined to die in battle'. They were the shield-maidens of Odin who chose the most heroic of the battle slain to join the gods in Valhalla and granted victory to the chieftain who won their favour. They either travelled through the air on winged horses, or they could fly through the air unaided as swan-maidens clothed in white feathers. But the conception of being looked after by a supernatural entity is better expressed in the form of the *fylgia* (or *fylgja*), who performed the role of personal and tribal protector, and who could also appear as an omen of death. In the *Lay of Helgi Hjörvarðsson*, Hedin encounters his brother Helgi's *fylgia* in the form of a woman riding a wolf with reins of serpents, which Helgi interprets, correctly as it turns out, as a sign of his impending death.[161]

There are many accounts of the actions of guardian angels. In 1847 John Mason Neale, better known for his Christmas carols such as 'Good King Wenceslas', told two stories of being saved by angels. In the first, a Derbyshire child falls into a stream

[160] Quoted in G. W. Hart, 'Guardian Angels', in L.P. (ed.), *A Book of Angels*, 1906, p. 243. Thomas Aquinas, *Summa*, Pt 1, quest. 113, §4.

[161] John Lindow, *Norse Mythology*, Oxford University Press, 2001, pp. 95–6, 167, 171; *New Larousse*, pp. 254, 283; Benjamin Thorpe, *Northern Mythology*, vol. 1, E. Lumley, 1851, pp. 113–14, referring to Helgakviða Hjörvarðssonar, Poetic Edda, various editions.

and is about to drown when she is pulled out by 'a beautiful lady, clad in white'. Nobody of that description could be found, so the thankful parents concluded that she must have been an angel. In the second, a widower and his two children visit the rambling old house of a friend. The children set off to explore and are about to stumble into a deep and uncovered well in the cellar when the figure of their deceased mother appears and prevents them. Neale was not sure whether to declare this spirit that of the mother, or of an angel in her shape.[162]

A story told by the Revd G. W. Hart in 1906 concerns a girl in America who was run over by a tram and thought to have been killed. She was taken home and though apparently unhurt, lay in some sort of comatose condition for a long time. Surprisingly, she regained consciousness and explained that a being in white had lifted the tram wheels one after the other as they passed over her, preventing them from crushing her. Two red lines were discernible on her body, apparently the course of the wheels.[163]

A similar story from the 1960s recounts how a young girl called Lucy was rushed into casualty at St Mary's Hospital, Paddington, after having been run over by a lorry. A policeman had seen both the front and rear wheels roll over her. The lorry driver had felt the bumps. Examining her, medical staff found only one small bruise on her shoulder. As they were about to send her off to be X-rayed, she opened her eyes and asked 'Where is that man in white?' Thinking she meant him, the doctor approached her bed. 'No, no,' said Lucy, 'the man in the long shiny dress.' She explained that this man had picked up the wheels as the lorry went over her. 'The wheels did not touch me,' she said. Lucy was discharged the next day.[164]

Another of Hart's stories begins with a deathbed confession.

---

[162] John Mason Neale, *The Unseen World: Communications with It, Real or Imaginary*, James Burns, 1847, p. 190.

[163] Hart, pp. 246–8.

[164] Told by Judith Shrimpton, GP, in Emma Heathcote-James, *Seeing Angels*, John Blake Publishing, 2001, pp. 74–5.

A Cornish collier, taken grievously ill, confesses in the presence of a priest to having planned to rob a well-to-do farmer on his return from market. The farmer was known to make the journey home by night, alone and with his purse bulging from the day's profits. As the miner and a confederate lay in ambush, the horse-drawn trap approaching, one of them cried out, 'Good God! There are two of them.' They fled. When asked about it later, the farmer stated that he was alone as always, but that he had on that night, as on many another, felt the presence of angels.[165]

According to research, about 18 per cent of reported angelic experiences involve some sort of guardian aspect, a life-saving act or the prevention of an accident. As with my own experience, many other people report hearing voices that impart information their conscious mind was unaware of at the time. For example, a woman is woken by a voice telling her that the water boiler is overheating and she is able to get help in time to prevent it exploding.[166]

Other accounts are more coincidental, often involving the apparent disappearance of, or inability to trace a human who renders (often unintentional) aid and is subsequently interpreted as an angel. A woman walking alone at night finds herself in a dangerous part of the city when another woman appears 'almost out of nowhere' and leads her through the danger only to vanish afterwards. A woman on crutches is harassed at a bus-stop by an aggressive drunk; she prays to God and a black sports car of 'unique design' pulls up from which a blond-haired driver warns the tramp off. Whatever the quality of these reports, they do demonstrate the continuing belief in personal guardian angels able to directly interfere in the mundane world.[167]

The darker side to this is that sometimes these heart-lifting stories of miraculous help in the hour of our greatest need are

---

[165] Hart, pp. 246–8.
[166] Heathcote-James, pp. 241–2; Judith White (1970) in Heathcote-James, pp. 115–17.
[167] Caroline Plant (undated), Vanessa Lillingston-Price (1986) in Heathcote-James, pp. 63–4, 66.

deliberately manufactured to propagate political or religious positions. Machen was one of the few honest enough to immediately disclaim that his story of the bowmen was based on anything other than his own imagination, but even then it was written to bolster public opinion that God was on the side of British in the war against 'the Hun'. An uplifting story widely circulated on the internet – and one that found its way into Heathcote-James' academic study – is that of 'A Dad's Story' (also known as 'The Birdies'). In this story a three-year-old boy called Brian is trapped under a garage door, but is saved from death by what he called 'the birdies', apparently angelic beings who prevent the automatic door from crushing him and bring his mother to the rescue. The story, originally entitled 'Free the Birdies' was apparently written in 1994 by a Mormon using the name Lloyd Glenn to promote temple attendance and observances amongst other members of the Church of Latter Day Saints. Attempts to contact Lloyd Glenn to verify his story have all failed, but the story continues to make the rounds.[168]

Experiencing Angels

Men's nerves and imagination play weird pranks in these strenuous times.

– Brigadier-General John Charteris[169]

From small beginnings the story of the Angels of Mons became an almost undeniable historical fact and unpatriotic to question. An apparently miraculous escape demanded a miraculous explanation. Machen was taken to task for his claims to have

---

[168] Heathcote-James (pp. 75–8) failed to find him, but reproduced the story as true anyway, against her own stated methodology (pp. 28–9). It was also reported that the producer for the US television programme 'Beyond Chance' had also tried with the same result (http://www.near-death.com/forum/fake/000/02.html, accessed 29 July 2010). See the analysis at http://www.snopes.com/glurge/birdies.asp.

[169] Charteris, pp. 25–6.

made the whole thing up. Soldiers and nurses swore blind that they knew someone who had seen the angels. As the years wore on, more 'evidence' was forthcoming despite the growing distance from the event itself. Even as the last of the surviving veterans passed away, stories were still coming out. Just after his 101st birthday in 1980, John Ewings, who had served in the Royal Inniskilling Fusiliers at Mons, told a BBC interviewer how 'I just looked up and the clouds parted [. . .] and this man came out with a flaming sword [. . .] what I thought I saw was an angel'. As late as 2000, Joyce Trott told of her father's experiences at the battle: '[there] was an eerie sound and there was a white light across the hill and they saw these crowds on horses riding across the top of the hill'.[170]

For the various writers and compilers of the Bible and other religious texts it was self-evident that angels were real and enacted God's will, either as messengers or in more hands-on roles, slaying unbelievers, saving prophets and preparing to decimate humanity at the Last Judgement. Like the Angels of Mons, these angels became undeniably factual and for the believer to question them was irreverent. However, when Charteris was looking into the Angels of Mons legend he was more ready to ascribe the phenomenon to psychological factors, but admitted that he could not find out how the story arose. The writer Arthur Machen claimed that the legend was created when he published *The Bowmen*, leading to a situation not unlike that of the Russian cosmonauts' supposed angel sighting onboard Salyut 7 in 1985. Originally reported – we should say *invented* – in the US tabloid *Weekly World News*, the story went on to become widely cited as a factual event.[171] The problem for Machen's version is that Charteris' comments are dated just

---

[170] John Ewings, BBC Northern Ireland, 22 May 1980, quoted in Clarke, pp. 52–3; Joyce Trott, BBC Everyman 'Angels', first broadcast on BBC1, 12 December 2000, quoted in Heathcote-James, pp. 70–1.
[171] 'Huge Angels Seen in Space', *Weekly World News*, 22 October 1985; for an analysis see Leo Ruickbie, 'Angels in Space', *Paranormal*, 56, February 2011, pp. 54–7.

days after the Battle of Mons and three weeks before the publication of 'The Bowmen'. Not only that, but the accounts that started coming back from the frontlines told of winged angels, supernatural cavalry, divine lights, mysterious clouds and not so much of ghostly archers from Agincourt as in Machen's tale. So what really did happen?

Other than broader surveys conducted by organizations like Gallup, the only serious in-depth study of angel experiences was carried out in the late 1990s by Emma Heathcote-James, then a PhD theology student at Birmingham University. After numerous calls for information on national television and in the press, including the BBC and *The Times*, she received 350 written replies from people claiming to have had some sort of angel experience.

Respondents' definitions of what constituted an 'angel' ranged from the traditional being in white with wings to any helpful incident with some sort of mysterious element, including strange smells and lights. Looking closely at her figures, we see that she found only 168 people who claimed to have seen an angel. Of these 109 reported seeing what we would traditionally think of as an angel. A typical experience ran along the following lines: '[He] looked like an angel with long flowing robes and wings'; or 'she looks rather like a Pre-Raphaelite goddess in a Burn[e]-Jones painting'. For a New Age angel-therapist like Doreen Virtue, 'Angels are glowing beings, filled with the inner radiance of God's love. Angels have soft, feathery wings'.[172]

Most people who claimed to have had an angel experience were aged thirty-one to fifty at the time and lived in the southeast of England – factors influenced by Heathcote-James's methodology and geography, as she acknowledged. More women than men reported such experiences and were generally more likely to see a traditional-style angel. This again is in line with demographic expectations. Virtue reported that about 80 to

---

[172] Heathcote-James, pp. 23–4, 32–3, 69, 248: describes 48 per cent as having seen a 'traditional' (31.1 per cent) or humanoid being (16.9 per cent); Doreen Virtue, http://www.angeltherapy.com/faq.php, accessed 23 July 2010.

85 per cent of her audience was female, seeing the male section split between a larger number of homosexual men and fewer of what she calls 'drag-alongs' – heterosexual men who reluctantly accompany wives or girlfriends. It would seem most probable that more women than men report angel experiences nowadays because more women are currently interested in angels. It is not surprising given their heritage that most people who see angels are Christians. The men unloading their bolt-action Lee-Enfield rifles with the speed of machine guns into the ranks of advancing Germans at Mons were Christians.[173]

The timing of the angels' fateful intervention at Mons is uncertain. Legend has fixed it at the height of the engagement, but a series of running battles was fought as the BEF tried to remove itself from the path of the German juggernaut. As well as various rearguard actions there was the retreat itself: a herculean marathon under blazing summer skies with an eighty-pound kit, little or no food and sometimes barely four hours of sleep. The first stage of the retreat from Mons to the regrouping point at Bavay involved a thirty-six-hour forced march with no sleep at all. The men of the Middlesex Regiment were described as 'stumbling along more like ghosts than living soldiers'. The Northumberland Fusiliers were 'a column of automatons that dragged along through the darkness of the night'. Private Frank Richards, 2 Royal Welsh Fusiliers, told how 'we retired all night with fixed bayonets, many sleeping as they marched'.[174]

In such conditions men reported seeing strange bright lights,

---

[173] Heathcote-James, pp. 233–4, 236, 240. Virtue quoted in 'Angel's Wings and Human Prayer', *New Age Retailer*, 20 July 2005, reproduced on http://www.angeltherapy.com/view_article.php?article_id=33, accessed 23 July 2010. According to Heathcote-James (p. 237), they were 53.1 per cent Christian, comprising: 39.1 per cent Protestant, 6.3 per cent Catholic, 3.4 per cent 'Christian Convert' and 4.3 per cent lapsed Christian of unspecified denomination. Buddhists, Jews, Muslims, New Agers, even agnostics and atheists, also reported angel type experiences.

[174] Regimental History, Middlesex Regiment, 24 August 1914; Regimental History, 5th Regiment, Northumberland Fusiliers, 24 August 1914; Frank Richards, *Old Soldiers Never Die*, Faber, 1964, p. 19; Clarke, pp. 48–50.

sheets of water along the roadside, bodies of soldiers on foot and horseback, trees turned into villages, castles appeared out of nothing, and one soldier kept ducking his head to avoid imaginary arches across the road. As Richards wrote, 'very nearly everyone were [sic] seeing things, we were all so dead beat'.[175]

It is a known fact that sleep deprivation causes hallucinations. Michael Golder, a professor of psychiatry at George Washington University, put it this way: 'a person who has been sleep-deprived for 72 hours is as susceptible to hallucinations as someone taking LSD'. Abnormally high body temperature, hunger and thirst have also been linked with hallucinations. Men marching without sleep, with little food in hot summer weather under stress of battle present ideal subjects for spontaneous hallucinations.[176]

Hallucinations are not as rare as we might think. When 500 people assessed as mentally 'normal' were questioned on the subject in the 1960s, 125 reported having had at least one hallucination. Included amongst these was 'seeing an angel in church during service'.[177] In his 1958 book, *Flying Saucers: A Modern Myth of Things Seen in the Skies*, Carl Gustav Jung specifically used the 'evidence' of the Angels of Mons to argue that the soldiers had experienced a 'non-pathological' vision, or what he would term a 'visionary rumour', simply, a rumour experienced in a visual as opposed to aural form. According to Jung, the extreme psychological stresses on these soldiers created a collective vision based on a shared symbolism reflecting unconscious wishes.

Psychologist Dr Susan Blackmore argued that angel experiences were produced by endorphins released during pain or shock. However, only a relatively few of Heathcote-James'

---

[175] Regimental History, 5th Regiment, Northumberland Fusiliers, 24 August 1914; A. Johnstone, letter to the *Evening News*, 11 August 1915; Richards, p. 19.
[176] Golder quoted in Rachel Horn, 'What Happens When We Hallucinate?', *Popular Science*, October 2006, p. 104; Peter D. Slade and Richard P. Bentall, *Sensory Deception: A Scientific Analysis of Hallucination*, Taylor & Francis, 1988, p. 33.
[177] Slade and Bentall, p. 70.

respondents reported an angel experience at the greatest moment of pain or shock, that is, during or after an accident.[178] According to Heathcote-James' research, the largest number of angelic experiences occurred in the bedroom rather than on the battlefield or at the scene of an accident. Although this is not specific enough to confirm that the people involved were actually asleep or on the point of sleep, this peak in the evidence does suggest typical hypnogogic (falling asleep) or hypopompic (waking up) states, that is, vivid sensory experiences associated with either falling asleep or waking up – a phenomenon medically described as early as 1848. People today seem to encounter angels in the same way that Daniel first encountered Gabriel: in their dreams, or dream-like states.[179]

Angels today are seen in an almost entirely positive aspect, but one of the abiding problems has always been deciding whose side they are on. They were clearly not on the side of the Assyrian armies when the 'chariots of fire' came to Elisha's assistance at the siege of Dothan. The Angels of Mons were no angels to the Germans, but when the first German soldiers were taken prisoner in the early days of WWI, guards were surprised to read *Gott mit uns* ('God is with us') on their belt buckles. As it says in the New Testament, 'Even Satan disguises himself as an angel of light' (2 Corinthians 11:14), and as we might add ourselves, even hell has its angels.

---

[178] Blackmore quoted in 'The Extraordinary Rise and Rise of Angels', *Cosmopolitan*, December 1997, p. 40, and Heathcote-James, p. 253; approx. 1.5 per cent reported an angel experience during or after an accident, although Heathcote-James does not give the exact figures.

[179] Slade and Bentall, p. 19; Heathcote-James, pp. 191, 239–40, 254 – 30 per cent of experiences occurred in the bedroom with another 9.5 per cent taking place in hospital rooms. Many more of the examples she quotes in her book involve relaxed states of mind, although she gives no analysis of this other than by location.

4. Demons

The priest approached the bed, a forced smile on his face. His words were kindly as he addressed the girl bound to the bed frame, trying to ignore the scratches and bruises mottling her puffy, beaten face.

'Hello, Regan. I'm a friend of your mother. I'd like to help you.'
The girl looked at him. 'You might loosen the straps then?'
'I'm afraid you might hurt yourself, Regan.'
'I'm not Regan.'
'I see. Well then, let's introduce ourselves. I'm Damien Karras.'
'And I'm the Devil. Now kindly undo these straps!'

It is an unforgettable encounter in a film that would be regarded as the scariest of all time.[180] As one of the taglines to *The Exorcist* put it 'Somewhere between science and superstition, there is another world. The world of darkness.' And millions of us have gone there – at least director William Friedkin's version of it.

This world of darkness is one in which swarming hordes of demons, ranked in innumerable legions under the command of mighty warlords of hell, press at the defences of our everyday lives. The fires burn below, white-hot in readiness for the damned, as fallen angels, wings singed and perfumed with brimstone, oil the machinery of destruction in preparation for the End Times. This is the theological reality. Sophisticated modern clerics may

---

[180] AMC/Harris Interactive poll, 2006.

play down the notion of the Devil, but the Church is founded upon the rock of resistance to the forces of (perceived) evil. Demonologists down the ages have analysed and classified them, sometimes fought them, and constantly warned us of their unceasing efforts to conquer our souls. If they are right, the thought alone is enough to drive us mad. The problem is that the subject of demons is far from straightforward.

What is a Demon?

Demons are divine. Literally. The word comes from the Greek *daimon* (δαίμων, Latin *daemon*), meaning 'divinity' from the age of Homer onward. It could refer to a specific god or goddess, or denote deity in general. Even in Ancient Greece they argued about its etymology. In the fifth century BCE the philosopher Plato said that the word originally meant 'knowing'. Some modern scholars prefer an origination from a root meaning 'to divide (destinies)', in the sense of distributing 'fate' or 'destiny', or the spirit controlling one's fate.[181]

Daimones, like other Classical supernatural entities, were morally ambivalent. *Daimones* caused *eudaimonia* (εὐδαιμονία), 'good fortune', as well as *kakodaimonia* (κακοδαιμονία), 'bad luck', or 'evil fate' – or even possession by an evil spirit. The poet Hesiod, who lived around 700 BCE, explained that these *daimones* were the souls of those who had lived during the Golden Age and who now watched over humankind as 'guardians of mortal men'. Plato later added that *daimones* were 'between gods and mortals' and, like angels, mediated between the two. Socrates' famous *daimon* seems to have been predisposed towards the good and was said to offer him advice. Also in the fifth century BCE, the philosopher Empedocles taught that the *daimon* was an 'occult self', or soul, that endured through successive incarnations.[182]

---

[181] Henry George Liddell and Robert Scott, *A Greek–English Lexicon*, Clarendon Press, 1940; K. van der Toorn, Bob Becking and Pieter Willem van der Horst (eds), *Dictionary of Deities and Demons in the Bible* [*DDD*], 2nd ed., Brill/Eerdmans, 1999, p. 235.

[182] Plato, *Cratylus* 398b, *Symposium* 202e; Hesiod, *Works and Days* 109–93;

Generally, *daimones* were seen as a class of spirit below the gods of Olympus, such as Zeus and Hera. Although in principle they could be either good or bad, this is not to say that the Greeks were lacking any conception of evil spirits. There was also a large number of entirely unpleasant *daimones*, euphemistically referred to as the 'other daimon', lurking in the shadows of the Greek worldview. Illness itself was a *daimon*, but also bore specific names such as Hepiales (also Epiales), the personification of fever, Enodius who caused diarrhoea and the fluttering, fairy-like Keres who loved to cause madness, blindness and even blisters, as well as stir up hate and discord. Like the Keres, other evil spirits were seen as responsible for social unrest, such as Eris ('strife'), 'insatiable in her fury', whilst others like Lamia ('gluttonous' or 'lecherous'), the blood-sucking child-killer and shark-like mother of the dog-headed sea monster Scylla, reigned over specific realms of human misery. Lamia, descended from the Akkadian demoness Lamashtu, was often counted amongst the Empusae ('forcers-in') who were said to frighten travellers on lonely roads and sexually assault men. Later a whole class of vampirizing she-devils came to be known as the lamiae, forerunners of the later succubi.[183]

Damaging or dangerous natural phenomena were also seen as spiritual entities. The three Gorgons – Stheino ('mighty'), Euryale ('wide wandering') and Medusa ('cunning') – represented the destroying power of the thunderstorm, their basilisk stare the lightning flash, whilst at the same time being the ultimate incarnation of the evil eye. The storm winds were also personified as the Harpies ('snatchers'). They were said to live in the entrance to the underworld called the Strophades, or in a

---

Liddell and Scott; E. R. Dodds, *The Greeks and the Irrational*, University of California Press, 1963, p. 153; *DDD*, p. 235.
[183] Walter Burkert, *Greek Religion*, Harvard University Press, 2000, pp. 180–1; Dodds, pp. 6–8; Cesidio R. Simboli, *Disease-Spirits and Divine Cures Among the Greeks and Romans*, Doctoral Thesis, Columbia University, 1921; Robert Graves, *The Greek Myths*, Penguin, 1992, pp. 189–90; *DDD*, p. 521.

cave on Crete, and were sent by the gods to carry people off to their doom or, paradoxically, bring life.[184]

One group of beings was so feared that they were known euphemistically as the Eumenides, the 'gracious' or 'kind ones'. Whilst everyone knew they were the Erinyes, 'the angry ones', they preferred not to name them out loud. The Romans would come to call them the Furies (*Furiae*). According to Hesiod, they were born of the blood of the primordial sky-god Uranus, murdered by his son Kronos. Aeschylus called them 'the children of Eternal Night'. Their eyes dripped blood, their skin was the colour of coal, sometimes with dog's faces, or Gorgon eyes, bat-winged to show the swiftness of their vengeance, serpents entwining their brows. They carried blazing torches and brass-studded whips. Despite their fearsome reputation their purpose was in itself not evil. They avenged perjury and murder, and upheld the moral order, embodying the judgement or curse pronounced upon a criminal.[185]

Vast ranks of the Nameless Ones of the underworld, tempting sirens, oracular and tomb-haunting sphinxes, sea-monsters, Ladon the dragon, the snake-woman Echidne, the 'goat-shanked *daimon*' Pan, and the corpse-eating Euronymous: many more such entities can be named, for the Ancient Greeks had a fully developed pantheon of horrors – gods, monsters and *daimones* – to account for all of the various destructive natural forces and human maladies that one could imagine. We should be careful in calling them personifications, since, in reality, this is how the Ancient Greeks actually understood these things: as *daimones*. They could be placated by ritual and even the Erinyes were known to have shown mercy at least once. The Greeks

[184] Homer, *Iliad*, 16.150; Hesiod, *Theogonia* 265; Aeschylus, *Eumenides*, 50, *Prometheus* 819; Ovid, *Metamorphoses*, 4.742; Virgil, *Aeneid*, 3, and *Georgia* 3.274. Felix Guirand (ed.), *New Larousse Encyclopedia of Mythology*, trans. Richard Aldington and Delano Ames, Crescent Books, 1987, p. 198; John Davidson Beazley, *The Development of Attic Black Figure*, University of California Press, 1986, p. 13; Graves, p. 244; Jane Ellen Harrison, *Prolegomena to the Study of Greek Religion*, Cambridge University Press, 1908, pp. 179–80, 187–8, 196.
[185] Also written Erinnyes. *New Larousse*, pp. 186–7; Graves, p. 122.

interacted with the *daimones*, seeing their inescapability and their functional necessity as supernatural agents (and, indeed, relatives) of the higher gods. Things would not stay that way.[186]

Demonization

Just as angels in the Judaeo-Christian tradition were both good and evil, so were *daimones* in the Greek. It was only in the politically charged culture-clash of the Hellenistic period that the Greek *daimones* became demonized and fixed in their entirely evil aspect. Alexander the Great had brought the ancient Near East under Greek control in the fourth century BCE. After his death, power was divided amongst his generals with Seleucus gaining control of Babylonia, instituting a monarchy and the succession of the line of the Seleucids. The defining moment was the suppression of Judaism under Antiochus Epiphanes, the Seleucid King of Judea, and the subsequent revolt led by Judas Maccabeus in 167 BCE. Antiochus had rededicated the temple of Jerusalem to Zeus; and Maccabeus destroyed the altar in 165. Greek culture was despised and hence the Greek *daimon* could only be evil. The Jews threw down Mount Olympus, home of the Greek gods, and made of it a hell, so that we read in the *Testament of Solomon* (first to fifth centuries CE) of seven female demons who spend part of their time on Olympus (8:4).[187]

---

[186] Aeschylus, *Eumenides*; Pausanius, *Description of Greece*, 10.28.1–10.29.1; Burkert, p. 421.

[187] David Albert Jones, *Angels: A History*, Oxford University Press, 2010, pp. 111–12; *DDD*, pp. 646, 938. The Old Testament contains no reference to Olympus. The Bible is a complex piece of literature that cannot be taken at face value. The earliest known biblical texts exist in fragments of the Greek Septuagint (Rahlfs 801, 819, 957) and Hebrew/Aramaic Dead Sea Scrolls (the Isaiah scroll: 1QIsa[a]) dating from the second century BCE. The earliest and most complete Christian Bible (Old and New Testaments) only dates from the fourth century CE, known in two forms as the Codex Sinaiticus and the Codex Vaticanus (LXX[B]), and is written in Greek. The earliest and most complete version of the Hebrew Bible in Hebrew is the so-called Masoretic Text and dates from the ninth and tenth centuries CE. The Hebrew Bible itself transmits the tradition that the Torah was written/assembled under divine inspiration by 'Ezra', in the fifth century BCE. The best evidence based on archaeology

The Greek translation of the Hebrew scriptures, the Septuagint, used the word 'demon' in a general masking of nuances into a homogenous evil. Where the Hebrew text talked of the national deities of non-Jews, tutelary spirits (*sedim*) and other pagan gods, the Greek talked only of demons. But even in the Old Testament the older sense of an intermediary performing the dictates of the divine will remained. Yahweh sends an evil spirit to torment Saul (1 Samuel 16:14), a lying spirit of false prophecy to lead Ahab astray (Exodus 12:23), a 'destroyer' (1 Corinthians 10:10), and a 'son of God' called Satan is sent to test Job.

Absorbing their religious ideas from regionally dominant cultures, the Hebrews inevitably acquired the rich demonology of Mesopotamia. Like the Greeks, the Mesopotamians saw natural forces and catastrophes – fire, hail, famine, pestilence – as spiritual entities sent by the gods, or themselves the offspring of the gods. The baby-snatching Pashittu, for example, was supposedly sent by the gods to control human population size. The plague god Resheph, represented in Ugarit as an archer, appears in Psalms (91:5–6) as 'the arrow flying by day' and the 'poisonous Qeteb' in Deuteronomy (32:24).[188]

Other spirits embody the inherent dangers of the desert and lonely places. In dark alleyways, Rabişu ('the croucher'), lay in ambush and we find him indirectly referred to in Genesis (4:7): sin crouching at Cain's door like a demon. Medical divination texts from the Old Babylonian period use phrases such as 'a *rabişu* has seized him' and 'he has walked in the path of a *rabişu*'. A typology of such demons developed, so we read of 'the *rabişu* of the road', 'the *rabişu* of the roof' and 'the *rabişu* of the lavatory'. Interestingly, *rabişu* was also the title of a high official in Mesopotamia as well as being applied as a title to some of the gods in a positive sense.[189]

---

would indicate that the oldest portions of the Bible, the Torah, were composed in the Hellenistic period and not in the second millennium BCE when they purport to have been written.

[188] *DDD*, pp. 572, 673.

[189] *DDD*, pp. 236, 682, 853. See W. G. Lambert and A. R. Millard, *Atra-hasis:*

Lilith makes her entry into the Old Testament as the 'screech owl' in Isaiah (34:14) and the 'terror of the night' in Psalms (91:5). The Hebrew *lîlît* is popularly believed to come from *laylâ*, 'night', although it actually derives from Akkadian *lilītu*, which itself comes from Sumerian *lil*. Evidence of belief in her is older than Yahweh, dating from the third millennium BCE. In the Epic of Gilgamesh we read of the demon *ki-sikil-lil-lá* who makes her lair in the trunk of a tree planted by the goddess Inanna (Ishtar). In Akkadian writings three related storm demons are often mentioned as *lilû*, *lilītu* and *(w)ardat lilî*. *Lilû* is the storm wind from the south-west. *Lilītu* is imagined flying like a bird and can escape from a house through the window. Lilith assimilated the similar Lamashtu during the Middle Babylonian period, leading to her migration to the Syrian region.[190]

In later Jewish traditions, Lilith is described as a demon with long hair and wings, and men are warned not to sleep alone in case she visits them. She is said to be Adam's first wife, or later mistress, with whom she conceived a vast brood of demons. She is even said to have been the Queen of Sheba (also called Zemargad): a beautiful woman from her head to her navel, flaming fire below. The lover of the demons Samael and Asmedai, she would also be called the Devil's grandmother and the progenitrix of witches and witchcraft. She was said to fly over the rooftops at night, sniffing for mothers' milk. She could take any form she desired in order to enter the house; mention is made of a black cat, a broom, or even a strand of black hair. Once inside she would either try and strangle the child or steal the afterbirth as food for her own children. In other stories she would steal newborn children and eat them. She appears as Obyzouth in the *Testament of Solomon*, 'a woman whose body and limbs were veiled by her long hair'.[191]

The Babylonian Story of the Flood, Clarendon Press, 1969, III, vii 3–4. For the medical texts see René Labat, *Traité akkadien de diagnostics et pronostics medicaux*, Brill, 1951, 34:23, 158:12, 182:40, 188:13 and 214:11.

[190] *DDD*, pp. 520–1, 851–2.

[191] Chester Charlton McCown, *The Testament of Solomon*, J. C. Hinrichs, 1922,

A thousand superstitions sprang up around this dangerous demoness. Special amulets could protect against her. In the *Testament of Solomon* she is counteracted by the angel Apharoph and if the new mother should write Obyzouth on a piece of paper and hang it up, then Lilith will avoid her. The blood of circumcision is said to be preserved by God as a ward against the injurious attentions of Lilith. If a child smiles on the night of the Sabbath, then Lilith is playing with it and it should be smacked three times on the nose. An old German baptism ritual went *Vivat Eva, foras Lilith* ('Long live Eve, out with Lilith'), apparently drawing on a Jewish exorcism formula. Today the tide has turned and brave or reckless magicians meet in smoky temples to invoke her:[192]

> Dark is she, but brilliant! Black are her wings, black on black! Her lips are red as rose, kissing all of the Universe! She is Lilith, who leadeth forth the hordes of the Abyss, and leadeth man to liberation![193]

Another demon who was always a demon curiously does not appear in the officially sanctioned version of the Bible. Asmodeus in the Apocryphal Book of Tobit (3:8–17) is a corruption of two words from the East Iranian language Avestan: *aēšma-*, 'wrath' and *daēuua*, 'threat, menace', which form the compound *xēšm-dēw* in Middle Persian (Pahlavi), meaning 'demon of wrath'

---

p. 13; *Shishim Sippurei Am* in Howard Schwartz, *Tree of Souls: The Mythology of Judaism*, Oxford University Press, 2007, p. 224.

[192] *DDD*, p. 521. For Talmudic references see Erubin 100b, Niddah 24b, and Shabbath 151b. Other traditions: *The Alphabet of Ben Sira*, c. eighth to tenth centuries CE; Herman Leberecht Strack, *The Jew and Human Sacrifice*, Bloch, 1909, p. 129, referring to the 'Zohar' to Leviticus 14 and 19; G. Lammert, *Volksmedizin und medizinischer Aberglaube*, F. A. Julien, 1869, p. 170; Schwartz, p. 221.

[193] Joseph Max and 'Lilith Darkchilde', 'Invocation of Lilith', 1994, revised 2002, http://home.comcast.net/~max555/rites/lilith_1.htm, accessed 12 August 2010, now widely disseminated on the internet. Max describes himself as an initiate of the Autonomatrix Guild of Chaos Magicians and 'Imperator General' of the Open Source Order of the Golden Dawn.

– usually transcribed as Aeshma Daeva. Aeshma first appears in the second millennium BCE in the collection of sacred Zoroastrian hymns called Gathas as the demon who brings illness and evil to mankind. In later texts he is described as wielding a 'bloody club' and additionally presides over drunkenness. In Tobit, Asmodeus kills seven successive husbands of Sara out of jealousy, leading to a reputation for conjugal discord that reappears in the *Testament of Solomon* (2:3). In other Jewish writings he acquires the title 'king of demons' and usurps the throne of Solomon. He finds his way into the books of magic (grimoires) as Asmoday. He plays a major role in the Solomonic grimoires (see the chapter on Magic). In the medieval *Key of Solomon* he leads the Golab, 'genii of wrath and sedition', as 'Samuel the Black'. He is the thirty-second spirit of the seventeenth century *Lesser Key of Solomon*, described as a 'great king', invoked for skill in mathematics and invisibility. However, lechery would become Asmodeus' special theological function by the sixteenth century. As a crowning achievement, the nineteenth-century French occultist Jacques Auguste Simon Collin de Plancy has Asmodeus seducing Eve.[194]

To this adopted demonology the Hebrews added a degradation and demonization of the gods of neighbouring peoples, so that the beliefs of their enemies became a swamp of stinking devils. Such was the fate of Beelzebub, in particular.

When the King of Israel, Ochozias (also Ahaziah), fell out of a window in Samaria and did himself an injury, he sent messengers to Ekron (Accaron) to find out from Beelzebub whether he would recover. Yahweh was understandably upset to be slighted

---

[194] Michael Arnoud Cor de Vaan, *The Avestan Vowels*, Rodopi, 2003, p. 351; *DDD*, pp. 106–8, 581–2; Kenneth McLeish, *Myth and Legends of the World Explored*, Bloomsbury, 1996, p. 87; Geoffrey W. Dennis, *The Encyclopedia of Jewish Myth, Magic and Mysticism*, Llewellyn, 2007, p. 22; Joseph H. Peterson (ed.), *The Lesser Key of Solomon*, Weiser, 2001, p. 21; S. Liddell MacGregor Mathers, *The Key of Solomon*, George Redway, 1888, p. 122; J. A. S. Collin de Plancy, *Dictionnaire infernal*, Société Nationale, 1845, p. 46. For the Zoroastrian references see the Gathas (Yasna 29:2 and 30:6), as well as Yasna 10:8, 97, 57:10–25.

like this and sent 'an angel of the Lord' to tell Elias to intercept the messengers and inform them that because of his actions Ochozias would not recover. As the Bible tells it he did not, of course, recover.

Worshipped at Ekron, one of the five major cities of the Philistines, Baal Zebub was clearly seen as an important oracular deity. The name is interpreted as Lord (Baal) of the Flies (Zebub) and the Greek Septuagint rendered the name as 'Baal the fly' (Βααλ μυῖα). However, the Greek translation by Symmachus in the second century CE, as well as references in the New Testament, give the name as Beezeboul and Beelzeboul (Βεελζεβουλ), suggesting an entirely different meaning. Beelzeboul finds accord with the titles *zbl* ('prince'), *zbl bʿl* ('prince Baal') and *zbl bʿl ʾars* ('prince, lord of the underworld') used in texts discovered at Ugarit. In the Old Testament *zebul* is used to mean 'residence' or 'high house'. In Ugaritic incantations Baal is called upon to dispel the demon of disease. What this shows is that 'Beelzebub' is in fact a derogatory pun on the god's real name of Baal Zebul ('Baal the Prince', or perhaps understood by the Jews as 'Lord of the High Place').[195]

There were plenty of other Baals around at the time. Meaning 'lord', *baʿal* was frequently attached to a number of other names, as well as being the particular name of a Canaanite god. The Old Testament uses the word about ninety times, but it is much older than that, dating back to the third millennium inscription from the ancient Mesopotamian city at Abu Ṣalabikh in what is now Iraq. From texts dated to around 1350 BCE, Baal is known to have been a god of the Ugaritic pantheon, being termed a son of El.[196] His known period of worship extends from the second millennium

---

[195] OT: 2 Kings 1;2–6. NT: Matthew 10:25, 12:24, 27; Mark 3:22; Luke 11:15, 18–19. M. Dietrich and O. Loretz, 'Die Baʿal-Titel *bʿl ars* und *aliy qrdm*', *Ugarit-Forschungen*, 12, 1980, pp. 391–3; *DDD* pp. 154–5. For the Ugaritic incantations see Ras-Ibn-Hani tablets, field numbers I.16, 1–3.

[196] See R. D. Biggs, *Inscriptions from Tell Abu Salabikh*, The University of Chicago Press, 1974; Dietrich and Loretz, pp. 391–3. Generally speaking, all the Ugarit gods were children of El.

BCE to about 200 BC. Baal found his way into the temples of Egypt and Phoenician colonization spread his cult throughout the Mediterranean. It is unsurprising that Baal was worshipped by the ancient Israelites in the early Iron Age, as we see in numerous Old Testament references to things like 'an altar of Baal in the house of Baal' (1 Kings 16:32) and 'the priest of Baal' (2 Kings 11:18) until suppressed by the adherents of the Yahweh cult – a fact that colours these various references to Baal.[197]

Baal and Baalim (plural) were worshipped in high places, including rooftops, as well as in temples. The shrine would comprise an image of the deity or a cone-shaped sacred stone, the *baetylion*, representing the abode of the god, or otherwise a sacred pole or pillar. Incense was burnt, libations poured, animals sacrificed. The priests led wild dances around the altar, working themselves into a frenzy so that they could cut themselves with knives until they ran with blood. The congregation would kiss the representations of Baal and indulge in immoral practices. At least that is the view presented in the Old Testament.[198]

As well as Baal Zebul, two other *ba'al* form names became demonized by the Yahweh cultists: Beelphegor and Baal-Berith. Beelphegor (Septuagint) or Baalpeor was the *ba'al* of Phogor/ Peor, a mountain in the land of the Moabites, lying in the highlands to the east of the Dead Sea. The Israelites also worshipped this god, again before suppression by the Yahwehists, with rites depicted as involving the familiar immoral practices. The tradition developed in the Rabbinical literature that these especially involved indecent exposure and a novel application of the act of defecation. He is generally known as Belphegor in the demonological and magical literature, so we find him in the *Key of Solomon* as chief of the disputers (*Tagaririm*).[199]

---

[197] *DDD*, pp. 132ff; Michael Jordan, *Dictionary of Gods and Goddesses*, Facts on File, 2004, p. 41.
[198] The OT references are numerous, but see especially 1 Kings 14, 16, 18, and 2 Kings 10–1, 17, 21, 23.
[199] Numbers 23:28, 25; Deuteronomy 3:29; Talmud: Sanhedrin 64a, 106a; Abodah Zarah, 44a; and Rashi's commentary on Numbers 25:3 (Sifrei Balak

Baal-Berith, 'Lord of the Covenant', was a Canaanite fertility god also worshipped by the Israelites (Judges 9:33). This covenant god provides the model for the later idea amongst the Jews that they had entered into a divine covenant with Yahweh. Stripped of the title 'Baal', Berith ended up as one of the seventy-two demons of the Solomon legend.[200]

Moloch (Molech), Milton's 'horrid King besmear'd with blood' is, like *ba'al*, an epithet, meaning in this case 'ruler, king' from the Semitic root *mlk*. A god *Mlk* was known in Ugarit with variations such as Malik at Ebla and the underworld god Muluk is also attested. In addition, entities called *maliku* received funerary offerings at Mari, either as spirits of the dead or chthonic (underworld) gods. All this points to an ancient underworld deity connected to a cult of the ancestral dead. Another god formerly worshipped by the Israelites, the Hebrew scriptures describe the Yahwehists' suppression of a cult of forbidden sexual relations with non-Jews (Leviticus 20:5) and/or a cult of child sacrifice (Leviticus 18:21): to 'make his son or his daughter to pass through the fire to Molech' (2 Kings 23:10). The Jewish centre of this cult was just outside Jerusalem at Tophet ('place of abomination') in the valley of Geennom; a temple erected by Solomon (1 Kings 11:7). He was denounced as an 'abomination' (1 Kings 11:7) and his followers were stoned to death (Leviticus 20:2). In the *Key of Solomon* he becomes with Satan one of the two chiefs of the Thamiel, or Double-Headed Ones, 'demons of revolt and anarchy', who are locked in battle against the Chaioth Ha-Qadesh, the Intelligences of the Divine Tetragram.[201]

1); 'Ancient Fragment of the Key of Solomon', in Mathers, p. 122.

[200] *DDD*, pp. 141–3. On the covenant question Mulder in the *DDD* argues contrary, but his position is unconvincing and somewhat overstated; see in support Yehezkel Kaufmann, *The Religion of Israel*, University of Chicago Press, 1960, pp. 138–9. At the very least, Baal-Berith demonstrates that the covenant was not a unique idea amongst the Jews.

[201] *DDD*, pp. 539–41, 581–5; John Milton, *Paradise Lost*, S. Simmons, 1674 [1667], Bk I, l. 392; Mathers, p. 121. Eissfeldt suggested that the name derived from the technical Punic term *molk/mulk* used in reference to a cult of child

Another Moloch, the sun god Adramelech (Semitic *'addir-melek)* of the city of Sepharvaim on the Euphrates, worshipped with the burnt offerings of children (2 Kings 17:31), becomes a demon in the Seventh Book of Moses. In Friedrich Gottlieb Klopstock's religious epic *The Messiah* (1748–73) he is described as 'the enemy of God, greater in malice, guile, ambition, and mischief than Satan, a fiend more curst'. In the nineteenth century Collin de Plancy assigned him the role of Grand-Chancellor of Hell, gentleman-in-waiting to the King of the Demons, and President of the High Council of Devils. He takes the form of a mule plumed with peacock's feathers.[202]

The ancient Hebrews angered Yahweh yet again, according to the Bible (Judges 2:13, 10:6; 1 Samuel 7:3–4, 12:10), by worshipping Ashtaroth. Solomon imported Ashtoreth 'the goddess of the Zidonians' to keep his 700 wives happy (1 Kings 11:5, 33; 2). Ranked alongside Baal and the Baalim, Ashtaroth (Ashtoreth) was in fact the great goddess Astarte (Ishtar in Akkadian) whom the Phoenicians ('Zidonians') equated with the Greek love goddess Aphrodite. She is generally thought to be a personification of the planet Venus (the Latin name for Aphrodite). Her name is found on texts recovered from Ugarit and ancient Egypt, and she is incorporated into the Greek pantheon as a wife of Kronos. She was the 'Queen of Heaven' with jurisdiction over procreation and to some extent healing. By the time Josiah came to destroy her shrine she was relegated to the status of 'abomination' (2 Kings 23:13). Strangely, the magical tradition took Ashtaroth over as male, whilst also preserving the female Astarte. Thus, according to Collin de Plancy, Ashtaroth (Astaroth) is a powerful grand-duke of hell, and Astarte retains her Venusian sex-goddess appeal. In the *Key of Solomon*, as 'the impure Venus of the Syrians', she leads the Gamchicoth, 'Disturbers of Souls'.[203]

---

sacrifice, but this is still controversial. See Otto Eissfeldt, *Molk als Opferbegriff im Punischen und Hebräischen und das Ende des Gottes Moloch*, Niemeyer, 1935.
[202] Klopstock quoted in Gustav Davidson, *A Dictionary of Angels*, The Free Press, 1971, p. 8; de Plancy, p. 6, pictured in the 1863 ed.
[203] *DDD*, pp. 109–14; de Plancy, pp. 47–8; Mathers, p. 122. Ashtaroth is also

To these lists of imported demons and demonized gods, the Hebrews had something to add that was uniquely their own. 'Wickedness' comes with the name of Belial (*bĕliyyaʻal*): 'a Spirit more lewd' said Milton, 'fell not from Heaven'. Biblical scholars argue over the origin and function of the word, but it seems most likely to be composed of *bĕlî* 'not', and **yaʻal*, 'to be worthy, to be of value'. Belial is 'not worthy'. He is 'the spirit of darkness'. He is impurity and lying. His wickedness is inducing people to worship other gods (Deuteronomy 13:14), perjury (e.g., 1 Kings 21:10), inhospitableness (e.g., Judges 19:22), getting women drunk in Yahweh's sanctuary (1 Samuel 1:13–17), priestly lechery (1 Samuel 2:12–22), and so on. He was the false messiah to the Samaritans. As Antichrist he came down from heaven to torment the world under the name of the Emperor Nero. From him come the seven spirits of seduction that enter humans at birth. He is so diabolical that he is sometimes called 'the Devil' himself, or else Belial is seen as the Devil's proper name. To the writer of the Book of Jubilees, all non-Jews are 'sons of Belial'. For later Christian writers, Belial stands in direct contrast to Christ.[204]

In the Qumran texts, *maśṭēmâ* ('hostility') is the destructive purpose of Belial as well as being the title 'Angel of Hostility' given to him. But in the Book of Jubilees *maśṭēmâ* develops as an independent entity. Here he is Mastemah, the prince of demons who leads his forces to destroy the sons of Noah. After Noah complains to his God, Mastemah's army is reduced to a tenth of its former size and the sons of Noah are taught medicine by the angels so that they might resist the remaining evil spirits. It is Mastemah who prompts the Hebrew God to test

---

the name of a city (Joshua 9:10, 12:4, 13:12, 31; 1 Chronicles 6:71). She was also worshipped as Atargatis, a compound of Astarte and Anat, *DDD*, p. 114.
[204] Milton, Bk I; *DDD*, pp. 169–71. Also called Beliar and Belior in the pseudographical *Testament of Levi* (18:4, 19:1). Rabbinical and Apocryphal references in order of mention: Levi 19; Joseph 7, 10; Reuben 4, 5; Simeon 5; Issachar 6–7; Daniel 5; Asher i, 3; Sibyllines 3:63, 4:2; Reuben 2; Levi 3; Jubilees 15:32. Belial is synonymous with the Devil in the Vulgate translation. 2 Corinthians 6:15.

Abraham through the sacrifice of his son Isaac. It is Mastemah who aids the Egyptians in trying to eliminate Moses. But he is still seen in the service of the Hebrew God as the spirit who kills the firstborn in Egypt. In Exodus (12:12) it is 'the Lord' himself who does this. The chosen people are saved because of the magical use of lambs' blood that turns Mastemah from their doors.[205]

Demonization was also the inevitable attitude of Christianity. In a book that set out to prove the superiority of Christianity over paganism, Eusebius of Caesarea (c. 263–339 CE) argued that the Greek *daimon* came from a word meaning 'to fear'. Although only a religio-political etymology at best, Eusebius nonetheless reflected the Christian view.[206] The New Testament is full of demons. They are the unclean spirits (Mark 5) who cruelly torment people (Matthew 15:22).

There were also some new additions. From being a place name in the Old Testament, Abaddon is recreated as demon in the New. From the common Semitic root meaning 'to destroy' found in Ugaritic and Aramaic as *'bd* and Akkadian as *abātu*, *'baddôn* is used in the Old Testament to mean 'place of destruction' and in the Babylonian Talmud is used as one of the names of Gehenna (hell). 1 Enoch (20:2) tells of a specific angel of *baddôn*, which in Revelation (9:11) becomes a proper name in itself. When the fifth angel blows his trumpet, 'a star' falls from heaven and is given the key of 'the bottomless pit' (Revelation 9:1). He unlocks hell, venting huge clouds of smoke and armoured locusts with lions' teeth and scorpions' tails (Revelation 9:2–10). The locusts 'had a king over them, which is the angel of the bottomless pit, whose name in the Hebrew tongue is Abaddon, but in the Greek tongue hath his name Apollyon' (Revelation 9:11). The Greek name alludes to Apollo who was worshipped from the eighth century BCE up to the

---

[205] *DDD*, pp. 553–4; Qumran 1QM 13:4, 1QM 13:11, 4Q 286 10 2:2; Jubilees, 10:1–13, 17:16, 48, 49, equated with Satan in Jub 10:11.
[206] Eusebius, *Praeparatio Evangelica*, 4.5.142.

sixth century CE as both a god of pestilence and destruction, and as a god of healing. Here we most likely see a fusing of Hebrew and Greek concepts, as opposed to outright demonization of an existing deity.[207]

Mammon, one of the most well-known of the demons, is also a later creation. The word is Aramaic meaning 'that in which one puts trust' with the sense of 'money, riches' with the negative connotation developing subsequently. It becomes the name of a demon only in the New Testament with the familiar line 'You cannot serve God and Mammon' attributed to Jesus (Luke 16:13, Matthew 6:24). His character is more fully realized in the late sixteenth century in Spenser's *The Faerie Queene* and Milton's *Paradise Lost* of 1667 as 'Mammon, the least erected Spirit that fell'. Spenser described him as 'an uncouth, savage, and uncivil wight', sooty-bearded, smoke-blackened and miserly hoarding his gold. According to Milton, he taught men to mine 'the bowels of their mother Earth for treasures better hid'. Collin de Plancy added a touch of satirical humour in 1845 when he described Mammon as Hell's ambassador to England.[208]

My Name is Legion

A complex demonology developed, attributing demons to a growing range of human activities and ailments, with various attempts to order and enumerate these swarming hordes of hell. The eleventh-century Byzantine writer, Michael Psellus, described six demonic species using the four-fold schema of the elements and augmenting them with underground and light-hating varieties. They are: Igneous, Aerial, Earthly, Aqueous, Subterranean and Lucifugus. In the sixteenth century Peter Binsfeld, suffragan bishop of Trier in Germany, witch-hunter

---

[207] *DDD*, pp. 1, 74–7. There are some foreshadowings of personification in Proverbs 27:20 and Job 26:5–6.

[208] *DDD*, pp. 542–3. Robert C. Fox, 'The Character of Mammon in *Paradise Lost*', *The Review of English Studies*, 1962, XIII.49, pp. 30–9; Edmund Spenser, *The Faerie Queen*, Bk II.7.3; Milton, Bk I, ll 679, 687–8; de Plancy, p. 145 – the ambassador ascription occurs only in this, the sixth edition.

and author of *De confessionibus maleficorum et sagarum* ('The Confessions of Evil-doers and Witches', 1589), matched the seven deadly sins to the seven deadliest demons: Pride is Lucifer, Avarice is Mammon, Lechery is Asmodeus, Anger is Satan, Gluttony is Beelzebub, Envy is Leviathan and Sloth is Belphegor. He was following something of a trend. There was a particular devil for everything imaginable, including wearing the then fashionable baggy trousers, according to a German sermon of the sixteenth century.[209]

Where the Old Testament knew only Satan and a colourful handful of demons and demonized gods, the New Testament would introduce the idea of a vast, numberless horde of demonic entities. According to Mark (5:1–9), Jesus encountered a possessed man 'dwelling among the tombs' in the 'country of the Gadarenes'. He demanded that the 'unclean spirit' reveal its name to him, but the answer was instead, 'My name is Legion: for we are many.' Around this time, a Roman legion would have numbered about 6,000 men. The apocryphal Gospel of Nicodemus added 'several legions of devils'. According to the usual interpretation of Revelation (12:4), a third of all the angels fell with Satan: 'And his tail drew the third part of the stars of heaven, and did cast them to the earth'. The Cistercian abbot Richalmus in the thirteenth century thought that the demons were as plentiful and incalculable as grains of sand. But with more ingenuity Johannes Wierus (c. 1515–88) came up with a precise reckoning. Each legion numbered 6,666 – a far more diabolical figure than the Romans could muster – and with 1,111 legions under the Satanic banner, the ranks of demons totalled 7,405,926. Professor Martinus Barrhaus, a theologian at Basel in the sixteenth century, went further still, counting 2,665,866,746,664 demons.[210]

---

[209] Michael Psellus, *Psellus' Dialogue on the Operation of Demons*, trans. Marcus Collisson, James Tegg, 1843; Andreas Musculus, *Vom Hosen Teuffel*, Johann Eichhorn, 1555.

[210] Maximilian Rudwin, *The Devil in Legend and Literature*, Open Court, 1931, pp. 17–25; Keith L. Roos, *The Devil in 16th Century German Literature*, Herbert Lang, 1972, p. 52.

Demonic Hierarchies: Kings of Demon[211]

1584 Scot, *Discoverie of Witchcraft*	17th c. *Lesser Key of Solomon*	1667 Milton, *Paradise Lost*	1690–1720 *Sacred Magic of Abramelin*	Dr Rudd, *Argel Magic*	1801 Barrett, *The Magus*
Amaymon	Amaymon	Satan	Lucifer	Beelzebub	Beelzebub
Gorson	Corson	Beelzebub	Leviathan	Python	Pytho
Zimimar	Zimimay (Ziminiar)	Mammon	Satan	Belial	Belial
Goap	Göap	Moloch	Belial	Asmodeus	Asmodeus
Baëll	Bael	Chemos (Peor)	Astarot (Ashtaroth)	Sathan	Satan
Purson (Curson)	Paimon	Baalim, Ashtaroth	Magot	Meririm	Meririm
Bileth	Beleth	Astoreth (Astarte)	Asmodee (Asmodeus)	Apollyon (Abaddon)	Apollyon (Abaddon)
Paimon	Purson	Thammuz	Belzebud (Beelzebub)	Astaroth	Astaroth
Beliall	Asmoday	Dagon	Oriens	Mammon	Mammon
Sidonay (Asmoday)	Viné	Rimmon	Paimon		
Vine	Balam	Ahaz	Ariton		
Zagan	Zagan	Osiris, Isis, [H]Orus	Amaimon		
Balam	Belial	Belial			

Prince of Demons: The Devil

The Demon and demons. The Devil and devils. It was the Fourth Lateran Council in 1215 that made the official distinction between 'the Devil and the other demons'. But the tendency had already been observed in the fourth century CE Latin version of the Bible known as the Vulgate. For a particular reason, as we shall see, *diabolus* was used of the chief of the evil forces, whilst *daemon* was used of his subordinates, although Christian tradition affirms that there is no difference of nature between them.[212]

The Devil, we should not forget, is a relative newcomer, a supernatural immigrant. Unlike the *daimones* he does not appear amongst the personnel of the Ancient Greek Underworld. The pagan peoples of Europe had their own bogies and beasties to

---

[211] Aleister Crowley (ed.), *The Goetia: The Lesser Key of Solomon the King*, trans. S. Liddel MacGregor Mathers, Weiser, 1997 [1904]. The seventy-two spirits of the Goetia are ruled over by 'the Four Great Kings', which are listed here together with spirits designated as kings amongst the seventy-two. The book claims to be compiled and edited from numerous manuscripts in diverse languages, four of which are listed, pp. 23–5, but undated and unreferenced. The editor of this volume, Hymenaeus Beta, mentions British Library Sloane 2731, p. 90, which is dated 1687; 'a manuscript codex by Dr Rudd' is also mentioned, p. 69. Some of the goetic manuscripts in the British Museum date back to the fourteenth century, but most survive from the seventeenth. Reginald Scot, *The Discoverie of Witchcraft*, 1584, Dover, 1972, pp. 217–25; p. 226 gives the four 'principall divels' that head this list. Scot's was the first English translation of a similar list appearing in Wierus' *De praestigiis daemonum*, 1583, as the *Pseudomonarchia daemonum* also identified as T.R., *Secretum secretorum*, 1570, by Scot. S. Liddel MacGregor Mathers, *The Book of the Sacred Magic of Abramelin the Mage*, J. M. Watkins, 1900, pp. 104, 110–11, dated 1458, but Mathers identifies the handwriting as being late seventeenth or early eighteenth century. Harley 6482, British Museum, published as Adam McLean (ed.), *A Treatise on Angel Magic*, Weiser, 2006, dated by McLean to 1699–1714, but argued to be the copy of an earlier manuscript. The spirits here mentioned are listed on pp. 69–70. Francis Barrett, *The Magus*, Lackington, Alley and Co., 1801, Bk II, pp. 46–7.

[212] 'Diabolus enim et alii daemones', Fourth Lateran Council, 1215, see Leonard E. Boyle, 'The Fourth Lateran Council and Manuals of Popular Theology', in Thomas J. Heffernan (ed.), *The Popular Literature of Medieval England*, University of Tennessee Press, 1985, pp. 30–43.

worry about, from Loki leading the *jötnar* and hordes of Hel into the last battle against the Norse gods, to the Morrigan and Caoránach, so-called mother of demons, and the whole race of Faery who bedevilled the Celts, and, as we saw, the *kakodaimones* who made life a misery for the Greeks. The Devil is one particular representation of the combat myth between good and evil found in many religious traditions.

The word *devil* only entered the English language in the eighth century coming via Latin from the Greek *diabolos* (διάβολος). From the verb *diaballo*, meaning 'to throw across' or 'to cross over', the word had the connotations of 'slanderous' and 'defamatory' as an adjective, and 'enmity' and 'quarrel' as a noun. In the sense of 'slanderer', the Greek was used in the third to first century BCE translations of the Hebrew Bible for *satan*.[213]

The Devil as we know him today began his career as Satan – the Accuser or Adversary – with the Hebrew deity Yahweh. We first find Satan in the Book of Job (1:6): 'when the sons of God came to present themselves before the Lord, and Satan came also among them'. Yahweh boasted that in Job he had an exemplary believer, but Satan suggested that God's protection was what kept Job in the fold. 'Does Job fear God in vain?' he asked. Here the classic role of tempter is first played out, tempting not man, but God.

Yahweh succumbed and granted Satan his commission: 'Behold, all that he hath is in thy power; only upon himself put not forth thine hand' (Job 1:12). Satan got to work. Job's oxen were stolen and his servants murdered, 'the fire of God' destroyed his sheep and some more servants, his camels were stolen and yet more servants were slaughtered, and a violent wind blew down the house where his brother and children were feasting, crushing them all to death.

Job was understandably distraught, but kept his faith. Satan was not one to give up easily and persuaded Yahweh to grant him further permission to abuse Job. A plague of boils followed and Job threw himself on a dunghill, wishing for death. His wife and friends all tried to turn him against Yahweh, but Job refused to blame him. Yahweh finally relented and decided Job should be rewarded for his loyalty. The spots cleared up, he had more children, amassed an even greater fortune and lived to 140.

Satan appears again in the Book of Zechariah (3:1–2), a text supposedly written by one of the so-called minor prophets Zechariah about the year 520 BCE. In a vision Zechariah saw 'Joshua the high priest standing before the angel of the Lord, and Satan standing at his right hand to resist him'. But Yahweh took a shine to the raggedly attired Joshua and said to Satan 'The Lord rebuke thee, O Satan!' Here Satan was clearly acting in his role of accuser and Joshua, like Job before him, is cleared of all charges.

In other supposedly sixth century BCE biblical texts we read of Satan standing up against Israel and inciting David to make a census (1 Chronicles 21) and Satan is equated with the 'Angel of Yahweh' who gave Balaam such a hard time about his ass (Numbers 22). Confusing matters, 'satan' in the more general sense of adversity or accusation also crops up in several other books of the Old Testament.

One of the more popular stories about the origin of the Devil as a fallen angel is told of the 'sons of God', whom we should understand as angels or 'the watchers' (1 Enoch 6:2), who, lusting after mortal women, descended from heaven and seduced them. A race of 'giants' (γίγαντες) was born – often thought to be the *nephilim*, 'the fallen ones', described in Genesis (6:3) and Numbers (13:33) – and then drowned in the Flood. Their spirits became the demons (1 Enoch 15:8–16:1), led by Azazel. Azazel – whose name might be derived from '*zz*, 'to be strong', and '*l*, 'god', or '*ez*, 'goat', and '*ozel*, 'to go away', as in 'scapegoat' – was a desert demon (Leviticus 16:8–10), who was both a messenger for Satan (1 Enoch 54:6), and the Devil himself (Jubilees 10:1–11). Then there is the tale of the angel who refused to revere Adam and was thrown out of heaven with his supporters.[214]

As similar sounding or acting beings the Devil enjoys further adventures in the non-canonical Apocrypha. He is the author of evil (Wisdom 2:24), he is Satanail who was thrown from heaven with his rebel angels (2 Enoch 19) and the seducer of Eve in the Garden of Eden (2 Enoch 31). He is equated with Mastemah in the Book of Jubilees. He is the licentious Asmodeus in the Book of Tobit. He is Sammael in the Martyrdom of Isaiah, bringing 'apostasy, sin, magic and the persecution of the righteous' (2:4–11). He becomes Samael, the angel of death and 'chief of satans' in the Jewish Talmud.

However, it was in Christianity that the Devil was to play his greatest role. In the New Testament the temptation in the wilderness is one of the keystones of Jesus' career, recounted in three of the four Gospels (Matthew 4, Mark 1, Luke 4). Jesus was specifically 'led up of the spirit into the wilderness to be tempted of the Devil' (Matthew 4:1). Dating from the first century CE these writings all tell the story of how the Devil appeared to Jesus during his forty days and nights of fasting in the desert. The brief details in Mark are fleshed out in Matthew and Luke with the addition of dialogue.

'The tempter' approached Jesus, saying 'If thou be the Son of God, command that these stones be made bread'. Jesus retorted with 'Man shall not live by bread alone'. The Devil then took him to the top of the Temple in Jerusalem and said 'If thou be the Son of God, cast thyself down: for it is written, He shall give his angels charge concerning thee: and in their hands they shall bear thee up'. Jesus replied 'Thou shalt not tempt the Lord thy God'. The Devil tried again, taking him to the summit of a high mountain, showing him the world stretched out below, saying

---

[214] *DDD*, pp. 128–31, 246, 344–5, 618–20. For the giant references see 1 Enoch 6–16, Genesis 6:1–4, Jude 6, 2 Peter 2:4. For the Adam story see The Life of Adam and Eve 13–15 in Hedley Frederick Davis Sparks, *The Apocryphal Old Testament*, Oxford University Press, 1984, p. 150, Tertullian, *De Patientia*, 5, and Qur'an 15:26–35.

'All these things will I give thee, if thou wilt fall down and worship me'. Jesus replied 'Get thee hence, Satan: for it is written, Thou shalt worship the Lord thy God, and only him shalt thou serve' (Matthew 4:3–11). Satan's role here is little different from that played out in the Old Testament, but it would not stay that way.

According to the Gospel of Luke (10:18), Jesus told his followers: 'I beheld Satan as lightning fall from heaven'. In the Book of Revelation, which only found its way into the Bible in 367 CE, we read: 'And the great dragon was cast out, that old serpent, called the Devil, and Satan, which deceiveth the whole world: he was cast out into the earth, and his angels were cast out with him' (12:9). Here the differing concepts and terminology of 'devil' and 'satan' are specifically equated. Both texts bring to the fore the ejection of evil from heaven, recalling the tradition of the Nephilim as 'the fallen ones'.

Later Church writers, such as Tertullian and Origen in the second and third centuries CE, identified Satan with a character called Lucifer (Isaiah 14:12): 'How thou art fallen from heaven, O Lucifer, son of the morning!' Isaiah was actually comparing the King of Babylon to the 'morning star' – *helel* in Hebrew, *lucifer* ('light-bearer') in Latin – which is the planet we call Venus. From this misinterpretation, and much influenced by the dramatic war in heaven depicted in The Secret Book of Enoch (2 Enoch), the Church Fathers developed the idea of Satan as Lucifer the Fallen Angel, as well as the original serpentine tempter in the Garden of Eden.[215]

After such a useful career with Yahweh why did Satan fall? We already had lust as a motivation in Enoch, but Eusebius of Caesarea said it was the worst of the Seven Deadly Sins: pride. For we read in John (1, 3:8) that 'the Devil sinneth from the beginning' and in Ecclesiasticus (10:15) that 'Pride is the beginning of all sin'. Misinterpreting another Old Testament passage

[215] Jeffrey Burton Russell, *The Devil: Perceptions of Evil from Antiquity to Primitive Christianity*, Cornell University Press, 1987, pp. 195, 229. Henry Angsar Kelly, *Satan: A Biography*, Cambridge University Press, 2006, pp. 178–9, 194ff.

concerning the King of Tyre, the Church Fathers thought they had found further reference to Satan when they read 'Thou hast been in Eden [. . .] Thou art the anointed cherub [. . .] Thou wast perfect [. . .] till iniquity was found in thee [. . .] I will cast thee to the ground' (Ezekiel 28:1–19). It read like a description of an angel cast out of heaven and we get further evidence of pride, or more precisely vanity: 'Thine heart was lifted up because of thy beauty'.[216]

But this beauty would not survive the fall from heaven. At the Council of Toledo in 447 CE we get the first official description of the Devil:

> A large black monstrous apparition with horns on his head, cloven hooves – or one cloven hoof – ass's ears, hair, claws, fiery eyes, terrible teeth, an immense phallus, and a sulphurous smell.[217]

It proved to be an enduring look. The medieval mystery plays scared their audiences with such monstrous and well-endowed devils. The Devil's large appendage and what he did with it would be a constant concern of the witch trials in the early modern period. The French demonologist Nicholas Remy noted that, at her trial in 1568, Alexée Drigie described it as being as 'long as some kitchen utensils' when only half erect. This demonic sexuality was heightened still further by the popular representation of naked witches and Freud would suggest characteristically that 'their great broomstick was probably the great lord Penis'. During the reign of James VI and I, the Devil still took an indecent form on the stage, appearing suchwise in Middleton and Rowley's play *A Courtly Masque* of 1620, for example. Black-faced phallic demons cavorted in the public streets during carnival in Germany. The

---

[216] Kelly, p. 193.
[217] Pennethorne Hughes, *Witchcraft*, Penguin, 1965, p. 104; and without the 'one cloven hoof' in Jeffrey Burton Russell, *Lucifer: The Devil in the Middle Ages*, Cornell University Press, 1986, p. 69.

influential French occultist Eliphas Lévi's depiction of the *Bouc de Sabbat* ('Sabbatic Goat') carried forward the idea of the Devil as a symbol of the generative powers into the nineteenth century, representing him with a fulsome bosom and a large rod entwined with serpents (caduceus) emerging from some cloth draped over the creature's loins, not to mention the horns and cloven hooves.[218]

When the authors of the infamous witch-hunters' manual, the *Malleus Maleficarum*, explicitly made the connection in the fifteenth century between the ancient fertility spirits, the 'Satyrs', 'Fauns' and 'Pans', and demonic 'Incubi', they were drawing on the authority of early Christian writers, such as Augustine of Hippo (354–430). There was clearly a continuing, centuries-long process of identifying the Christian demonic with elements of classical mythology. But the process did not end there.[219]

As Christianity spread through Europe its missionaries identified every god and goddess they came across as so many disguises of the Devil sent to lead people from the Gospel. For example, the Council of Leptinnes (744) added a new clause to the rite of baptism to 'renounce all the works of the demon, and all his words, and Thor, and Odin, and Saxnot, and all evil beings that are like them'. Egbert, first Archbishop of York in the eighth century, prohibited what were called 'offerings to devils'. The Canon Episcopi (dated to 906) described how 'some

---

[218] Nicholas Remy, *Demonolatry*, trans. E. A. Aswin, John Rodker, 1930[1595], Bk I, Ch. VI, p. 14; Thomas Middleton and William Rowley, *A Courtly Masque: The Device Called, The World Tost at Tennis*, Edward Wright, 1620; Maximilian Rudwin, *The Origin of the German Carnival Comedy*, Stechert & Co., 1920, pp. 35–6, 43–4; Eliphas Lévi, *Transcendental Magic: Its Doctrine and Ritual*, trans. A. E. Waite. William Rider & Son, 1923, description p. xxii, depiction p. 180 – first published as *Dogme et rituel de la haute magie*, G. Baillière, 1861; Montague Summers, *The History of Witchcraft and Demonology*, pp. 277–8 and see also 98–100; Robert Muchembled, *A History of the Devil: From the Middle Ages to the Present*, Polity Press, 2003, pp. 17, 46–51, 66, Freud quoted on p. 209; Leo Ruickbie, 'Witchcraft: The Naked Truth', paper presented to Miller's Academy, 21 April 2009.

[219] Heinrich Institoris and Jakob Sprenger, *Malleus Maleficarum*, trans. Montague Summers, Dover, 1928 [1487], Pt 1, Q. 3, p. 24.

wicked women, perverted by the Devil [. . .] ride upon certain beasts with Diana, the goddess of pagans'. Thus the Church assembled its own theological Frankenstein's monster and sparked it into life with the raw current of fear.[220]

The Devil's image, too, began to change. In a strange turn towards decency he would take to wearing human clothes. Innumerable witch trial records would describe someone attired in the fashions of the day. The descriptions from the late sixteenth century into the seventeenth century largely agree that he most often appeared as a large black man dressed in black. He had other colours to his wardrobe, but black was his favourite; 'as proof,' said the demonologist Henri Boguet, 'that his study is only to do evil; for evil [. . .] is symbolised by black'. He was sometimes young, sometimes old, sometimes female, usually male, sometimes crippled and frequently unable to conceal his cloven hooves. He could take animal form, even appear as a priest, the Virgin Mary, or Jesus himself, but his most alarming manifestation is undoubtedly in cases of possession.[221]

Possession

'I believe this was a genuine case of possession,' Father Walter Halloran told *The Kansas City Star* newspaper in 1995 when they asked about an exorcism that had taken place at the Alexian Brothers Hospital, St Louis, Maryland, USA, in 1949. It was the case that had inspired twenty-year-old English Literature student William Peter Blatty to write *The Exorcist* years later. Possession, the belief that the human personality has been taken over by another entity, is a universal social experience recorded throughout history. It manifests in diverse ways with multiple symptoms, often of a terrifying and violent nature, but the fundamental aspect is the loss of conscious control of one's mind and body. Within Western culture it is

---

[220] Leo Ruickbie, *Witchcraft Out of the Shadows*, Robert Hale, 2004, pp. 61, 65.

[221] Henri Boguet, *Discours Exécrable des Sorciers*, Romain de Beauvais, 1603.

most usual to see this experience in terms of Christianity and talk of 'demonic possession' and being 'possessed by the Devil'. In the fifteenth century the *Malleus Maleficarum* stated that 'devils can enter the heads and other parts of the body of men, and can move the inner mental images from place to place'. Possession is still defined by the Catholic Church as 'the domination by the demon over man's bodily organs and his lower spiritual faculties'. According to research, 41 per cent of Americans today believe that this can actually happen and the Church has reported a huge rise in requests for exorcism.[222]

The Church identifies three signs of possession that particularly distinguish it from psychological disorders: the ability to speak in a language unknown to the possessed individual, or to understand it when it is spoken; to be able to see into the future, or discover 'hidden events'; and having any other powers that are 'beyond the subject's age and natural condition'. However, others have counted many more, such as nineteenth-century French writer P. L. Jacob:[223]

1. Believing that one is possessed
2. Leading a bad life
3. Living beyond society
4. Being ill for a long time with unusual symptoms

---

[222] Mark Opsasnick, 'The Haunted Boy of Cottage City: The Cold Hard Facts Behind the Story that Inspired *The Exorcist*', *Strange Magazine*, 20, December 1998; Halloran quoted in '*The Exorcist* Fairly Close to the Mark', *National Catholic Reporter*, 1 September 2000; William Peter Blatty, *The Exorcist*, Harper & Row, 1971; *Malleus Maleficarum*, Pt 2, Ch. X; *De Exorcismis et Supplicationibus Quibusdam*, Libreria Editrice Vaticana, 2003; Frank Newport and Maura Strausberg, 'Americans' Belief in Psychic and Paranormal Phenomena is Up Over Last Decade', Gallup, 8 June 2001, http://www.gallup.com/poll/4483/americans-belief-psychic-paranormal-phenomena-over-last-decade.aspx, accessed 18 January 2011 – a further 16 per cent were unsure; 'Huge Rise in Calls to Cast Out Demons', *Paranormal*, 56, February 2011, p. 8.

[223] *The Roman Ritual: Complete Edition*, trans. Philip T. Weller, Bruce Publishing Co., 1964.

5. Blaspheming the name of God and speaking often of the Devil
6. Making a pact with the Devil
7. Having dealings with spirits
8. Having a terrible and horrible facial expression
9. Being tired of life and despairing
10. Being furious and doing violence
11. Screaming and crying like a beast[224]

Some of the most dramatic manifestations of possession occurred in several French convents during the seventeenth century. In Aix-en-Provence in 1611 two possessions cost Father Louis Gaufridi his life. At Louviers in 1647 more than fourteen possessions led to the imprisonment of Sister Madeleine Bavent and the execution of Father Thomas Boullé. The Mother Superior, Barbara Buvée, was lucky enough to be acquitted at Auxonne in 1650 following her trial for the possession of eight people. The most infamous case, however, was the mass possession of Ursuline nuns at Loudun in 1634 which saw Father Urbain Grandier being burnt to death, along with the pacts and magical writings he was alleged to have made. An eye-witness to the possessions, Monsieur des Niau, Counsellor at la Flèche, described the scene:[225]

When the Exorcist gave some order to the Devil, the nuns suddenly passed from a state of quiet into the most terrible convulsions [. . .] They struck their chests and backs with their heads, as if they had had their neck broken, and with inconceivable rapidity [. . .] their faces became so frightful one could not bear to look at them [. . .] they threw themselves back till their heads touched their feet and walked in this position [. . .] They uttered cries so horrible and so loud

---

[224] P. L. Jacob, *Curiosités Infernales*, Garnier, 1886, my translation.
[225] Leo Ruickbie, *La Sorcellerie en France: Catalogue de l'Exposition*, Witchology, 2009, n.p.

that nothing like it was ever heard before; they made use of expressions so indecent as to shame the most debauched men, while their acts, both in exposing themselves and inviting lewd behaviour from those present, would have astonished the inmates of the lowest brothel in the country.[226]

Whilst religious and popular explanations continue to draw on the spirit world, modern psychiatry explains possession as a dissociative state with the alarming physical displays categorized as psychogenic seizures or pseudoseizures, that is, non-epileptic, stress-related fits. However, psychiatrists themselves do not always make that diagnosis. With many years' experience in psychiatry, the late Dr Arthur Guirdham came to the conclusion that 'people who insist that possession cannot exist have never seen a case or, if they have, have been so blinkered by prejudice that they have temporarily lost the capacity to assess symptoms'.[227]

Demons Today

The Church today has moved away from such crude personifications as 'demons' and 'the Devil'. Neither he nor his imps should be thought of as the horned and cloven-hooved fiends we are so familiar with, but instead as an abstract force for evil. Likewise, God himself should not be thought of as a white-bearded old man, but as a nebulous supreme good. In a confidential poll of Catholic priests conducted in 1960, 80 per cent said they did not believe in the Devil.[228]

It is an example of what an episcopal conference in Italy organized by the Theological Institute of Assisi would warn against: the 'extreme rationalism that denies the existence of the Devil'.[229] This development caused the Vatican's chief exorcist,

---

[226] Edmund Goldsmith (ed.), *The History of the Devils of Loudun*, 3 vols, privately published, 1887, vol. 2, pp. 35–44.
[227] Arthur Guirdham, *The Psyche in Medicine*, Spearman, 1978, p. 55.
[228] Morgan Scott Peck, *Glimpses of the Devil*, Free Press, 2005, p. 2.
[229] ZENIT, 11 May 2000.

Father Gabriel Amorth, to express his deep concern. After claiming to have performed an incredible 70,000 exorcisms, Amorth is convinced that the Devil exists. He even went so far as to state recently that 'the Devil is at work inside the Vatican'.[230] 'We have a clergy and an Episcopate who no longer believe in the Devil,' he said in another interview, adding, 'meanwhile, the Satanic sects prosper'.[231]

So what of the supposed 'Satanic sects'? Surely they believe in the Devil and his demons? It came as a shock to find myself included in that last category when the Jesus-is-Savior.com website 'reviewed' my first book on witchcraft, *Witchcraft Out of the Shadows*. Under the heading of 'Wicca = Satan' , Wicca – a modern witchcraft-inspired religion – was denounced as the 'false religion of the Devil'. It is a common enough charge made by Christian fundamentalists, but it is not the way the Wiccans themselves see it.

Most books on Wicca by Wiccans or sympathizers categorically state that Wiccans neither worship nor believe in the Devil. According to Gerald Gardner, the founder of Wicca, 'The Devil' was the medieval honorific for the leader of a coven of witches, now obsolete, or a term of disparagement for the same used by the Church – he argued both ends. The first was an idea he got from Margaret Murray's *The Witch-Cult in Western Europe* – a book that sought to prove that witchcraft was an organized pagan religion antecedent to Christianity. Gardner went to great lengths to stress that as a supernatural entity 'The Devil is, or rather was, an invention of the Church'. Of course, the press immediately denounced him as a 'whitewasher of witchcraft'.[232]

It would have surprised Gardner to find himself in agreement with a real Satanist. When Anton Szandor LaVey founded the

[230] *The Times*, 11 March 2010.
[231] *30 Days*, June 2000.
[232] Gerald B. Gardner, *Witchcraft Today*, Rider and Co., 1954, pp. 43–4; Margaret Murray, *The Witch-Cult in Western Europe*, Clarendon Press, 1921; *Sunday Pictorial*, 12 June 1955.

Church of Satan in 1966 and proclaimed himself the Black Pope he had no intention of actually worshipping Satan. Like Gardner, he turned things on their head. In one of his Nine Satanic Statements he asserted that 'Satan has been the best friend the [Christian] church has ever had, as he has kept it in business all these years!'[233]

For LaVey, Satan was symbolic of his rejection of Christianity and 1960s counter-culture values, and representative of his own philosophy of life rather than an actual entity. In *The Satanic Bible* he made it clear that 'most Satanists do not accept Satan as an anthropomorphic being with cloven hooves, a barbed tail, and horns'. Forty years on, the current High Priest of the Church of Satan, Peter H. Gilmore, continues this interpretation: 'Satanists do not believe in the supernatural, in neither God nor the Devil . . . Satan is not a conscious entity to be worshipped'. Instead, Gilmore says that 'Satan is a symbol of Man living as his prideful, carnal nature dictates'.[234]

With the Church, witches and even Satanists withdrawing from the idea of a supreme personality of evil, just who does believe in the Devil? Research has shown that around two in three ordinary Americans believe in the Devil and that more than one in three believe that they have been tempted by him. About one in five people – again in America – believe that 'most evil in the world is caused by the Devil' and a little fewer than one in two believe that he has an army of demons to help him.[235]

[233] Anton Szandor LaVey, *The Satanic Bible*, Avon Books, 1969, p. 25.

[234] Peter H. Gilmore, 'Satanism: The Feared Religion', churchofsatan.com, no date, stated to have been first published in *A New Age: Essays on Current Religious Beliefs and Practices*, Merrimac Books, 1992.

[235] Jennifer Robinson, 'The Devil and the Demographic Details', Gallup, 25 February 2003, http://www.gallup.com/poll/7858/devil-demographic-details.aspx, accessed 30 March 2010; Frank Newport, 'Americans More Likely to Believe in God Than Devil, Heaven More Than Hell', Gallup, 13 June 2007, http://www.gallup.com/poll/27877/americans-more-likely-believe-god-than-devil-heaven-more-than-hell.aspx, accessed 30 March 2010; Princeton Survey Research Associates for *Newsweek*, published as Kenneth L. Woodward, 'Do We Need Satan?', *Newsweek*, 13 November, 1995; Christopher Bader, F. Carson Mencken and Joseph Baker, *Paranormal*

Many health professionals also believe. Dealing directly with alleged cases of possession, psychiatrists M. Scott Peck and Richard E. Gallagher both came to the conclusion that the condition was real with the inevitable implication that there must be a Devil and/or demons. 'I would never again doubt the existence of Satan,' wrote Peck. 'Even those who doubt such a phenomenon exists,' said Gallagher, 'may find the following example rather persuasive'. They documented a range of extraordinary events, including levitation, psychokinesis and clairvoyance.[236]

After years of working with violent criminals, Rex Beaber, professor of medicine at the University of California, began to wonder if there really was 'an extra force, a dark force, that works through humans and perpetrates terror'.[237] Certainly this is something some violent criminals themselves believe. 'I believe in Satan,' said serial killer Richard Ramirez in a 1994 interview. 'I believe evil is a force that is beyond us and that we just have to invite him in.' Ramirez was a petty burglar with a drug addiction who terrified Los Angeles in 1984–5 as the sadistic 'Night Stalker'. During one of his attacks, he forced the victim to repeat 'I love Satan' as he raped her. At his preliminary court hearings, Richard Ramirez flashed a reversed pentagram on the palm of his hand to reporters and shouted 'Hail Satan!' Ramirez was eventually convicted on thirteen counts of murder in 1989.[238]

Other murderers have believed that they were actually trying to kill the Devil himself. When police found mixed martial arts fighter Jarrod Wyatt on 21 March 2010, covered in blood and standing over the body of his friend Taylor Powell, he told them

America, New York University Press, 2010, pp. 161–3, quoting from the Baylor Religion Survey, Wave 2, 2007.

[236] Peck, p. 238; Richard E. Gallagher, 'A Case of Demonic Possession', *New Oxford Review*, March 2008.

[237] Rex Julian Beaber, 'The Pathology of Evil', *Los Angeles Times*, 6 January 1985.

[238] 'Interview with Richard Ramirez', *Feast of Hate and Fear*, 6, 1996, http://feastofhateandfear.com/archives/night_stalker.html, accessed 15 December 2010; Michael Newton, *Raising Hell*, Warner, 1994, pp. 305–9; Peter Vronsky, *Serial Killers: The Method and Madness of Monsters*, Penguin, 2004.

'Satan was in that dude'. Wyatt had allegedly ripped out Powell's still beating heart and cooked it, as well as tearing off his tongue and a large part of his face, because he believed that his friend was the Devil. It was thought that they had been experimenting with hallucinogenic mushrooms. Speaking in his defence, lawyer James Fallman said 'My client was trying to silence the Devil.' Three psychiatrists have declared him sane.[239]

A demon was originally the morally neutral *daimon*, but underlying the Greek word there was always a universal concep-tion of destroying forces, often invisible – disease, famine, natural catastrophe – whose restless, indiscriminate actions seemed like the work of evil supernatural powers. Demons became a way to explain these events and a means by which they could be magically controlled.

Whilst a rich demonology inherited from Babylonia contin-ued to be developed and expounded with the incorporation of imagery from Classical mythology and European paganism, the Christian Church tended towards centralizing the powers of darkness in the single figure of the Devil. Jesus is tempted by the Devil. Martin Luther sees the Devil. They did not toy with mere demons. Even in modern culture, the character of Regan in *The Exorcist* is possessed by the Devil.

Towards the end of the film *The Exorcist* the priest-hero Karras asks the older Father Merrin, 'Why her? Why this girl?' Merrin replies, 'I think the point is to make us despair. To see ourselves as [. . .] animal and ugly. To make us reject the possi-bility that God could love us.' It was Satan and Job all over again. Only this time there would be no happy ending. Merrin dies of a heart attack and Karras, suddenly possessed himself, throws himself out of a window, tumbling down those infamous long narrow steps to his death.

As Joseph Conrad once wrote, 'The belief in a supernatural source of evil is not necessary; men alone are quite capable of

---

[239] John Driscoll, 'Klamath Suspect Wyatt Will Answer to Murder Charges', *The Times-Standard*, 27 May 2010; Anthony Skeens, 'DA Wants Death Penalty Option', *The Daily Triplicate*, 9 May 2011.

every wickedness'. Where stories like *The Exorcist* reinforce the Christian worldview, history shows us that the Devil and his demons will always be things we create ourselves, whether as an explanation for the misfortunes of life, a projection of our guilt for causing some of those misfortunes, or simply the face our mind gives to our innermost fears. The apparent evidence of possession cases and the efficacy of exorcism is suggestive, tempting, but ultimately not conclusive. As we understand more about the human mind we claim more of the territory that was once held by the diabolical, but the question and hence the possibility will long remain. As the French Decadent poet Charles Baudelaire once wrote, 'the greatest trick of the Devil is to persuade you that he does not exist'. And surely 200 million Americans cannot be wrong?[240]

---

[240] Charles Baudelaire, 'Le Joueur généreux', Le Spleen de Paris, *le Figaro*, 7–14 February 1864; Joseph Conrad, *Under Western Eyes*, 1911, Part Second, IV.

5. Extraterrestrials

It was a clear summer's afternoon on Tuesday, 24 June 1947, as Kenneth Arnold (1915–84) flew over the jagged Cascade mountain range, Washington State, USA. He was making a routine business flight from Chehalis to Yakima, but there was a $10,000 reward being offered to find a missing C-46 US Marine Corps transport. He veered his three-seater, single-engined Callair off course and headed towards Mount Rainier, the 4,392-metre-high stratovolcano that dominated the skyline. After an hour he turned back on course. 'The air was so smooth that day that it was a real pleasure flying,' he recalled. He sat back in his seat and enjoyed the view. A bright flash caught his attention. Off to his left he spotted nine objects flying at high speed. He described them as 'shaped like a pie plate', or 'flat like a pie pan and somewhat bat shaped', and 'saucer-like'. They moved 'like fish flipping in the sun'. They were so highly reflective that it was 'as if someone had started an arc light in front of my eyes'. He estimated that they were travelling at something like 1,200 miles an hour at an altitude of 10,000 feet.[241]

[241] Bill Bequette, 'Boise Flyer Maintains He Saw 'Em', *East Oregonian*, 26 June 1947; *Chicago Daily Tribune*, 26 June 1947; Frank M. Brown, Confidential Memorandum, Incident 4AF 1208 I, 16 July 1947; Ted Bloecher, *The UFO Wave of 1947*, NICAP, 1967, http://nicap.org/waves/Wave47Rpt/ReportUFOWave1947_Cover.htm, accessed 30 September 2010. The original newspaper articles and other documents for 1947 have been archived by Jan L. Aldrich, 'Project 1947', http://www.project1947.com.

Arnold was a successful businessman. He ran his own company, Great Western Fire Control Supply, selling and installing a range of fire-fighting equipment. His aeroplane had just cost him $5,000. He was also a thirty-two-year-old family man – married with two children – and had recently bought a new house on the outskirts of Boise. He was an Eagle Scout, a college football star and a Red Cross Life Saving Examiner, liked and respected in the community. He had three years' flying experience, regularly clocking up to a 100 hours a month. He could land his 'crate' in a cow pasture and the worst mishap had been a flat tyre. Arnold was what constituted a reliable witness and an experienced flyer. And now, flying across the mountains, he was about to be plunged into a celebrity he had never sought and change the face of history.[242]

Arnold ran through the likely explanations for the mysterious objects. Perhaps they were snow geese? 'But geese don't fly that high – and, anyway, what would geese be doing going south for this time of year?' Perhaps they were jet-engined planes? But 'their motion was wrong for jet jobs'. Perhaps the window was causing the reflections? He rolled down his window, but could still see the objects.[243]

They were also too fast. The Americans' new Lockheed P-80 Shooting Star jet fighter had only clocked 623 mph at Muroc Army Air Field, California, and Chuck Yeager was yet to make his historic flight in the experimental Bell X-1. Although two German pilots during WWII – Hans Guido Mutke in a Messerschmitt Me 262 and Heini Dittmar in a Messerschmitt Me 163 – had reportedly broken the sound barrier with speeds in excess of 1,062km/h (670m/h), this had only been achieved in a steep dive. Whatever Arnold had seen, supposing his calculations were correct, defied what was then technologically possible for a piloted aircraft.[244]

---

[242] Brown, Memorandum.

[243] Bequette, *East Oregonian*, 26 June 1947.

[244] Michael David Hall and Wendy Ann Connors, *Alfred Loedding and the Great Flying Saucer Wave of 1947*, Rose Press, 1998, p. 25. Muroc was later renamed

The local press quickly picked up the story. As news spread, apparently confirmatory reports started coming in. A Mr Savage from Oklahoma City saw something streak overhead: 'The machine, or whatever it was, was a shiny silvery color – very big – and was moving at a terrific rate of speed.' W. I. Davenport, a carpenter in the Midwest, said he saw nine fast moving objects from the roof of a house he was working on. E. H. Sprinkle of Eugene claimed to have photographed seven strange objects. George Clover of Bellingham saw three fast moving, shiny objects 'like kites'. Some time later prospector Fred Johnson reported to both the Air Force and the FBI that he had observed flying objects near Mt Adams on the 24th, estimated at an altitude of 300m (1,000 feet) and of 9m (30 feet) diameter. As they passed over-head, his compass needle swung wildly from side to side.[245]

In all, at least twenty sightings were reported for 24 June 1947. As excitement mounted, Arnold found himself at the centre of increasing interest, most of it unwanted. A preacher telephoned to tell him that his sighting was a forewarning of the end of the world. A woman rushed out of a café after seeing Arnold inside, shrieking, 'There's the man who saw the men from Mars.' One of the newspapers said Arnold 'would like to get on one of his 1200-mile-an-hour "flying saucers" and escape from the furor.' The flying saucer had been born.[246]

Arnold's encounter is often seen as the beginning of the modern UFO phenomenon.[247] In some ways it was, although

---

Edwards Air Force Base. Ferdinand C. W. Käsmann, *Die schnellsten Jets der Welt*, Aviatic-Verlag, 1999, pp. 17, 122. At 20°C, sea level, the speed of sound is 1,236 km/h (768m/h), but as temperature and molecular mass decrease at higher altitudes the speed of sound also decreases.

[245] Savage and Davenport quoted in 'Flying Disk Mystery Grows', *Oregon Journal*, 26 June 1947; Sprinkle and Clover quoted in 'Flying Saucer Story Grows', *The Oregonian*, 28 June 1947; Johnson in Bruce Maccabee, 'Strong Magnetic Field Detected Following a Sighting of an Unidentified Flying Object', *Journal of Scientific Exploration*, 8, 1994, p. 359.

[246] Bloecher, §I–3; 'Harassed Saucer-Sighter Would Like to Escape Fuss', *Statesman Journal*, 28 June 1947.

[247] See Gordon Stein (ed.), *The Encyclopedia of the Paranormal*, Prometheus Books, 1996, p. 767; or Stuart Gordon, *The Paranormal: An Illustrated Encyclopedia*, Head-

there were earlier sightings noted without having to reinterpret religious experiences or meteorological phenomena. Between the years 1890 and 1945 there were two peaks in the UFO-type events reported for which date, time, latitude and longitude were known: 1896–7 saw a wave of 'airship' sightings; in 1909 there was a 'phantom aircraft' wave.[248] June to July 1947 also exhibited a surge of sightings, with the highest number of eighty-two separate reports logged for 7 July alone. American ufologist Ted Bloecher (1929–) would document more than 850 cases for these two months.[249]

The sightings go on. Three soldiers at Tern Hill barracks, Shropshire, reported strange lights 'like rotating cubes with multiple colours' in June 2008, only hours before a police helicopter gave chase to an unidentified craft near Cardiff some eighty miles away.[250] Four UFOs were supposedly photographed over London in March 2009.[251] A 'comet-like fireball' or 'twinkling spotlight' closed Xiaoshan airport in Hangzhou, China, when it showed up on radar on 7 July 2010.[252] A 'hyperdimensional UFO' was reported as firing 'a ray of light or directed energy beam' in the vicinity of the White House, Washington, D.C., on 20 July 2010.[253] The number of UFO reports is over-

line, 1992, p. 672, for example. According to Hall and Connors, p. 144, the USAF also dates the UFO phenomenon from this time.

[248] Peter A. Sturrock, 'Time-Series Analysis of a Catalog of UFO Events: Evidence of a Local-Sidereal-Time Modulation', *Journal of Scientific Exploration*, 18, 2004, p. 401.

[249] Larry Hatch, *U* UFO Database, http://web.archive.org/web/20060701162649/www.larryhatch.net/YDAY47.html, accessed 29 September 2010; Bloecher, abstract.

[250] 'Soldier Spots 13 UFOs Above Barracks', *Daily Telegraph*, 25 June 2008; 'Invasion of the Bobby Snatchers: Police Helicopter has Close Encounter with a UFO', *Daily Mail*, 20 June 2008.

[251] Sarah Knapton, 'UFOs Photographed Over London', *Daily Telegraph*, 18 March 2009.

[252] Wang Xiang, 'Experts Probe Hangzhou UFO Sighting', ShanghaiDaily.com, 14 July 2010; 'Chinese Airport Closed After Fiery UFO is Spotted Flying Over City', *Daily Mail*, 16 July 2010.

[253] Mark Fraser, 'Sightings', *Paranormal*, 52, October 2010, p. 13.

whelming. By June 2006 Larry Hatch had documented 18,552 UFO-type events, even filtering out known hoaxes and misidentified meteorological phenomena. Are extraterrestrials really out there?[254] Even Arnold had difficulty accepting what he saw, but as he said, 'I must believe my eyes.'[255]

Closer Encounters

Worried that the saucers posed a threat to national security, Arnold immediately reported his sightings to the military. Ignoring almost all of what Arnold had said, the newspapers had already found their explanations. A Lieutenant Colonel Harold E. Turner, Army Air Force, was on record as saying that the discs were the circular exhaust pipes of jets. The science editor for Associated Press, Howard W. Blakeslee, said that what Arnold saw was simply sunlight reflecting from ordinary aircraft.[256]

With everyone trying to explain it all away, Arnold stuck to his story, only complaining that neither the FBI nor the military seemed to be taking his report seriously. 'If I was running the country,' he told reporters, 'and someone reported something unusual, I'd certainly want to know more about it.'[257]

However, some quarters of the military had taken Arnold's report seriously. Two intelligence officers from Hamilton Field, California – Captain William Davidson and Lieutenant Frank Brown – were assigned to investigate the case. After questioning Arnold in a hotel room for six hours, their official report read:

---

[254] http://web.archive.org/web/20060701162858/www.larryhatch.net/ALLABOUT.html, accessed 29 September 2010.

[255] 'Bug-Eyed Salesman Reports Fast-Flying Mystery Planes', *The Norman Transcript*, 26 June 1947.

[256] Bill Bequette, 'Experts Reach Deep Into Bag to Explain "Flying Discs"', *East Oregonian*, 28 June 1947.

[257] '"Flying Saucer" Observer Says No One Can Change His Mind', *Idaho Statesman*, 28 June 1947.

It is the personal opinion of the interviewer that Mr Arnold actually saw what he stated he saw. It is difficult to believe that a man of [his] character and apparent integrity would state that he saw objects and write up a report to the extent that he did if he did not see them.[258]

Forced to accept that Arnold was a reliable witness, military intelligence were left with a troubling conclusion: he *had* seen flying discs. But events were about to move to another level. Fifteen days after Arnold's sighting, on Tuesday, 8 July 1947, the *Roswell Daily Record* ran a front-page story under the headline 'RAAF Captures Flying Saucer on Ranch in Roswell Region':

The intelligence office of the 509th Bombardment group at Roswell Army Field announced at noon today, that the field has come into possession of a flying saucer. According to information released by the department, over authority of Maj. J. A. Marcel, intelligence officer, the disk was recovered on a ranch in the Roswell vicinity, after an unidentified rancher had notified Sheriff Geo. Wilcox, here, that he had found the instrument on his premises. Major Marcel and a detail from his department went to the ranch and recovered the disk, it was stated. After the intelligence officer here had inspected the instrument it was flown to higher headquarters. The intelligence office stated that no details of the saucer's construction or its appearance had been revealed.[259]

The 509th had flown the Boeing B-29 Superfortresses that dropped the atomic bomb on Hiroshima and Nagasaki. It was then the world's only operational atomic bomber squadron, so at the very least, the area around their base was highly sensitive

---

[258] Quoted in Bloecher, I–2.
[259] Transcription of the article at http://ufologie.net/rw/p/rdr8jul1947.htm, accessed 13 October 2010.

and the possibility that their airspace had been penetrated by unidentified craft must have been extremely worrying.

The newspaper went on to suggest that events unfolded on the night of Wednesday, 2 July 1947, when Mr and Mrs Dan Wilmot saw 'a large glowing object' speed across the sky at around 10 o'clock. Mr Wilmot estimated that it was travelling at about 400 to 500 miles an hour at an altitude of 1,500 feet. It was oval shaped and about 15 to 20 feet in diameter. Others said that they had seen a strange blue light at about 3 a.m. The evening edition of the *Los Angeles Herald-Express* for 8 July 1947 was already printing the official explanation that the object was a 'radar weather target'. The *Seattle Daily Times* quoted Brigadier General Roger Ramey as saying the object was of 'flimsy construction; almost like a box kite' and covered with something like tinfoil. The next day the newspapers were printing reports that the object had been discovered three weeks earlier and even that unnamed Army Air Force sources had ruled out the possibility that it was some sort of weather kite.[260]

The unidentified rancher had meanwhile been identified as William Ware Brazel and now gave his account of the story. He told the *Roswell Daily Record* that, on 14 June, he and his eight-year-old son Vernon were about seven or eight miles out from the J. B. Foster Ranch when they discovered 'a large area of bright wreckage made up of rubber strips, tinfoil, a rather tough paper and sticks'. It was only on 4 July that he went back to the spot to recover the debris. When he heard about the flying discs he wondered whether he had accidentally found one. In town some days later he mentioned his find to Sheriff George Wilcox. Wilcox contacted the Roswell Army Air Field (RAAF) and Major Marcel, accompanied by

---

[260] 'Army Finds "Flying Saucer", General believes it is radar weather target', *Los Angeles Herald-Express*, 8 July 1947; 'Disk lands on ranch in N.M. – is held by Army', *Seattle Daily Times*, 8 July 1947; 'Only Meager Details of Flying Disc Given – Kite-Like Device Found in N.M. Studied by Army', *The Wyoming Eagle*, 9 July 1947.

a man in plain clothes, went back with Brazel to examine and remove the evidence.[261]

Brazel had found weather balloons on his ranch before. 'I am sure,' he told the newspaper, 'that what I found was not any weather observation balloon.' But on the same day the *Roswell Daily Record* also published Brigadier General Ramey's conclusion that the mysterious object was, after all, just a high-altitude weather balloon. A reward of $3,000 was offered for evidence of alien activity. Soon people were handing in 'a spinning gadget of aluminium' and 'a piece of metal' that allegedly 'took 6300 degrees of heat to melt'. By 10 July 1947 the French newspaper *L'Aurore* was already suggesting a cover-up. So what had been found?[262]

Foo-Files

On 23 September 1947 the commanding officer of Air Materiel [*sic*] Command (AMC), General Nathan F. Twining, wrote to the commanding officer of the US Air Force (USAF), Brigadier General George Schulgen.[263] The word SECRET was stamped in large letters on all three pages of the memo. As Twining indicated, he had already conducted a preliminary investigation of the 'so-called "Flying Disks"', involving Intelligence T-2 and Aircraft Laboratory Engineering Division T-3, and was now submitting his findings. He detailed the discs' commonly reported characteristics:[264]

---

[261] 'Harassed Rancher Who Located "Saucer" Sorry He Told About It', *Roswell Daily Record*, 9 July 1947.

[262] 'Gen. Ramey Empties Roswell Saucer', *Roswell Daily Record*, 9 July 1947; 'AAF "Flying Saucer" Merely Weather Box-Kite', *The Washington Post*, 9 July 1947; '"Disk" Near Bomb Test Site is Just a Weather Balloon', *The New York Times*, 9 July 1947; 'Les "Soucoupes Volantes" Gardent Leur Mystère', *L'Aurore*, 10 July 1947.

[263] The US Army Air Forces (USAAF) had been redesignated the US Air Force (USAF) from 18 September 1947, becoming a separate military service under the terms of the National Security Act, 1947.

[264] Edward J. Ruppelt, *The Report on Unidentified Flying Objects*, Doubleday & Company,1956, pp. 15–16, gives Air Technical Intelligence Center; Curtis

1. Metallic or light reflecting surface.
2. Absence of trail, except in a few instances when the object apparently was operating under high performance conditions.
3. Circular or elliptical in shape, flat on bottom and domed on top.
4. Several reports of well kept formation flights varying from three to nine objects.
5. Normally no associated sound, except in three instances a substantial rumbling roar was noted.
6. Level flight speeds normally above 300 knots are estimated.[265]

'The phenomenon reported,' Twining concluded, 'is something real and not visionary or fictitious.' He recommended that Army Air Force Headquarters instigate a 'detailed study'. This became Air Materiel Command's Project XS-304, codename 'Project Sign'. The Allied military had been receiving reports of mysterious craft – dubbed 'foo fighters' by US pilots – towards the end of WWII and 'ghost rockets' had haunted Scandinavian skies in the summer of 1946, but only now would a systematic study be undertaken. Although there has been some controversy over the existence of an earlier investigation into UFOs called Majestic 12 (also Majic-12 and MJ-12), Project Sign was the first documented (and uncontested) official investigation by the USAF.[266]

Initiated on 22 January 1948 and conducted at Wright-Patterson Air Force Base, Dayton, Ohio, by the Technical

---

Peebles, *Watch the Skies*, Smithsonian Institution Press, 1994, p. 250; Stanton T. Friedman, *Flying Saucers and Science*, Career Press, 2008, p. 115. So-called Twining Memo, 'AMC Opinion Concerning "Flying Discs"', TSDIN/HMM/ig/6-4100, 23 September 1947.

[265] Twining Memo.

[266] Hall and Conors gave the project number as HT-304, but Project Sign's own Technical Report, February 1949, gives XS-304; 'Science: Foo-Fighter', *Time*, 15 January 1945; on 'ghost rockets' see USAFE Item 14, TT 1524, (Top Secret), 4 November 1948, declassified 1997, National Archives, Washington, D.C. Reports of so-called 'ghost rockets' became widespread across Europe during the course of 1946.

Intelligence Division, Project Sign was classified 'restricted' and given priority 2A – 1A being the highest rating. The Air Force were serious about this one. Most of that concern was around the possibility that the UFOs could be some new Soviet aircraft or guided rocketry, especially utilizing captured Nazi technology. But as they examined the cases, it seemed less and less likely that the Soviets could be behind them – they were simply too extraordinary.[267]

Among the many cases investigated, several stood out. Captain Thomas F. Mantell, Jr, flying an Air National Guard F-51, intercepted a UFO over Kentucky on 7 January 1948. As Mantell took the pursuit above the safety limit of 15,000 feet for flying without oxygen, radio contact with the pilot was lost. His crashed F-51 was recovered from the William J. Phillips farm near Franklin, Kentucky. First Venus, then a US Navy Skyhook research balloon were blamed for the incident. First Lieutenant Robert W. Meyers was leading a flight of P-47s of the 67th Fighter Group, Central Philippines, when he encountered something like a silver 'half-moon' with a 'turtle back' flying beneath him. He too lost radio contact as he attempted pursuit, but the UFO easily outmanoeuvred him and escaped at high speed. It sounded like an experimental 'flying wing', but nothing fitting that description was known to be operating in the region. On 24 July 1948, Eastern Airlines DC-3 Flight 576 narrowly avoided a mid-air collision as a UFO travelling at 800 mph closed to within 700 feet of the aeroplane as it flew over Alabama. Captain Clarence S. Chiles and First Officer John B. Whitted clearly observed a wingless cylindrical object with two rows of windows, trailing 50 feet of flame behind it. Passenger Clarence L. McKelvie also reported seeing a 'strange, eerie

[267] Ruppelt, pp. 16, 30. Hall and Connors, p. 117. Hall and Connors give a start date of 11 February 1948, whilst the Technical Report and Project 'Saucer' Press Release both give 22 January 1948. According to the Project Blue Book, 'History of the Project', 1 February 1966, NARA Blue Book, Roll 87, T1206-87, the Technical Intelligence Division, AMC, issued Technical Instruction No. 2185 on 11 February 1948 relating to the creation of Sign.

streak of light'. Sign investigators told the pilots that they had seen a fireball, but Chiles and Whitted insisted that it had been a craft of some sort.[268]

By early 1949, Project Sign was ready to report. Technical Report No. F-TR-2274-IA was prepared by missile specialist Lawrence H. Treuttnet and reserve Army Air Force colonel Albert B. Deyarmond and released in February 1949. It was based on analysis of 243 US and 30 non-US cases, of which only 20 per cent had been positively identified as 'conventional aerial objects'. Treuttnet and Deyarmond concluded that 'No definite evidence is yet available to confirm or disprove the actual existence of unidentified flying objects as new and unknown types of aircraft', although they noted that because the study was still ongoing, no definitive conclusion could yet be reached.[269]

On 27 April 1949 the National Military Establishment Office of Public Information in Washington, D.C., issued a press release entitled 'Project "Saucer"', detailing the work and findings of then still classified Project Sign. Claiming to have identified about 30 per cent of cases investigated as weather balloons, aircraft, birds, flares, astronomical phenomena, optical illusions and mass hallucinations, the press release still conceded that the final answer had not been reached. But this apparent honesty belied the real purpose of the release, which was to assuage public fears: 'The "saucers" are not a joke. Neither are they cause for alarm to the population.' It was the equivalent of *The Hitchhiker's Guide to the Galaxy*'s 'Don't Panic'.[270]

But the USAF had panicked, although for different reasons. With Project Sign leaning closer to an extraterrestrial explanation, essentially as the only explanation left, the top brass deemed it necessary to shake things up. A Top Secret 'Estimate

---

[268] Hall and Connors, pp. 133–40; Ruppelt, pp. 31–40.

[269] http://www.bluebookarchive.org/page.aspx?PageCode=MAXW-PBB1-8, accessed 21 October 2010.

[270] 'Project "Saucer"', Memorandum to the Press No. M 26 – 49, National Military Establishment Office of Public Information, Washington, D.C., 27 April 1949.

of the Situation' had been made, apparently concluding that UFOs were real, but as Captain Edward J. Ruppelt, later director of UFO research, explained, 'it was kicked back'. No copies of this Estimate have so far been unearthed by ufologists. On 11 February 1949, Sign was redesignated Project Grudge and new personnel were assigned to conduct the research. In his *Report on Unidentified Flying Objects*, Ruppelt called this period 'the Dark Ages'. The name Grudge was evidently more than just a random moniker.[271]

In August 1949 Grudge released the 600-page-long 'Unidentified Flying Objects – Project Grudge', Technical Report No. 102-AC-49/15-100 – the 'Grudge Report'. After analysing 244 cases it concluded that UFOs were one of four things:[272]

a) misinterpretation of conventional objects,
b) mass hysteria or 'War Nerves',
c) hoaxes and/or
d) psychopathological persons.[273]

Writer John A. Keel, famous for *The Mothman Prophecies*, described Grudge as 'hundreds of pages of irrelevant nonsense'.[274] Based on Grudge's findings the AMC recommended that research be reduced in scope. Grudge quickly stagnated. It was finally announced on 27 December 1949 in a USAF press conference that the project had been terminated. Work continued on the possibly paranormal 'green fireballs', codenamed Project Twinkle, and even Grudge was still lingering in the background. According to Ruppelt, when the USAF's Director of Intelligence, Major General (later Lieutenant General) Charles P. Cabell got the full measure of the sorry

---

[271] Ruppelt, p. 59; 'History of the Project', n.p., gives 16 December 1948 as the date of redesignation.
[272] Ruppelt, pp. 65–8; 'History of the Project', n.p.
[273] 'History of the Project', n.p.
[274] John A. Keel, 'The Man Who Invented Flying Saucers', *Fortean Times*, 41, 1983, pp. 52–7.

state Grudge was in he demanded that a new project be set up. In September 1951, Ruppelt took over Grudge and a new series of monthly reports started appearing from November 1951. In March 1952, Grudge was redesignated Project Blue Book.[275]

An area of about 13m³ (42 cubic feet) in the US National Archives is occupied by the text records of Project Blue Book. This is estimated to contain about 84,000 pages, all of which can be read on 94 rolls of 35mm microfilm. Luckily, the Public Affairs Division of the Wright-Patterson Air Force Base produced a fact sheet in 1985 that summarized the findings. In the period from 1947 to 1969 a total of 12,618 sightings had been reported: 701 remained unidentified.[276]

Despite the initial impetus from General Cabell, the official line from the Pentagon continued to be less than constructive. Ruppelt applied for a transfer. In 1956 he published his landmark book *The Report on Unidentified Flying Objects* documenting the many incredible contacts he had investigated, yet Ruppelt remained agnostic. He was not a believer, he said, but also added:

> Every time I begin to get skeptical I think of the other reports, the many reports made by experienced pilots and radar operators, scientists, and other people who know what they're looking at. These reports were thoroughly investigated and they are still unknowns.[277]

Strictly speaking, then, he had to admit that there were unidentified flying objects and only tentatively raised the possibility that 'Maybe the earth is being visited by interplanetary spaceships'. Even with such an even-handed approach he seems to

---

[275] Ruppelt, p. 65; Status Report No. 1, Project Grudge, 30 November 1951, http://www.bluebookarchive.org/page.aspx?PageCode=MAXW-PBB1-498, accessed 21 October 2010; 'History of the Project', n.p.

[276] US National Archives, http://www.archives.gov/foia/ufos.html, accessed 13 October 2010. The Blue Book Archive website at http://www.bluebookarchive. org/ has about 10 per cent of this material online.

[277] Ruppelt, p. 242.

have ruffled a few feathers. The Commander, ATIC, wrote to the Secretary of the Air Force in 1958 concerning the book. Undermining Ruppelt's credibility as an expert, he dismissed his conclusions as 'questionable'. He had proved Ruppelt's oft made point: the Air Force only wanted *identified* flying objects and certainly did not want to hear about extraterrestrials.[278]

UFO sightings and radar contacts continued and were just as remarkable as before, and Blue Book was just as far away from solving the problem. Not long after Ruppelt left, Blue Book Special Report No. 14 had to concede that 'It can never be absolutely proven that "flying saucers" do not exist'. Completed on 17 March 1954, it was declassified and released to the public on 5 May 1955. The USAF on its own could not get rid of the unidentifieds, but they were adamant that it was 'highly improbable' that they were the product of 'technological developments outside the range of present-day scientific knowledge'. By 1966 the USAF were receiving more than 2,000 letters a year from people demanding to know more about the UFO investigations.[279]

As part of Blue Book, the USAF had contracted the University of Colorado to conduct an independent Scientific Study of Unidentified Objects, the 'Colorado Project' or 'Condon Committee', under the direction of Edward U. Condon.[280] With admirable restraint, Karl Pflock characterized this study as 'not so independent and not so scientific'.[281] Evidence was later

---

[278] Ruppelt, p. 243; Cmdr, ATIC, to Sec[retar]y of Air Force, OIS, 23 May 1958, Document T1206-87, NARA Blue Book Roll No. 87, Page ID: NARA-PBB87-335-339, http://www.bluebookarchive.org/page.aspx?PageCode=NARA-PBB87-336, accessed 27 October 2010.

[279] 'History of the Report', n.p.; 'Extract from Special Report #14', Document T1206-86, NARA Blue Book Roll No. 86, Page ID: NARA-PBB86-881, http://www.bluebookarchive.org/page.aspx?PageCode=NARA-PBB86-881, accessed 27 October 2010.

[280] Reproduced online at http://www.project1947.com/shg/condon/index.html and http://files.ncas.org/condon/ with the permission of the Regents of the University of Colorado.

[281] Karl T. Pflock, Review of Richard H. Hall, *Alien Invasion or Human Fantasy?*, Mount Rainier, 2004, *Journal of Scientific Exploration*, 18, 2004, p. 710.

forthcoming that Condon and others had held secret meetings with the CIA and that the CIA contributed to the project, neither facts being mentioned in the Condon Report itself. The project's much touted scientific methodology also met with serious criticism.[282] But the USAF had what it wanted: a way out of the UFO maze. Shored up by Condon they could now confidently state:

> The conclusions of Project BLUE BOOK are: (1) no UFO reported, investigated, and evaluated by the Air Force has ever given any indication of threat to our national security; (2) there has been no evidence submitted to or discovered by the Air Force that sightings categorized as "unidentified" represent technological developments or principles beyond the range of present-day scientific knowledge; and (3) there has been no evidence indicating that sightings categorized as "unidentified" are extraterrestrial vehicles.[283]

On 17 December 1969, the Secretary of the Air Force terminated Project Blue Book. There would be no further plans to investigate UFOs again. But the Americans were not the only ones to investigate the UFO phenomenon. With news of the Argentinian Air Force forming a commission to investigate UFOs and the New Zealand Defence Force declassifying its UFO files, the search is far from over.[284]

---

[282] Peter A. Sturrock, 'An Analysis of the Condon Report on the Colorado UFO Project', *Journal of Scientific Exploration*, 1.1, 1987, pp. 75ff.

[283] 'U.S. Air Force Fact Sheet Concerning UFOs and Project BLUE BOOK', January 1985, US National Archives, http://www.archives.gov/foia/ufos.html, accessed 13 October 2010.

[284] 'USAF Fact Sheet'; 'Argentina to Record UFO Sightings', *AFP*, 29 December 2010; 'New Zealand Releases UFO Files', *Daily Telegraph*, 23 December 2010.

Official UFO Investigations

Name	Country	Organization	Period Active
Majestic 12 (contested)	USA	Inter-governmental	1946–54?
Project Sign	USA	US Air Force (USAF)	1948
Project Grudge	USA	US Air Force (USAF)	1949–1
Project Magnet	Canada	Dept of Transport	1950–4
Flying Saucer Working Party	UK	Ministry of Defence (MoD)	1950–51
Robertson Panel	USA	Central Intelligence Agency (CIA)	1952, 1953
Project Blue Book	USA	US Air Force (USAF)	1952–69
Condon Committee (Condon Report)	USA	University of Colorado	1966–8
GEPAN/SEPRA/GEIPAN	France	Centre National d'Études Spatiales (CNES)	1977–
Project Condign	UK	Defence Intelligence Staff (DIS)	1997–2000

In 1999 the French public woke up to an astounding report published by weekly news and entertainment magazine *VSD*. In 'Les OVNI et la Defense: A quoi doit-on se préparer?' ('UFOS and Defence: What Must We Be Prepared For?') about 200,000 people read of hundreds of UFO cases with the conclusion that aliens were probably out there and 'critical vigilance' was required. Specifically, the report argued that the UFO phenomenon was worthy of continued serious investigation because it could not be ruled out that some sort of non-human technology was involved and that this necessarily had ramifications for national security. The implication was also there that the US government was being less than open with its information, particularly as regards Roswell. The report was produced by a group calling itself COMETA – the 'Committee for In-Depth Studies' – comprised of twelve private individuals formerly involved with the prestigious Institut des Hautes Études de Défense Nationale (IHEDN), including generals, an admiral and a police superintendent, amongst others, under retired air force general Denis Letty. It was endorsed by heavyweight figures such as General Bernard Norlain of the French Air Force and a former director of IHEDN, as well as André Lebeau, former president of Centre National d'Études Spatiales (CNES). Originally only sent to top officials, including then President Jacques Chirac and Prime Minister Lionel Jospin, the report garnered the reputation of being an official document. However, as a private initiative it did not carry the weight that many had hoped for it.[285]

On 22 March 2007 the French space agency CNES released via its website the equivalent of 100,000 A4 pages of eye-witness

---

[285] Bruce Maccabee, 'DVD Review: *Out of the Blue: The Definitive Investigation of the UFO Phenomenon*', 2004, *Journal of Scientific Exploration*, 22, 2008, p. 453; Mark Rodeghier, 'The 1999 French Report on UFOs and Defense', *International UFO Reporter*, Summer 2000, pp. 20–3; Claude Maugé 'A Commentary on COMETA', trans. Jacques Vallée, *Journal of Scientific Exploration*, 15, 2001, pp. 139–42; Gildas Bourdais, 'The French Report on UFOs and Defense: A Summary', CUFOS, http://www.cufos.org/cometa.html, accessed 21 December 2010.

reports, photographs, film footage and audio recordings of some 1,650 sightings documented since 1954. Printed out and piled high this amount would stand as tall as a three-storey building. Within three hours demand crashed the CNES servers.

Jacques Patenet, head of the Group d'Études et d'Information sur les Phénomènes Aérospatiaux Non Identifiés (GEIPAN), the CNES UFO team, was equivocal: 'The data that we are releasing doesn't demonstrate the presence of extraterrestrial beings, but it doesn't demonstrate the impossibility of such presence either'. Of the 1,650 cases he said, 'a few dozen are very intriguing and can be called UFOs', or about 28 per cent according to their figures. CNES still receives about a hundred new reports every year.[286]

When the UK's Ministry of Defence (MoD) declassified files in 2006 it was discovered that they had collected more than 10,000 eye-witness accounts. In 2007 Dr David Clarke, Dr Joe McGonagle and Gary Anthony campaigned to have the MoD release all of its UFO files to the public. In 2008 the British Government released its most comprehensive files on UFO sightings. Compiled by the Ministry of Defence between 1978 and 2002 the files were made available under the Freedom of Information Act (FOIA) with further releases planned for following years. The Flying Saucer Working Party (FSWP) had already reported on the problem as long ago as 1951. It came to entirely negative conclusions as to whether UFOs were of extraterrestrial origin. But then the FSWP had relied on the USAF's entirely negative Project Grudge. However, the MoD continued to operate a UFO 'desk' until 2009 before a round of budgetry cuts deemed its

---

[286] Molly Moore, 'French Get a Look at Nation's UFO Files', *Washington Post*, 23 March 2007. 'The Plain Truth of the Matter', CNES, March 2007, http://www.cnes.fr/web/CNES-en/5871-the-plain-truth-of-the-matter.php, accessed 24 March 2010. 'GEIPAN UAP Investigation Unit Opens its Files', CNES, 26 March 2007, http://www.cnes.fr/web/CNES-en/5866-geipan-uap-investigation-unit-opens-its-files.php, accessed 24 March 2010. See www.cnes-geipan.fr.

cost of £50,000 a year an expendable luxury. The MoD, whilst stating that it has no opinion on extraterrestrials, said that 'in over fifty years, no UFO report has revealed any evidence of a potential threat to the United Kingdom'. The last recorded entry, dated 30 November 2009, took place at 19:40 in Wilnecote, Staffordshire: 'Strange orange light coming from the North, clear night, no port and starboard indicators, translucent halo, lasted 1 min 20 secs, constant speed, straight line.'[287]

Roswell today is no longer the sleepy rural town that it was. It is now a major tourist attraction with an annual UFO festival, the Roswell International UFO Museum and Research Center and at least three competing crash sites. The museum was founded by Lieutenant Walter Haut, who had issued the fateful press release on 8 July 1947, and Glenn Dennis. Registered as a non-profit educational organization in 1991, it opened to visitors in autumn 1992. The museum claims to attract upwards of 150,000 people a year.[288]

As well as the tourism, additional evidence or interpretations continue to surface, keeping the Roswell controversy alive and kicking. Bible code hunters even found the word

---

[287] David Clarke and Andy Roberts, *Out of the Shadows: UFOs, the Establishment and Official Cover Up*, Piatkus Books, 2002; Finlo Rohrer, 'Saucers in the Sky', BBC News Magazine, 4 July 2007; Graham Tibbetts, 'British Government Releases UFO Files', *Daily Telegraph*, 13 May 2008; Andrew Hough, 'MoD Department that Investigated UFO Sightings "Closed"', *Daily Telegraph*, 4 December 2009; HQ Air Command, 'Closure of UFO Hotline', MoD, 31 December 2008/1 March 2010, http://www.mod.uk/DefenceInternet/Freedom-mOfInformation/PublicationScheme/SearchPublicationScheme/ClosureOf UfoHelpdesk.htm, accessed 23 October 2010; Air Command, 'UFO Reports 2009', MoD, p. 39, http://www.mod.uk/NR/rdonlyres/41A2F229-95B9-47E5-99C6-CB242838A03C/0/ufo_report_2009.pdf, accessed 23 October 2010.
[288] Dennis Stacey, Review of Karl T. Pflock, *Roswell: Inconvenient Facts and the Will to Believe*, Prometheus, 2001, *Journal of Scientific Exploration*, 15, 2001, p. 429; http://www.roswellufomuseum.com/about.htm, accessed 23 October 2010.

Top 10 UFO Encounters

Case	Date	Location	Alleged Occurrence
Kenneth Arnold	1947	Washington State, USA	nine 'flying discs' sighted
Roswell	1947	New Mexico, USA	UFO crash
Mantell	1948	Kentucky, USA	UFO pursuit
Chiles-Whitted	1948	Alabama, USA	UFO near-collision
Washington D.C.	1952	District of Columbia, USA	sightings and radar contacts
1966–7 UFO Wave	1966–7	USA and Canada	mass sightings documented
Shag Harbour	1967	Nova Scotia, Canada	UFO crash
Tehran	1976	Tehran, Iran	jets scrambled to intercept UFO
Rendlesham Forest	1980	Suffolk, UK	RAF base close encounter
Belgian UFO Wave	1989–90	Wallonia, Belgium	mass black triangle sightings

'Roswell' hidden in Genesis 31:28, adding to the aura.[289] But the significant new findings came from an alleged crash eye-witness, new analysis of a 1947 photograph, and archaeological digs in the supposed crash area.

In 1996 the deathbed confession of Jim Ragsdale was published along with a sworn affidavit attesting to its authenticity. He claimed not only to have seen the alleged flying disc crash, but also to have investigated the wreckage. He described seeing an instrument panel, chairs and four dead alien bodies through a hole in the fuselage. It looked like the truth was finally out. However, using the forensic psychology procedures of Statement Validity Analysis and Fact Pattern Analysis, James Houran and Stephen Porter found that Ragdale's statement did not resemble true memory recall and was factually inconsistent.[290]

A photograph taken of Brigadier General Ramey and Colonel Thomas J. DuBose examining the remains of a balloon was released to quiet the public. But even this has become evidence of proof, at least for some. Ramey is shown holding a piece of paper, which some people have said makes clear reference to a crashed UFO of alien origins. The piece of paper is barely, if at all, legible and experiments by James Houran and Kevin Randle have shown that interpretations of its contents are entirely due to the reader's expectations.[291]

---

[289] Matt Lamy, *100 Strangest Mysteries*, Barnes & Nobles 2007, p. 100. Using equidistant letter sequencing you can find almost anything in the Bible, or any long text such as *Moby Dick*, *War and Peace*, etc.

[290] Jim Ragsdale, *The Jim Ragsdale Story: A Closer Look at the Roswell Incident*, Jim Ragsdale Productions, 1996; James Houran and Stephen Porter, 'Statement Validity Analysis of "The Jim Ragsdale Story": Implication for the Roswell Incident', *Journal of Scientific Exploration*, 12.1, 1998, pp. 57–71.

[291] James Houran and Kevin Randle, '"A Message in a Bottle:" Confounds in Deciphering the Ramey Memo from the Roswell UFO Case', *Journal of Scientific Exploration*, 16.1, 2002, pp. 45–66. The photograph is held by the Fort Worth-Star Telegram Photograph Collection, The University of Texas at Arlington Libraries. As a reader of *Journal of Scientific Exploration* (16, 2002, pp. 662–3), James Westwood, pointed out, if this letter was in any way an official military communication then it should have been recorded and filed. Randle had indeed searched for the document, but to no avail.

In 2002 the SCI FI Channel sponsored archaeologists from the University of New Mexico to excavate at the alleged crash site. Working under project leader Dr William Doleman, they reputedly discovered 'historical materials of uncertain origin' and suggestive furrows. Some members of the team were certain that they were under government surveillance and feared that there might be a sabotage attempt. In the end, the nine-day excavation went ahead unmolested. Aerial photographs of the region from 1946 may indicate that at least one of the features discovered was already present before the supposed crash event took place.[292]

Area 51

Area 51 is a US Air Force base in Nevada, about 800 miles away from Roswell, New Mexico. It is primarily a testing site for secret aircraft and weapons projects. For example, the U-2 spy plane of the 1950s was tested and developed here. It is a restricted area with the 'use of deadly force' authorized to protect it. Largely because of this secrecy, Area 51 is rumoured to house wreckage from the alleged Roswell UFO crash and other crashes, as well as the bodies of extraterrestrials.

About 20,000 people signed the Roswell Declaration demanding that the US government release all its files on the Roswell Incident. It was sent to the US Congress in 1997. Kent Jeffrey was one of those instrumental in organizing the campaign, but after studying all of the evidence that has since become available he has reversed his earlier position on Roswell. Twining also noted that there was a 'lack of physical evidence in the shape of crash-recovered exhibits'. This was a secret memo from one high-ranking officer to another; if any evidence of a crashed UFO had been recovered at Roswell, he would surely

---

[292] William H. Doleman, Thomas J. Carey and Donald R. Schmitt, *The Roswell Dig Diaries*, Pocket Books, 2004; reviewed by Kevin Randle in *Journal of Scientific Exploration*, 18, 2004, pp. 706–10.

have mentioned it. Many have challenged such conflicting evidence as signs of deception. Karl Pflock, for one, argued that there was a cover-up, but that what was being covered up was not an extraterrestrial crash but the government's own top-secret balloon experiment to detect Soviet nuclear testing called Project Mogul. This was certainly one of the explanations being forwarded by the USAF itself.[293]

Project Blue Book wrote off Kenneth Arnold's sighting as a mirage. The USAF fact sheet ended on tetchy note, pointing to the ongoing public interest in the question: 'There are not now nor ever have been, any extraterrestrial visitors or equipment on Wright-Patterson Air Force Base'. Of course, this could lead some to deduce that any extraterrestrial visitors or equipment that the USAF did have must have been taken somewhere else.[294]

Closest Encounters

Do you remember hearing or seeing the word TRONDANT and knowing that it has a secret meaning for you?

'I saw a glimmer of silver reflecting from the metal frame between the door and the windscreen and then to the left over my head was this massive craft.' Bridget Grant, described by the *Sun* as a 'UFO magnet', claims to have had seventeen close

---

[293] Twining Memo. Others remain convinced that a UFO had crashed and was examined at Roswell, e.g., Philip Corso and William Birnes, *The Day After Roswell*, Pocket Books/Simon & Schuster, 1997.

[294] 'USAF Fact Sheet'. See Kent Jeffrey, 'Roswell – Anatomy of a Myth', *Journal of Scientific Exploration*, 12.1, 1998, pp. 79–101, for an argument against a UFO crash at Roswell and the replies from Michael Swords and Robert M. Wood in that same issue. For the final official position see USAF, *The Roswell Report: Fact Versus Fiction in the New Mexico Desert*, US Government Printing Office, 1995, and USAF, *The Roswell Report: Case Closed*, Barnes & Noble, 1997. As a further guide, the bibliography for Randle's *Roswell Encyclopedia*, although omitted from the book, has been published in *Journal of Scientific Exploration*, 15, 2001, pp. 425ff.

Hynek's UFO Classification System

I – Long Range (more than 500 feet)

Nocturnal Lights	N	Light seen at night
Daylight Discs	D	Light seen during the day
Radar-Visual	R	Sighting with radar contact

II – Close Range (less than 500 feet)

Close Encounter of the First Kind	CE1	Close range sighting of a UFO
Close Encounter of the Second Kind	CE2	Physical evidence after a UFO sighting
Close Encounter of the Third Kind	CE3	Contact with the occupant of a UFO

Dr J. Allen Hynek (1910–86) was a prominent astronomer and the director of the Lindheimer Astronomical Research Center at Northwestern University, USA. After serving as scientific adviser to the US Air Force UFO projects Sign, Grudge and Blue Book, he founded the Center for UFO Studies (CUFOS). He presented his classification in *The UFO Experience: A Scientific Enquiry*, Corgi Books, 1972, and *The Hynek UFO Report*, Sphere Books, 1977.

encounters with aliens in the last forty years. She is not alone. It is said that *The X-Files* creator Chris Carter got the idea for the series after reading the 1991 Roper Survey claiming that 3.7 million people in the USA believe that they have been abducted by aliens. If he had waited a year Carter could have read the more astonishing estimate that as many as 15 million Americans may believe that they have been abducted by aliens.[295]

The classic abduction case is that of American couple Betty and Barney Hill who claimed to have been kidnapped by aliens in 1961. Abductees differ from contactees – people who claim to have made contact with extraterrestrials. The abductee is usually forcibly captured and may be subjected to invasive techniques that would be illegal under almost all earthling legal systems. The contactee, in contrast, usually makes contact with benign entities who have some message for humanity, typically involving world peace. Whilst abduction always involves the report of a physical process, 'contact' can be broadly defined from 'telepathic' communication to actual physical meeting. Several contactees, such as George King and Claude Vorilhon, have gone on to found religious movements based on their experiences.

A large number of supposed alien abduction claims are based on memories said to have been recalled under hypnosis. The problem is that most clinical researchers are coming to the conclusion that memories are not recalled under hypnosis but created; that is, they are false but have the full weight of apparent past experience to convince the subject. Investigating abductees, Susan Clancy, then a postdoctoral fellow at Harvard, found that her sample group of eleven exhibited a tendency to develop false memories (using the Deese/Reodiger-McDermott paradigm) and had a higher than average score on a test for schizotopy. She concluded that abductees were virtually schizophrenic with a marked tendency towards 'magical thinking' and 'perceptual aberration'. It was later said, rather cruelly, of Betty Hill that she was 'unable to distinguish between a landed UFO and a streetlight'. 'As far as science knows,' Clancy concluded, 'no one is being abducted by aliens.'[296]

---

[295] David M. Jacobs, *Secret Life: Firsthand Accounts of UFO Abductions*, Simon & Schuster, 1992; Tim Spanton, 'Brit Housewife is UFO Magnet', the *Sun*, 11 November 2010; 'X Appeal: The X-Files Builds a Cult Following by Following the Occult', *Entertainment Weekly*, 214, 18 March 1994.

[296] Susan Clancy, *Abducted: How People Come to Believe They were Kidnapped*

By the way, if you did remember hearing or seeing the word TRONDANT then your return for the 1991 Roper Survey would have been discarded on the grounds of 'positive response bias', meaning that you will agree to anything. That immediately disqualified 1 per cent of the sample. The problem is that the survey's dramatic claims were based on answers from only 2 per cent of the remaining sample. In 1981 the psychologists Sheryl C. Wilson and Theodore X. Barber identified the fantasy-prone personality – the type of person who has intense fantasies often to the point where they cannot tell them apart from reality. Their research showed that 4 per cent of the general population fell into this category.[297]

The classic experiment on abduction was conducted in 1977 by Professor Alvin 'Corky' Lawson (1929–2010) of California State University. Recruiting a group of sixteen volunteers with little or no knowledge of abductions, he hypnotized them and asked them a set of eight questions. Almost all of his subjects 'gave us interesting narratives with many specific incidents about getting onboard, seeing alien creatures, having an examination, interacting with the aliens, and being returned'. Comparing these artificially created abduction accounts with those purporting to be real he discovered that there was very little significant difference between them. If correct, Lawson's research suggests that, although only 4 per cent of people are fantasy prone, almost

by Aliens, Harvard University Press, 2005, p. 129; David M. Jacobs, review of Clancy's *Abducted*, *Journal of Scientific Exploration*, 20, 2006, pp. 307, 309: Beth Potier, 'Starship Memories', *Harvard University Gazette*, 31 October 2002; Bruce Grierson, 'A Bad Trip Down Memory Lane', *The New York Times*, 27 July 2003; Leonard S. Newman and Roy F. Baumeister, 'Toward an Explanation of the UFO Abduction Phenomenon: Hypnotic Elaboration, Extraterrestrial Sado-masochism, and Spurious Memories', *Psychological Inquiry*, 7, 1996, pp. 99–126. Betty Hill comment in Robert Sheaffer, 'Over the Hill on UFO Abductions', *Skeptical Inquirer*, 31.6, November/December 2007.

[297] Sheryl C. Wilson and Theodore X. Barber, 'The Fantasy-Prone Personality: Implications for Understanding Imagery, Hypnosis, and Parapsychological Phenomena', in Anees A. Sheikh (ed.), *Imagery: Current Theory, Research and Application*, John Wiley and Sons, 1983, pp. 340–90.

everyone will develop a relevant fantasy narrative under the right circumstances.[298]

However, before we dismiss alien abduction on these grounds, long-standing researcher Associate Professor David M. Jacobs of Temple University, Philadelphia, noted that abductees were reporting a range of obscure procedures (which they themselves did not understand) that had not been reported by the press and which found agreement with other abduction accounts of which they were unaware. When people are allegedly abducted their absence is often noted by others: the police might be called out, search parties organized, etc. When they return they often have unaccounted for marks on their bodies, broken bones, stains on their clothing – clothing which may even be on inside out, back to front or be someone else's entirely. Sometimes there are even eye-witnesses. In-depth psychological testing by Budd Hopkins in 1983 has also demonstrated an absence of mental illness among abductees. Some researchers, such as Clancy and psychologist Dr Susan Blackmore, have explained many more of these claims as the product of sleep paralysis hallucinations. That was not what Jacobs discovered. Out of approximately 700 cases, Jacobs found that only 40 per cent took place in bed at night, and that not all of these people were asleep. Jenny Randles conducted a similar experiment to Lawson's in 1987 and with twenty subjects using creative visualization produced none of the classic abduction motifs. Even Clancy had to admit, 'you can't disprove alien abductions'.[299]

---

[298] Peter Brookesmith, 'Necrolog: Alvin Lawson', *Fortean Times*, 270, January 2010, pp. 28–9.

[299] Jacobs, review of Clancy's *Abducted*, pp. 305–6, 311; William J. Cromie, 'Alien Abduction Claims Explained', *Harvard University Gazette*, 22 September 2005; Brookesmith, p. 29. See also Kevin D. Randle, et al., *The Abduction Enigma*, Forge, 1999, who argue that there is no scientific evidence for alien abductions. James Houran, Review of Kevin D. Randle, *The Abduction Enigma*, *Journal of Scientific Exploration*, 14, 2000, pp. 476–7. In reviewing Clancy's *Abducted*, the reviewer argued that all debunkers make one or more mistakes in not knowing the evidence, ignoring it, or distorting it, see *Journal of Scientific Exploration*, 20, 2006, p. 303. Susan Blackmore and Marcus Cox, 'Alien Abductions, Sleep Paralysis and the Temporal Lobe', *European Journal of UFO and Abduction Studies*, 1, 2000, pp. 113–18.

Notable Abductees

Name	Date	Location(s)	Further Reading
Elizabeth Klarer	1954–63	Kwa-Zulu Natal, South Africa	—, *Beyond the Light Barrier* (1980)
Antonio Villas Boas	1957	Minas Gerais, Brazil	
Betty and Barney Hill	1961	New Hampshire, USA	—, *The Interrupted Journey* (1966)
Herbert Schirmer	1967	Nebraska, USA	
Charles Hickson and Calvin Parker	1973	Mississippi, USA	William Mendez, *UFO Contact at Pascagoula* (1983)
Travis Walton	1975	Arizona, USA	—, *The Walton Experience* (1978)
Jack and Jim Weiner, Chuck Rak, and Charlie Foltz	1976	Maine, USA	Raymond E. Fowler, *The Allagash Abductions* (1993)
Robert Taylor	1979	Scotland, UK	
Bridget Grant	1970s?–93	Various, UK and USA	— and Nick Pope, *The Alien Within* (forthcoming)
Louis Whitley Strieber	1985	New York State, USA	—, *Communion: A True Story* (1987)
Kirsan Ilyumzhinov	1997	Kalmykia, Russian Federation	—, *The President's Crown of Thorns* (1998)

The evidence is unexplained. The interpretations are conflicting. There is clearly still a mystery here, even if it turns out to be more psychological than extraterrestrial. As James Houran noted, 'even if humankind is not being abducted by aliens [. . .] the abduction phenomenon has value outside the immediate context of ufology'.[300]

For those concerned about the problem, or simply wishing to hedge their bets, alien abduction insurance is provided by the UFO Abduction Insurance Company, also known as the St Lawrence Agency, based in Florida. Their $10 million policy is available for $19.95, although any successful claimants are only entitled to receive $1 a year for the next ten million years. Goodfellow Rebecca Ingrams Pearson Ltd of London apparently sold suicide cult Heaven's Gate just such a policy in 1996. For $1,000 a year the insured would receive a $1 million payout in the event of abduction, impregnation or death caused by aliens. The thirty-nine members of Heaven's Gate committed mass suicide, believing that a UFO travelling alongside the Hale-Bopp comet was sent to collect them. Under the terms of the policy, suicide rendered the contract null and void. Managing director Simon Burgess is reported as saying 'There has never been a genuine claim for alien abduction'. According to *Investment News*, the company has sold some 4,000 alien protection policies.[301]

---

[300] Houran, p. 477. See also the important contribution by A. Pritchard, et. al. (eds), *Alien Discussions: Proceedings of the Abduction Study Conference*, North Cambridge Press, 1994.

[301] Vicki Haddock, 'Don't Sweat Alien Threat', *San Francisco Chronicle*, 18 October 1998; Louise Jury, 'Cult Insured Against Aliens', the *Independent*, 31 March 1997; Gary S. Mogel, 'Antidote to Alien Impregnation? Insurance', *Investment News*, 21 May 2007. Kimberly Lankford, 'Weird Insurance', *CBS MoneyWatch*, October 1998, stated that 20,000 such policies had been sold. The UFO Abduction Insurance Co., offers what are essentially novelty documents payable to Comp-Pay Services, Inc., see www.ufo2001.com, accessed 26 October 2010. There are other websites, such as www.abductioninsurance. net, offering similar products. Goodfellow Rebecca Ingrams Pearson Ltd, is now registered as British Insurance Limited based in Maidstone, Kent, according to Companies House records accessed 26 October 2010.

Notable Contactees[302]

Name	Contact	Founder of	Author of
Daniel Fry	1949	Understanding, Inc.	*The White Sands Incident* (1954)
George Van Tassel	1951	The Giant Rock Spacecraft Convention	*I Rode a Flying Saucer* (1952)
George Adamski	1952	Adamski Foundation	*Flying Saucers Have Landed*, with Desmond Leslie (1953)
Truman Bethurum	c. 1953	Sanctuary of Thought	*The Voice of the Planet Clarion* (1957)
Gloria Lee	1953	Cosmon Research Foundation	*Why We Are Here!* (1959)
George King	1954	Aetherius Society	*You Are Responsible!* (1961)
Allen Noonan, aka Allen Michael	1954	Universal Industrial Church of the New World Comforter	*The Everlasting Gospel* (1973)
Gabriel Green	c. 1957	Amalgamated Flying Saucer Clubs of America, Inc., Universal Flying Saucer Party	*Let's Face Facts About Flying Saucers* (1967)
Claude Vorilhon, aka Raël	1973	The Raël Movement (Raëlism)	*Le Livre qui dit la vérité* ('The Book Which Tells the Truth') (1974)
Eduard 'Billy' Meier	1975	*Freie Interessengemeinschaft für Grenz- und Geisteswissenschaften und Ufologiestudien* ('Free Community of Interests for the Fringe and Spiritual Sciences and Ufological Studies')	*Talmud Jmmanuel* (2005)
Ivo A. Benda	1997	Universe People, Cosmic People of Light Powers	*Rozhovory s poučením od mých přátel z vesmíru* ('Interviews with Instructions from my Friends from the Universe') (1997)

---

[302] These are dates of alleged contact provided by or for the individuals listed.

Final Frontiers

Chrononauts from the future. Hypoterrestrials from inner space. Ultraterrestrials from other dimensions or the collective unconscious. Unidentified Flying Angels or demonic fallen angels from Hell. It might even be suggested that UFO should stand for Unidentified Flying Organism. That UFOs are alien spacecraft is only the least exotic explanation that has been proposed for the phenomenon.[303]

In the March 1945 issue of the sci-fi magazine *Amazing Stories*, editor Raymond Palmer published a rewritten account by a psychologically troubled welder called Richard Sharpe Shaver (1907–c. 1975) of his encounters with a race of underground beings, the 'Abandondero' or simply Dero for short, in 'I Remember Lemuria'. A supposedly abandoned remnant of a race of giants who left earth thousands of years ago, the Dero delight in dangerously depraved sexual orgies and the harassment of top-dwellers. The story was a massive success, boosting *Amazing Stories*' circulation from 25,000 to 250,000 a month by the end of the year. Palmer bought up everything Shaver had on the Dero – reams and reams of it, apparently – and commissioned more, sitting up into the wee small hours rewriting it all as what would become known as 'The Shaver Mystery'. Soon people were writing in with their own horrifying experiences. One reader – later identified as self-described 'disruption agent' Fred Lee Crisman – pleaded 'For heaven's sake, drop the whole thing! You are playing with dynamite'. Crisman claimed that in the final months of World War II he had narrowly escaped with his life from a cave in the northern foothills of the Karakoram after a deadly firefight with unidentified subterranean assailants.[304]

---

[303] Nick Redfern, 'What is a UFO?', *Paranormal*, 50, August 2010, pp. 58–63; Brad Steiger, 'Are UFOs Alive?', *UFO Digest*, 19 August 2008, http://www.ufodigest.com/news/0808/areufosalive.html, accessed 6 November 2010; Nick Redfern, 'From the Heavens or from Hell?' *Paranormal*, 54, December 2010, pp. 58-63; Leo Ruickbie, 'Angels in Space', *Paranormal*, 56, February 2011, pp. 54–7.

[304] John A. Keel, 'The Man Who Invented Flying Saucers', *Fortean Times*, 41, 1983, pp. 52–7. See also Michael Barkun, *A Culture of Conspiracy: Apocalyptic*

Robert Ernst Dickhoff, founder of the American Buddhist Society and Fellowship, described in his 1951 book *Agharta:The Subterranean World*, how Martians had established colonies on earth, creating a vast network of underground tunnels. Milinko S. Stevic, an engineer from what was then Yugoslavia, toured the USA in the 1970s telling all who would listen that a world of cities and tunnels existed below the surface, and that Adolf Hitler had even used them to escape war-torn Germany and take up residence in New Jersey. This innerverse was the Atlantean Empire of a race so advanced that they cruised our wildest dreams (particularly Stevic's) in their UFOs.[305] So when E. A. Guest later claimed that whilst working for the US military his father had seen a classified briefing on Roswell as the crash site of a craft from inner, not outer, space, the scene had already been set. The late Mac Tonnies took the theme further, arguing that what we had previously thought of as fairies, ghosts, demons, or even extraterrestrials, were so many manifestations of the subterraneans' psychological warfare and advanced technology. Abductions are their harvesting of human DNA in an attempt to treat a debilitating genetic syndrome. Roswell he explained as the crash of one of their surveillance devices. Eoin Colfer's *Artemis Fowl* fantasy world of techno-fairies never sounded more plausible.[306]

In the 1970s the shadow of the Devil fell across ufology. John Godwin, author of *Occult America* (1972), had already seen the connection between the Dero and the traditional religious idea of demons. In 1975 John Keel also argued that there was a more than suggestive parallel between the experiences of UFO

Visions in Contemporary America, University of California Press, 2003.

[305] John Godwin, 'The Lost Worlds of Mysticism', the *Oakland Tribune*, 12 August 1972, excerpted from John Godwin, *Occult America*, Doubleday & Company, 1972.

[306] E. A. Guest, 'The Other Paradigm', *Fate*, April 2005, republished in *The Best of Roswell: From the Files of Fate Magazine*, Galde Press, 2007; Redfern, 'What is a UFO?' p. 60; Nigel Watson, 'They Came from Planet Earth', *Paranormal*, 49, July 2010, pp. 25–9; Mac Tonnies, *The Cryptoterrestrials*, Anomalist Books, 2010.

eye-witnesses and possession cases. Like Tonnies he also saw a broader picture. Of UFO eye-witnesses he said:

> Many, I found, suffered certain medical symptoms such as temporary amnesia, severe headaches, muscular spasms, excessive thirst and other effects, all of which have been observed throughout history in religious miracles, demonology, occult phenomena, and contact with fairies. All of these manifestations clearly share a common source or cause.[307]

Others were convinced that the common source or cause was the Devil. By the end of the 1970s, George Knewstub and Roger Stanway, leading figures in the British UFO Research Organization (BUFORA), had reached this conclusion. Stanway himself based this on personal experience. After a sudden and unwanted desire to throw himself in front of a train deep within the bowels of the earth in London's Underground, overcome by reciting a prayer from St John's Gospel, he became convinced that the forces of evil were at work.[308]

The rumoured Collins Elite – a secret conclave of top US government, military and intelligence staff – would agree. When ufologist Nick Redfern tracked down Anglican priest Ray Boeche in 2006 he uncovered an astonishing twist in the UFO conspiracy theory. Boeche was not just any Anglican priest, he had founded the Fortean Research Center and was a former regional director for the Mutual UFO Network (MUFON). Perhaps this was why two Department of Defense (DoD) physicists arranged a clandestine meeting with him. According to Boeche's story they gave him information that not only confirmed the presence of what they called 'non-human entities', but also that many within the DoD believe that they are in actuality demonic beings. Kennedy Space

---

[307] Quoted in Redfern, 'What is a UFO?', p. 63.
[308] Redfern, 'What is a UFO?', p. 63. See also Nick Redfern, *Final Events and the Secret Government Group on Demonic UFOs and the Afterlife*, Anomalist Books, 2010.

Center researcher Joe Jordan is on record as saying 'we're dealing with fallen angels'.[309]

The 'aliens', whatever their provenance, come in all manner of guises. Over the years people have reported seeing blond-haired 'Space-Brothers', hairy dwarfs, flying jellyfish, huge bananas, scaly-skinned reptilians, giant humanoids, as well as the familiar 'little green men' and 'greys'.[310]

With so much apparent evidence of *something*, at least, and so many strange and conflicting theories, what is the answer? Veteran UFO expert Professor Michael D. Swords characterized UFO research as an 'intellectual vortex which can easily addict you, draw you in, and still tell you very little about the fundamentals which lie below'.[311] Despite the problems, he was still willing to come to at least one very definite conclusion about the phenomenon.

'They're here,' said Swords in 2006, adding 'They've been here in some force at least since World War Two.'[312] But that is not something you will hear from the authorities. Most official governmental investigations into UFOs have now been terminated after reaching the conclusion that there are no UFOs. This is a conclusion that many people are unwilling to accept. There are millions in the USA alone, where almost one in four people believe that UFOs are alien spacecraft and nearly one in five claim to have seen one. Even the official investigations had to admit that they could not explain everything. Then there are the many sightings from reliable witnesses, experienced enough

---

[309] Redfern, 'From the Heavens or from Hell?', pp. 59–60, 63.

[310] Nick Redfern, 'Know Your Aliens', *Paranormal*, 53, November 2010, pp. 40–5. On jellyfish see, for example, the 13 October sighting reported by Lisa Karpova, 'New Yorkers Wave "Hi" to Jellyfish UFOs', *Pravda*, 21 October 2010 – children later claimed that the UFOs were balloons that had escaped from a surprise party for their unfortunately named teacher Andrea Craparo: 'UFO? NYC Kids Say No [. . .]', *New York Daily News*, 14 October 2010.

[311] Michael D. Swords, 'A Guide to UFO Research', *Journal of Scientific Exploration*, 7, 1993, p. 68.

[312] Michael D. Swords, 'Ufology', *Journal of Scientific Exploration*, 20, 2006, p. 572.

SETI

In 1961 the astronomer Frank Drake formulated the so-called Drake Equation that appeared to show that, logically, there must be many extraterrestrial civilizations in the universe. But it did not answer the obvious question. In 1950 the physicist Enrico Fermi had made an off-the-cuff remark that 'if there are extraterrestrials, then where are they?' – the so-called Fermi Paradox. To tackle the problem, Drake was instrumental in organizing a meeting to discuss the ways and means of finding the missing extraterrestrials and the Search for Extraterrestrial Intelligence (SETI) was born. Today it is the name for a number of different projects with the common aim of finding evidence that we are not alone in the universe. For example, one project called SETI@home is a computer programme that uses idle processing power to analyse radio signals. A SETI Institute was founded in 1984 to further advance the search. Currently, it has a staff of over 150 scientists and others. In October 2010 it was reported that a signal discovered two years earlier by scientists at the University of Western Sydney had originated from the solar system of red dwarf star Gliese 581 in the constellation of Libra, which may contain the habitable planet Gliese 581g.

with aerial phenomena to know when they are seeing something out of the ordinary. Decades after Roswell, 80 per cent of Americans believe that their government is hiding evidence of extraterrestrial life.[313]

On 27 September 2010, seasoned UFO investigator Robert Hastings held a conference at the National Press Club in Washington, D.C., on UFO interference with nuclear weapons facilities. He had talked to 120 US military personnel about the

---

[313] Christopher Bader, F. Carson Mencken and Joseph Baker, *Paranormal America*, New York University Press, 2010, p. 73; 'Poll: U.S. Hiding Knowledge of Aliens', CNN, 15 June 1997.

problem and seven of them were now willing to go public with their experiences. One of them, former ICBM (Inter-Continental Ballistic Missile) launch officer Captain Robert Salas, described how ten nuclear Minuteman missiles under his command became unlaunchable after a perimeter guard reported a UFO hovering over the Malmstrom Air Force Base, Montana, in 1967. Colonel Charles Halt recalled his UFO encounter at RAF Bentwaters near Ipswich in 1980. 'I believe – these gentlemen believe,' Hastings told reporters, 'that this planet is being visited by beings from another world.'[314]

After scoffing at Hastings' press conference, *The Washington Post*'s columnist John Kelly drew an entirely warranted flurry of abusive emails. Among them was one from 'Art' in Olney. His father had been a US Navy fighter pilot in World War II and one of the first recruits to the fledgling National Security Agency (NSA). He recalled sitting down to dinner with his family as a boy. At the time the media was full of news about UFO sightings. 'You see all those UFO reports in the news?' asked his father. 'Believe it.' Art added that he never spoke of it again.[315]

[314] 'Robert Hastings Presents Major UFO Press Conference in Washington, DC, September 27th 2010', Press Release, 15 September 2010; 'UFOs Eyed Nukes, Ex-Air Force Personnel Say', http://news.blogs.cnn.com/2010/09/27/ufos-showed-interest-in-nukes-ex-air-force-personnel-say/, 27 September 2010; Tony Harnden, 'Aliens "Tried to Warn US and Russia They Were Playing With Fire During Cold War"', *Daily Telegraph*, 28 September 2010.

[315] John Kelly, 'UFO Visits to Nuclear Facilities? Hmmmm', *Washington Post*, 27 September 2010; John Kelly 'Close Encounters with UFOs (Unexpectedly Furious Observers)', *Washington Post*, 5 October 2010.

Part II: Approaches to the Supernatural

Do you believe then that the sciences would have arisen and grown up if the sorcerers, alchemists, astrologers and witches had not been their forerunners; those who, with their promisings and foreshadowings had first to create a thirst, a hunger, and a taste for *hidden and forbidden* powers?
— Nietzsche, *Die fröhliche Wissenschaft*, 1882

The most beautiful thing we can experience is the mysterious. It is the source of all true art and science.
— Albert Einstein, 'What I Believe', 1930

If the doors of perception were cleansed, every thing would appear to man as it is, infinite.
— William Blake, *The Marriage of Heaven and Hell*, c. 1793

6. Magic

He made with a wand a Circle in the dust, and within that many more Circles and Characters: [. . .] then began Doctor Faustus to call for Mephostophiles [*sic*] the Spirit, and to charge him in the name of Beelzebub to appear.[316]

So begins the legend of Doctor Faustus, the infamous sixteenth-century magician, with his descent into diabolism to take an everlasting place in literature. According to the 'History of Dr Johann Faust, the far-bestriding Magician and Black Artist' – the almost contemporary book that claimed to be biographical, even autobiographical in parts – there is a cry 'as if hell had been opened' and Mephistopheles (to use the usual spelling) falls to earth like a bolt of lightning. Although the book is a Protestant morality tale – perhaps even a retrospective witch-craft trial – in which Faustus is punished with a gratuitously violent death and eternal damnation for his unchristian curios-ity, it comes from an age in which most people believed in the actual existence of demons, devils and a supreme evil being. The real Dr Faustus' contemporary, the German theologian Martin Luther, famously threw his inkpot at the Devil, such was his belief in the Archfiend's actual and tangible existence. Here,

---

[316] 'P.F.', *The Historie of the Damnable Life, and the Deserved Death of Doctor Iohn Faustus*, Thomas Orwin, 1592, p. 2, English translation of the anonymous *Historia von D. Johann Fausten, dem weitbeschreyten Zauberer und Schwarzkünstler*, Johann Spies, 1587.

178 *The Supernatural*

however, evil spirits are not enough – Faustus must invoke them using magic, a strange interplay of wand, circles, characters, and words. Magic is the bizarre science of the supernatural.[317]

Magic in Theory

There are many definitions and theories of what magic is. Aleister Crowley, the British occultist almost as legendary as Faustus, most famously said that 'Magick' – the 'k' was important, but that is another story – was 'The Science and Art of causing Change to occur in conformity with Will'. Certainly, the successful invocation of Mephistopheles was in conformity with Faustus' supposed will, but it is still a long way off from explaining how it is all meant to work. Crowley spent another 500 pages in *Magick in Theory and Practice* talking about it and telling us how to do it, but he still did not *explain* it.[318]

It was instead one of Crowley's contemporaries, a Scotsman called James George Frazer (later 'Sir'), who came up with quite possibly the most influential explanation of how magic is believed to work. Born in Glasgow in 1854, Frazer left for Cambridge to study the classics and, inspired by Sir Edward Tylor's *Primitive Culture*, social anthropology. His researches led to the publication of *The Golden Bough: A Study in Comparative Religion* in several editions and eventually twelve volumes from 1890 to 1915. He admitted himself that the book was 'one of the hothouse plants of the Victorian age [. . .] it grew and grew and grew'.[319]

The Golden Bough was a hit, particularly after the twelve massive volumes were edited into one with the slightly snappier subtitle *A Study in Magic and Religion*. It influenced such eminent people as

[317] See Leo Ruickbie, *Faustus: The Life and Times of a Renaissance Magician*, The History Press, 2009.

[318] Aleister Crowley, *Magick*, privately published, 1929.

[319] Sir J. G. Frazer, *The Golden Bough: A Study in Comparative Religion*, 2 vols, Macmillan & Co., 1890, and other editions. Due to the number of editions, I shall refer to the 1922 abridged edition by chapter and section number. Frazer on *The Golden Bough* quoted in George W. Stocking, 'Introduction', in Sir J. G. Frazer, *The Golden Bough*, Penguin, 1998. Sir Edward Tylor, *Primitive Culture: Researches into the Development of Mythology, Philosophy, Religion, Art, and Custom*, 2 vols, J. Murray, 1871.

the writers A. E. Housman, D. H. Lawrence and T. S. Eliot. Crowley, another Cambridge man, quoted a large chunk in support of his theories in *Magick*. H. P. Lovecraft mentioned it in 'The Call of Cthulhu'. And director Francis Ford Coppola slipped a copy of the book into his 1979 masterpiece *Apocalypse Now*.[320]

Frazer's general theory was that civilization progresses from magic to religion to science. It was a typical nineteenth-century viewpoint, much out of fashion nowadays, especially as quantum physics almost seems to have taken us back to magic. However, what inspired people about Frazer's work was his romantic theory of the Sacred King. The Sacred King represents the solar god as the principal of vegetation who must be seasonally sacrificed to ensure the continuing fertility of the land. This was the idea behind the 1973 cult film *The Wicker Man*. It was this that Coppola was referring to in the showdown between Martin Sheen's character and Marlon Brando as the crazed jungle warlord he is sent to assassinate.

In order to get to this idea, Frazer first had to deal with magic. Frazer ranged across the known universe of the imagination revealed in classical literature, ethnographies and travellers' accounts of strange peoples in distant lands, in forgotten times, in search of the answer. He wondered why among certain North American tribes, a figure drawn in sand, ashes or clay and then stabbed was believed to affect the physical body of the victim. He discovered that the Peruvian Indians had a spell called 'burning the soul' that involved making images out of fat and grain to resemble the intended victim which were then burnt on the road he or she was expected to take. He read of a Malay charm instructing the magician to take something of the victim: nail-pairings, hair and eyebrow clippings, spittle – enough to represent every part of him – to mix these with wax taken from an abandoned beehive and shape it to a human likeness. The magician should then roast the wax figure over a flame for seven nights, saying:[321]

[320] H. P. Lovecraft, 'The Call of Cthulhu', *Weird Tales*, February 1928.
[321] Frazer, Ch. 3, §. 2.

It is not the wax that I am scorching,
It is the liver, heart, and spleen of so-and-so that I scorch.[322]

Frazer wondered why, in darkest Sussex, only fifty years before, a maid had remonstrated with her mistress against throwing away the baby-teeth of the children. The maid had believed that they would be gnawed by wild beasts and that the harm done to the teeth would strike their former owners. As proof, she pointed to the example of poor old Master Simmons, who, it was said, had grown a pig's tooth in his upper jaw because his mother had thrown one of his baby-teeth into the pigs' trough.[323]

The answer to all this, Frazer decided, was sympathy. Not the sort of sympathy you got from your mother when, as a child, you fell over and grazed your knee. More, as Frazer put it, 'that things act on each other at a distance through a secret sympathy', hence his general term 'sympathetic magic'. Sympathetic magic, he said, operated according to either (or both) of two principles: the Law of Similarity and the Law of Contagion. According to the Law of Similarity, the magician believes he can produce an effect by imitating it, hence stabbing figures in the sand. He also called this homoeopathic magic, that like affects like. According to the Law of Contagion, the magician, or Sussex maid, believes that things that have once been in contact with each other remain in contact even when separated.[324]

In his *Confessions*, Crowley neatly summed up Frazer's theory: 'magic he defines as science which does not work'. Frazer's theory was not so very different from that of his hero Edward Tylor. Tylor had earlier argued that magic was an error in thinking of the 'lowest known stages of civilization' where an imagined connection between things was mistaken as a real one. This has been the general interpretation ever since, although Crowley preferred to look at science as magic that worked.[325]

---

[322] Frazer, Ch. 3, §. 2.

[323] Frazer, Ch. 3, §. 3.

[324] Frazer, Ch. 3, §. 1.

[325] Aleister Crowley, *The Confessions of Aleister Crowley: An Autohagiography*,

Frazer was far from sympathetic himself when he said that these principles were readily familiar 'to the crude intelligence not only of the savage, but of ignorant and dull-witted people everywhere'. Frazer was surely wrong to attribute the idea of sympathetic magic solely to 'the savage' and simple-minded. Sigmund Freud – 'that creature Freud', as Frazer called him – labelled it 'magical thinking' and his observations led him to believe that it was a universal developmental stage exhibited by children and retained by certain types of neurotics. He did not believe that it worked either.[326]

Of course, if you start out with the preconception that magic does not work, then your theory is going to reflect that and you naturally have to account for it in terms of human failing or under-development. Even in 1900 the great pioneering psychologist William James was surprised that Frazer had not considered, indeed knew nothing about, psychical research. When Crowley – according to the well-known story told by Dennis Wheatley – made a wax figure of the Master of John's (not Frazer) and stabbed it in the leg, he did not think that he was either ignorant or stupid when the same tutor later fell down some steps and broke his ankle. He thought magic worked; at least he did with regard to his better-documented experiments. And he is not alone.[327]

When a group of psychologists from Harvard and Princeton got together to try some fiendish experiments on unwitting students – presumably neither savage nor stupid – they made some surprising discoveries. They got the voodoo dolls out, made the subjects watch basketball (twice), and American football. In all four studies they found that the students believed that their magical actions or thoughts had influenced the target. When participants stuck pins in a doll representing a confederate of the researchers who then complained of spontaneous symptoms,

Routledge & Kegan Paul, 1979 [1929], pp. 127, 517. Tylor, vol. 1, pp. 112, 116.
[326] Frazer, Ch. 3, §. 1; Stocking, 'Introduction' and *Delimiting Anthropology: Occasional Essays and Reflections*, University of Wisconsin Press, 2001, p. 159; Sigmund Freud, *Totem und Tabu*, Hugo Heller & Cie, 1913.
[327] Dennis Wheatley, *The Devil And All His Works*, Hutchinson, 1971, p. 273.

they believed that they had caused them; and when the participants were told to imagine positive outcomes for both staged and real-life sports scenarios, they again believed that they had caused them when they occurred. Even when a positive outcome was not forthcoming, the participants felt responsible for that, too. The students thought they had paranormal powers, but not the psychologists of course.[328]

Like Tylor and Frazer more than a hundred years before them, the psychologists also talked about 'common cognitive errors', 'apparent mental causation' and even cited *The Golden Bough*. But again their premise was that magic does not work and their experimental design reflected this. It could be argued that what they had done was prove you can trick people into thinking magically. Even Frazer conceded that 'imagination acts upon man as really as does gravitation, and may kill him as certainly as a dose of prussic acid'. Was he admitting that magic could, in effect, work?

Magic in Writing
The aspiring magician today is well-served by a vast publishing industry supplying everything from the most obscure and rare titles to common-or-garden DIY manuals on the magic arts, but it was not always so. The magician Faustus lived during the beginning of the great print revolution, but even then the materials of greatest interest to him were not yet part of that revolution. The books of magic, or grimoires, that he sought were handwritten and circulated in secret to avoid the hostile attentions of the Church. For these reasons and because of the nature of the material within, such grimoires acquired the reputation, not just as books on magic, but as magical books in themselves.

In cataloguing what he called 'the forbidden arts', the Bavarian physician, writer and diplomat, Johannes Hartlieb (c. 1400–68), was concerned that his own book, in the wrong hands, could be used as a grimoire. Hartlieb was detailed

---

[328] Emily Pronin, et al., 'Everyday Magical Powers', *Journal of Personality and Social Psychology*, 2006, 91.2, pp. 218–31.

enough in his descriptions, but stopped short of giving practical instructions. Even if it fell into the wrong hands, little harm could come of it. Hartlieb only served to whet the appetite.[329]

Despite this coyness, Hartlieb had himself given some pointers when he named the various texts being used in black magic: *Sigillum Salomonis*, *Clavicula Salomonis*, *Hierarchia* and *Schemhamphoras*. The *Sigillum* (Seal) and *Clavicula* (Key) were of a genre fancifully ascribed to King Solomon, generally thought to have reigned from around 970 to 928 BCE. Out of the legendary wisdom of Solomon, spiced with his dabbling in exotic cults, grew a tradition of Solomon the magician, perhaps as early as the second century BCE, but no earlier.[330] It was rather the Jewish historian Flavius Josephus who first alluded to a Solomonic magic text in the first century CE, describing the alleged powers of the legendary king:[331]

> God also enabled him to learn that skill which expels demons, which is a science useful and sanative to men. He composed such incantations also by which distempers are alleviated. And he left behind him the manner of using exorcisms, by which they drive away demons, so that they never return; and this method of cure is of great force unto this day.[332]

This was the Solomon who used a magic ring to compel legions of demons to build the Temple in Jerusalem, as we read in the pseudepigraphical *Testament of Solomon*. It is the earliest magical book attributed to Solomon despite being composed some time during the first to fifth centuries CE by authors unknown. It is a description of the various demons, their particular sphere of

---

[329] Hartlieb, p. 125.

[330] Owen Davies, *Grimoires: A History of Magic Books*, Oxford University Press, 2009, p. 12.

[331] Flavius Josephus, *Antiquities of the Jews*, trans. William Whiston, Applegate, 1855, p. 216. Reginald Scot, *The Discoverie of Witchcraft*, William Brome, 1584, Dover reprint, 1972, p. 264; S. Liddel MacGregor Mathers (ed. and trans.), *The Key of Solomon*, George Redway, 1888, pp. v, viii.

[332] Josephus, Ch. 2, §. 5.

mischief, and the correct angel to invoke against them. For example, Asmodeus causes strife between newly weds, but may be defeated by invoking Raphael and smoking the liver and gall of a fish over hot ashes. According to the Book of Tobit (6:7), Raphael himself teaches Tobias a similar exorcism ritual: 'Touching the heart and the liver [of a fish], if a devil or an evil spirit trouble any, we must make a smoke thereof before the man or the woman, and the party shall be no more vexed'. From the beginning, Solomonic magic was essentially about controlling spiritual entities. Far from being an ineffectual science it was theologically logical.[333]

We find Solomon and the power of his seal in the medieval *Picatrix* (see below) and whispers of his mysterious book (or books) are to be found in the writings of the Byzantine scholars Michael Psellus, Nicetas Choniates and Michael Glycas in the eleventh to twelfth centuries CE, as well as Roger Bacon in the thirteenth century, for example. Still in the thirteenth century, William of Auvergne, the Bishop of Paris, roundly condemned Solomonic magic, showing its pervasive influence, and singled out the *Liber sacer* as 'a cursed and execrable book'. Johannes Trithemius, occult scholar and sometime abbot of Sponheim in Germany, later catalogued a *Clavicula Solomonis* in 1508 amongst other magical texts. Another German scholar, Johannes Reuchlin, in his great work on the cabbala of 1517, mentioned a book 'inscribed "to Solomon" under Raziel's name'. Several manuscripts dated 1564 in the British Library also make this connection between Solomon and Raziel. But there are few surviving early examples. Of the manuscripts in the British Library catalogued under the name of Solomon (Salomon) the earliest *Key* texts are from the second half of the sixteenth century. Elements of Solomonic magic – the 'Almadel' and the ring of Solomon – survive in fifteenth-century manuscripts found in Florence and Paris, and there is also an 'Ars notoria Salomonis' dating from the thirteenth century in the British Library.[334]

---

[333] Chester Charlton McCown, *The Testament of Solomon*, J. C. Hinrichs, 1922.
[334] Lynn Thorndike, *A History of Magic and Experimental Science*, 8 vols,

A text like the late-sixteenth-century *Kay* [*sic*] *of Knowledge* attributed to Solomon described a complete system of magic.[335] The full procedure is made explicit. Instructions on when and how to conjure the spirits are illustrated with diagrams of the magical circles and signs pertinent to each operation and descriptions of the tools needed. One reads of the right way to extract the blood of a bat and consecrate virgin parchment. A Solomonic grimoire was a working manual of magic.

The *Schemhamphoras* is also part of this Solomonic genre. This 'Schemhamphoras' (also 'Shemhamphorash') is *Shem ham-M'forash*, the great cabbalistic name of God. Out of this name are derived seventy-two spirits – the spirits said to have been commanded by Solomon. These are the spirits we find in Johannes Wierus's *Pseudomonarchia Daemonum* ('The False Monarchy of Demons') of 1577 and Reginald Scot's *Discoverie of Witchcraft* of 1584, although neither Wierus nor Scot listed all seventy-two. Wierus said he had taken his list from an older text called the *Book of the Offices of Spirits, or the Book of Sayings of Emperor Solomon Concerning the Princes and Kings of the Demons*.[336] In 1508 Trithemius had also mentioned a *De officio spirituum* attributed to Solomon and it is possible that the two are, if not the same, then certainly similar. Hartlieb's *Hierarchia* is an otherwise unknown text, but by its name would seem to indicate some sort of table of spirits, perhaps similar to the *Schemhamphoras* and *De officio*.

Columbia University Press, 1923–58, vol. 1, pp. 279ff; Johannes Trithemius, *Antipalus maleficiorum*, c.1500, in Johannes Busaeus, ed., *Paralipomena opusculum Petri Blesensis et Joannis Trithemii aliorumque*, Ioannem Wulffrath, 1605, pp. 291–311; Johannes Reuchlin, *On the Art of the Kabbalah*, trans. Martin and Sarah Goodman, Bison Books, 1993, p. 95 – cf. London, British Library, Sloane 3826, fol. 1ʳ-57ʳ; 'Salomon. King of Israel. Sepher Raziel: A Magical Treatise 1564', London, British Library, Sloane MSS 3826, 3846, 3847; 'Ars Notoria', British Library, Sloane 1712.
[335] London, British Library, Additional MS 36674.
[336] Wierus of course knew it by its Latin title *Liber officiorum spirituum, seu Liber dictus Empto. Salomonis, de principibus & regibus dæmoniorum*. See Johannes Wierus, *De praestigiis daemonum*, Joannem Oporinum, 1577.

Famous Grimoires

Title	Quotation	Example Spell	Dating
Testament of Solomon	Testament of Solomon, son of David, who was king in Jerusalem, and mastered and controlled all spirits of the air, on the earth, and under the earth.	The liver of the fish and its gall I hung on the spike of a reed, and burned it over Asmodeus	1st–5th centuries CE
Picatrix ('The Goal of the Wise')	I set forth such miraculous and confusing matters from all the sciences for this reason only, that you may be purified for the earnest study of these marvellous arts and may achieve what the ancient sages achieved.	Of examples of figures, and the forms of imagery that call down the help of the planets	11th century
The Sworn Book of Honorius (Liber Juratus, or Liber Sacer/Sacratus)	One whose name was Honorius, the son of Euclid, master of the Thebians, [. . .] through the council of a certain angel whose name was Hocroel, did write seven volumes of art magic.	How a man should obtain his will by every angel	13th/14th century
The Key of Solomon (Clavicula Salomonis)	The secret of secrets [. . .] I have written them in this Key, so that like as a key openeth a treasure-house, so this alone may open the knowledge and understanding of magical arts and sciences.	Experiment of invisibility	14th–16th centuries
Arbatel de Magia Veterum ('Arbatel of the Magic of the Ancients')	The greatest precept of Magic is, to know what every man ought to receive for his use from the assisting Spirit, and what to refuse.	n/a	1575

The Lesser Key of Solomon (*Lemegeton Clavicula Salomonis*, also *The Goetia*)	This Book contains all the names, orders, and offices of all the spirits Salomon ever conversed with. The seals and characters belonging to each spirit, and the manner of calling them forth to visible appearance.	Zepar . . . his office is to cause women to love men and to bring them together in love	17th century
The Sacred Magic of Abramelin the Mage	The sacred mystery by which I entered into the knowledge of the holy angels, enjoying their sight and their sacred conversation, from whom at length I received afterwards the foundation of the Veritable Magic, and how to command and dominate the evil spirits.	To find and take possession of all kinds of treasures, provided that they be not at all (magically) guarded	17th/18th century
The Sixth and Seventh Books of Moses	Revealed by God the Almighty to his faithful servant Moses, on Mount Sinai, *intervalle lucis*, and in this manner they also came into the hands of Aaron, Caleb, Joshua, and finally to David and his son Solomon and their high priest Zadoc.	The Eleventh Table gives luck and fortune; its spirits give the treasures of the sea	18th century
Le Petit Albert ('The Little Albert')	It may well be called a universal treasure, because in its small size it contains marvellous capabilities of rewarding all mankind.	To remove rotten teeth without pain	1782
Grimorium Verum ('The True Grimoire')	The most approved Keys of Solomon the Hebrew Rabbin, wherein the most hidden secrets, both natural and supernatural, are immediately exhibited.	To make a girl dance in the nude	19th century
Le Grand Grimoire	This great book is most rare, most sought after in our lands, which for its rarity is called after the Rabbis, the true Great Work.	To win anytime one plays the lottery	19th century

Picatrix

When the late-fourteenth-century Arab historian Ibn Khaldun spoke out against magic he had one book to hand, a book whose author the satirist Rabelais later called 'the reverend father in the Devil [. . .] rector of the Diabolical faculty'. It was called in Arabic *Ghâyat al-Hakîm fi'l-sihr* ('The Goal of the Wise') or, as it was known in Europe, *Picatrix*. As Ibn Khaldun wrote:[337]

> These are sciences showing how human souls may become prepared to exercise an influence upon the world of the elements, either without or with the aid of celestial matters. The first kind is sorcery, the second kind is talismans. These sciences are forbidden by the various religious laws, because they are harmful and require [their practitioners] to direct themselves to [beings] other than God, such as stars and other things.[338]

It was written in Arabic sometime between 1047 and 1051, somewhere in Spain. King Alfonso X of Castile later commanded a translation into Spanish in 1256, possibly by the King's personal physician Rabbi Yehuda ben Moshe, and from this came the Latin translation, the most influential of which was thought to have been produced by Aegidius de Thebaldis, translator of Ptolemy's *Tetrabiblos*. The manuscript was copied and re-copied, but only published in the twentieth century. Today some seventeen copies have survived the ravages of time and the fires of the Inquisition. The important Renaissance humanist Giovanni Pico della Mirandola was known to possess a copy. His son Gian Francesco Pico may also have seen it, although he called it 'a most vain book, full of superstitions'. Trithemius denounced it as being full of 'many things that are frivolous, superstitious, and diabolical' – and he would not be the last. Its

---

[337] Eugenio Garin, *Astrology in the Renaissance: The Zodiac of Life*, Arkana, 1983, pp. 46–7.
[338] Quoted in Garin, p. 42.

influence can be seen in the work of the influential occultist Agrippa von Nettesheim, a contemporary of Faustus.[339]

But what is it about the *Picatrix* that gave it such a subterranean reputation? It is a confused, disordered mass, divided haphazardly into four books. It begins dramatically enough by revealing the reasons for writing the book: to illuminate a closely kept secret of the ancient philosophers, the secret of magic. The reader is admonished to preserve the secret from the uneducated. The text interweaves astrology, astronomy and magic, moving from Greek stellar theory to practical advice on how to influence the cosmos. Religion makes its appearance, but seen through a magician's lens. We are immersed in the legendary prehistory of Egypt and the astro-magical aphorisms of a mysterious Babylonian called 'Utârid, as well as the philosophy of Plato, Aristotle and Hippocrates, and the divinatory uses of the Qur'an.

The *Picatrix* attempts to divide its subject into talismanic magic, celestial worship and incantatory practices, but the barriers between them are porous and the forms intermingle. Instructions are given on the correct constellations to be used in making talismans with examples of incantations to make them effective. The signs of the zodiac are considered in great depth with a reverent personification of the planets that raises them to the level of gods to be worshipped and, as the book is written by a magician, invoked. There is talk of djinn, demons and angels, of love magic and the correct method of attracting the planetary energies. Details are given of how the planets should be worshipped according to the ways of the Sabians, including child sacrifice. There are Nabatean prayers to Saturn and the Sun, descriptions of the ceremonies for each planet with examples of amulets and talismans. There are formulae and

[339] Helmut Ritter and Martin Plessner, trans., *'Picatrix.' Das Ziel der Weisen von Pseudo-Magriti*, Warburg Institute, 1962; Elizabeth M. Butler, *Ritual Magic*, Cambridge University Press, 1949, p. 48; Garin, pp. 48, 50; Trithemius, *Antipaulus Maleficiorum* quoted in Noel L. Brann, *Trithemius and Magical Theology*, State University of New York Press, 1999, p. 67; Daniel Pickering Walker, *Spiritual and Demonic Magic*, Sutton, 2000, pp. 147, 182, n. 5.

ceremonies for incense to honour the planets said to have been devised by Buddha, perfumes given by God to Moses and 'Indian' enchantments. There are extracts from the *Book of Poisons* and an ancient temple book said to have been discovered in the days of Cleopatra.

The Moorish influence is unmistakable and the Spanish origin would seem vouchsafed. Celestial mysticism and the violent rites of the Sabians are clearly heretical to the Church, but it is undoubtedly the practical instructions given on the manufacture and correct use of talismans that gives this book the sulphurous reputation that so quickly accrued to it. With a manual such as this the magician could do a brisk trade in talismans.

Whilst the text may at times be confused and disjointed a clear picture emerges of a magical astrology designed not only to interpret the stars, but to harness their power. 'The roots of magic,' says *Picatrix*, 'are the movements of the planets'. Drawing on the ninth of the *Karpos* from the Ptolemaic *Centiloquium*, the *Picatrix* states 'All things in this world obey the celestial forms'.[340] With such a manual the whole world would be at the magician's feet, or so he – and his clients – might think.

The *Picatrix* goes beyond even the promise of ultimate power. It offers an all-embracing conception of reality. It is a conception that sharply differs from that of orthodox Christianity. It is a challenge to and refutation of Christianity, and it offers an alternative. No wonder, then, that the *Picatrix* was so feared and its reputation tarred with the accusation of black magic.

Owning the Grimoires

A few years before Hartlieb came to serve Albrecht III, Duke of Bavaria, in Munich, a court case heard in Briançon in 1437 threw some light on the sort of people who owned grimoires. The trial concerned one Jubertus of Bavaria, a sixty-year-old man from Regensburg in the east of that province, arraigned before the judge on charges of flying to nocturnal assemblies,

---

[340] Quotations from Garin, p. 49.

murdering children and black magic. In his confession Jubertus spoke of a man called Johannes Cunalis, a priest and plebian of Munich. Jubertus had served Cunalis for ten years and witnessed how he kept a book of necromancy, which when opened by him brought forth three demons. Cunalis was a Satanist of the first rank. He worshipped the Devil as his god with sacrilegious rites, showing his buttocks to the east before making a cross on the floor that he spat on, stamped on, urinated and finally defecated on. Cunalis had also made a pact with his demons, leaving them his body and soul after death. The use of torture in extracting this confession is not mentioned, but as it was commonplace it cannot be ruled out. Cunalis was also just the kind of man to have written or compiled a grimoire.[341]

Jubertus had also been in Vienna about the year 1435 where he had been causing a commotion. He had cursed someone called Johannes Fabri of Vienna and had been boasting about it just before his arrest. He had also set Cunalis' three demons on three drunken cooks who had refused to let him drink in a tavern. The demons seized them as they staggered out into the night after their revelry, throwing one down a well, another into the privy of the Dominicans and the other into the privy of the Franciscans. The one they pitched down the well died, but the other two were discovered by the friars at matins – one can imagine the looks on their faces – and rescued.

Here Cunalis' book had already reached such magical proportions that the simple act of opening it unleashed three demons that had been seemingly bound within. Other grim-oires, such as the *Enchiridion of Pope Leo* conferred magical powers in other ways. According to legend, Pope Leo III gave Charlemagne a collection of prayers – the *Enchiridion* – as he was leaving Rome in 800 CE with the instructions to always carry it with him and recite it daily. It would confer divine

[341] Joseph Hansen (ed.), *Quellen und Untersuchungen zur Geschichte des Hexen-wahns und der grossen Hexenverfolgung im Mittelalter*, Georgi, 1901, pp. 539–44; Richard Kieckhefer, *Forbidden Rites: A Necromancer's Manual of the Fifteenth Century*, Sutton, 1997, pp. 30–2.

protection so that Charlemagne might pass through all dangers unharmed and triumph over his enemies.

Picatrix and the other grimoires belong to that genre that would have fed every Christian book-burning for a thousand years. The number of survivals is low, but given the extent of that book-burning it is likely that at one time a great number of such texts was in circulation. Indeed, one scholar investigating the matter of German *Loosbücher* (lot or divination books) in the late nineteenth century thought that, from the number of examples surviving in the libraries of his day, the fifteenth century must have been 'rich in such books'. Certainly, when the Visitation of the Saxon Church peered into the activities of village pastors and churchwardens in Germany during 1527–8 it uncovered an embarrassing hoard of magical books.[342]

In the twentieth century, the German Lutheran minister and anti-magical campaigner Kurt Koch was still warning that grimoires 'circulate among people like poisonous gases, poisoning their very minds and souls' and complained about the 'flood of magical conjuration which washes the Alps'. Such concerns led to Planet-Verlag, the German publisher of the *Sixth and Seventh Books of Moses*, being taken to court in 1956. Found guilty of being 'a danger to the general public', they were fined and ordered to destroy their remaining stock. Reactions were no less strong to J. K. Rowling's *Harry Potter* books. However, the demand is so high that such determined persecution has failed to prevent the continued dissemination of magical literature.[343]

---

[342] Johann Sotzmann, 'Die Loosbücher des Mittelalters', *Serapeum*, 20, 1851, pp. 307–8; R. Po-chia Hsia, *The Myth of Ritual Murder: Jews and Magic in Reformation Germany,* Yale University Press, 1988, p. 135.

[343] A. E. Waite, *The Book of Ceremonial Magic*, pp. 40–2; Kurt Koch, *Between Christ and Satan*, Kregel, 1962, p. 131; Davies, pp. 256–60; Leo Ruickbie, '"Either Must Die at the Hand of the Other": Religious Reactions to Harry Potter', in Jennifer P. Sims (ed.), *The Sociology of Harry Potter*, Zossima, forthcoming.

Magic with Spirits

The spirit or soul, the animating, personalizing 'thing' that drives and defines the human being always seemed like a thing apart, a 'ghost in the machine'. When we sleep, where does it go? When we die, where does it go? In folklore, custom and magic there is a long tradition of what Frazer called 'the external soul'. Traditionally, the shaman had the power to send forth his soul at will and to conjure the souls of others out of their bodies. The Siberian Yakuts, for example, say that every shaman puts his soul (or one of his souls) in an animal and hides it away. The weakest must take dogs, the strongest may choose the stallion, elk, black bear, wild boar, or eagle. Here, and in similar accounts from the Americas, Africa and Australia, we have the origin of the witch's familiar. Such spirits did not only belong to individuals. Recalling shamanistic notions of tribal spirits, the Lachlan clan of Rum in the Western Isles had a taboo on deer-stalking as it was believed that family and animal shared the same fate.[344]

The shaman, the witch and the werewolf have long been thought to be able to venture out of the physical human body and travel this world or others as spirit. It is a shamanic idea that we find in tales of witches and sorcerers turning into cats and wolves, that the spirit can take an animal form, which when harmed causes reciprocal damage to the physical body. Among the Koryak people of north-eastern Siberia it was said that in days of old 'there was no sharp distinction between men, animals, and other objects' and everyone could transform themselves into animals – a practice since reserved for shamans. It is still a superstition not to suddenly awake a dreaming sleeper for fear that their soul, thought to be beyond the body and participating in the dreamworld, may not return in time. The Yakut shaman Tyusypyut boasted that 'nobody can find my *ie-kyla* [external soul], it lies hidden far away in

---

[344] Frazer, Ch. 67, §. 1; James M. MacKinlay, *Folklore of Scottish Lochs and Springs*, William Hodge & Co., 1893, ch. XIV.

the stony mountains of Edzhigansk'. Many folktales preserve this idea.[345]

From Norway 'the giant who had no heart in his body' devises a complicated concealment to ensure his invulnerability. 'Far, far away in a lake,' explains the giant, 'lies an island, on that island stands a church, in that church is a well, in that well swims a duck, in that duck there is an egg, and in that egg there lies my heart.' The hero, of course, manages to get the egg and, crushing it, destroys the giant. In Scotland we find the story of another giant who kept his soul out of harm's way in an egg, and of the Uille Bheist, the monstrous sea-maiden, who did likewise. From Russia comes the story of Koshchei the Deathless whose 'death' is again hidden in an egg.[346]

There are many more examples from across Europe. A soul is kept 'in a stone, in the head of a bird, in the head of a leveret, in the middle head of a seven-headed hydra' in Rome; 'in a pigeon, in a hare, in the silver tusk of a wild boar' in Albania; 'in a board, in the heart of a fox, in a mountain' in Serbia; 'in an egg, which is within a duck, which is within a stag, which is under a tree' in old Bohemia; 'in a light, in an egg, in a duck, in a pond, in a mountain' in Transylvania. The Indian folktale of the evil magician Punchkin proceeds along similar lines. Needless to say, the hero in these tales manages to overcome the obstacles and lay his hands on the magician's or monster's soul and, with the typical bloodthirstiness of the old fairy-tales, proceeds to rip it apart or crush it in front of the villain.[347]

---

[345] A. E. Crawley, *The Idea of the Soul*, Adam and Charles Black, 1909, p. 148; M. A. Czaplicka, *Aboriginal Siberia: A Study in Social Anthropology*, Clarendon Press, 1914, Pt III, Ch. 13, §. 2.

[346] Sir George Webbe Dasent, *Popular Tales from the Norse*, 2nd ed., David Douglas, 1912 [1859], p. 66; J. F. Campbell, *Popular Tales of the West Highlands*, 2 vols, Edmonston and Douglas, 1860, vol. 1, p. 11; Campbell, vol. 1, p. 82; William Ralston Shedden Ralston, *Russian Fairy Tales: A Choice Collection of Muscovite Folk-Lore*, Hurst & Co., 1873, p. 114.

[347] Mary Frere, *Old Deccan Days; or Hindoo Fairy Legends, Current in Southern India. Collected from Oral Tradition*, John Murray, 1868, pp. 1–12; Joseph Jacobs, *Indian Fairy Tales*, David Nutt, 1912, n.p., 'Story Notes, IV. Punchkin';

The shaman could also extract the soul for beneficial ends. When a family moves into a new house, an event of spiritual peril on the island of Sulawesi, the witchdoctor collects their souls in a bag to safeguard them, returning them when they are safely installed. Among the Dyaks of south-eastern Borneo, the witchdoctor preserves the soul of a newborn infant in half a coconut which he covers with a cloth and places on a small platform suspended from the rafters. The souls of the newly born are also temporarily kept in coconuts on the Kei Islands. In Alaska, the Eskimo medicine-man takes the soul of a sick child and places it in an amulet – a 'soul-box' – which he then further protects by stowing in his medicine-bag. The North American Haida shaman tempts the soul of an invalid into a hollow bone and keeps it safe until the body is well again. In 1995 the ethnologist Elizabeth McAlister reported that this form of magic was still practised in Haiti. Country people might put the *nanm*, 'soul', of their children in a bottle before sending them to school in Port-au-Prince to magically protect them. Birth, moving, illness – and, indeed, going to school – these were critical moments requiring additional magical security.[348]

The soul could also be united with another living thing, to thrive as it thrives, or wither as it withers. Only part externalized, the soul is shared between human and plant, or human and animal. Uniting with a plant usually served as an external indicator of health. In many parts of the world – from Europe to Papua New Guinea to West Africa – a tree is planted at the birth of a child and serves to act as a barometer of its fate. The Edgewell Tree near Dalhousie Castle in Scotland was a portent

Ralston, p. 120. See also E. Clodd, 'The Philosophy of Punchkin', *Folk-Lore Journal*, vol. 2, and George W. Cox, *Mythology of the Aryan Nations*, vol. 1, Longmans, Green & Co., 1870, pp. 135–42.

[348] Frazer, Ch. 67, §. 1; Frederick Starr, 'Dress and Adornment: IV. Religious Dress', *Popular Science*, December 1891, p. 196; Elizabeth McAlister, 'A Sorcerer's Bottle: The Visual Art of Magic in Haiti', in Donald J. Cosentino, (ed.), *Sacred Arts of Haitian Vodou*, UCLA Fowler Museum of Cultural History, 1995, p. 317.

for the welfare of a whole family line and, as Sir Walter Scott's visit in 1829 showed, something of a tourist attraction.[349]

Various forms of black magic could also be used to attack the soul or spirit by forcing or luring it out of the body. The *Tjilaiyu* ceremony of the Kakadu tribe aims at capturing a victim's *yalmuru*, 'spirit', and causing him to thus come into harm's way. The charm involves securing some of the victim's excrement to lure the *yalmuru* into a fire pit. A Malay charm to steal someone's soul involves taking sand or earth from the person's footprint. In the third century BCE, Clearchus, a pupil of Aristotle's, reported an incident in which a magician tapped a boy with his 'soul-drawing wand' (*psychoulkos rhabdos*) and drew out his soul for a time, leaving the body insensible to pain as if dead. However, as any good shaman will tell you, it is not just the souls of the living that can be captured.[350]

Necromagia

When Avie Woodbury had had enough of the two ghosts that were haunting her home in Christchurch, New Zealand, she called in an exorcist. This 'exorcist' from her local Spiritualist church identified one of the spirits as that of Les Graham, who had died in the house in the 1920s. Les was mischievous, but weak. The other spirit was that of a little girl and was much stronger, able to move objects and activate appliances, according to Woodbury. The exorcist was apparently able to trap the two spirits in bottles of what was said to be holy water. 'The holy water dulls the spirits' energy,' explained Woodbury, 'sort of puts them to sleep.' She added that 'We have had no activity since they were bottled on July 15th 2009. So I believe they are in the bottles.'

---

[349] Frazer, Ch. 67, §. 2; Sir Walter Scott, entry for 13 May 1829, *The Journal of Sir Walter Scott from the Original Manuscript at Abbotsford*, vol. 2, Burt Franklin, 1890.
[350] Sir Baldwin Spencer, *Native Tribes of the Northern Territory of Australia*, Macmillan, 1914; [Sir] R. O. Winstedt, *Shaman, Saiva and Sufi*, Constable & Company, 1925; Daniel Ogden, *Magic, Witchcraft and Ghosts in the Greek and Roman Worlds: A Sourcebook*, Oxford University Press, 2002, p. 171.

Sleeping or not, she still felt scared by their presence and put the two little bottles, half-filled with blue liquid, up for sale on the New Zealand auction site TradeMe. Worldwide press coverage helped draw almost 215,000 page views and boost the winning bid to NZ$5,000 (£2,339 approx.). John Deese of Florida used to sell his bottled ghosts for a more affordable US$20 (£13) and such items occasionally surface on eBay.[351]

In October 2010, in a small village in Malaysia, hundreds of people gathered outside the home of Siti Balqis Mohd Nor when they heard that her possessing spirits were about to be exorcised. The twenty-two-year-old had for the past two months been allegedly vanishing and re-appearing in unusual locations, once inside a cement mixer. Her parents had spent thousands of *ringgit*, employing around a hundred native shamans, or *bomoh*, to try and cure their daughter. After a newspaper highlighted her story, two *bomoh* came forward, waiving their fee. With onlookers jostling to take photographs and video outside, the *bomoh* emerged to say that they had cast out nine djinns and imprisoned them in special containers – large, ordinary-looking jars with a layer of mixed material in the bottom. As one *bomoh* chanted inside, the other waited by the door, catching the spirits as they tried to flee. It is not reported whether anyone in the crowd managed to capture this on film, but the jars were lined up on the bonnet of a car afterwards to the delight of snappers. The *bomoh* said that they would finally dispose of the djinns by throwing the containers into the sea. Siti Balqis told reporters that 'I am relieved to be able to live without fear of suddenly finding myself alone in strange places'. Clearly, it was believed that the djinns, like Woodbury's ghosts, could be extracted and relocated by

---

[351] 'For Sale: "Two Captured Ghosts, Trapped Inside Bottles of Holy Water to Make Them Sleepy"', *Daily Mail*, 8 March 2010; 'TradeMe: Ghost Auction Involved Bogus Bidders', *3 News*, 9 March 2010; 'Fla. Man Selling Ghosts', http://www.clickorlando.com/news/16388581/detail.html, 25 May 2008, accessed 3 January 2011; 'Purported Exorcised Poltergeist Ghost in a Bottle/ Wicca' being sold on eBay.co.uk, accessed 13 May 2011.

magical means, prompting us to wonder what the essential difference between the two might be.[352]

TheHouseofVoodoo.com offers a nice line in Zombie Spirit Bottles. According to their website, Bianca, 'the powerful New Orleans Voodoo Queen', uses a 'voodoo hoodoo ritual spell' known only to her to capture the spirits and force them into the bottles. Without making any guarantees, Bianca 'does acknowledge that strange things have been known to happen when one is in possession of one of these unique fetishes'. As we saw in the chapter on 'The Undead', the word 'zombie' comes from *nzambi*, 'god, spirit', or *zumbi*, 'fetish', in the Kongo language. To make such a bottle, according to the website, one ties a colourful glass receptacle to a tree, cobalt blue being traditional. As sunlight sparkles and shines through the glass, evil spirits are attracted to it and, entering, find themselves so seduced by the dazzling refractions that they remain within. Highly decorative works of art in themselves, Bianca's Zombie Spirit Bottles are currently retailing at US$350.[353]

Quite accidentally it seems, Elizabeth McAlister found herself being given a spirit bottle as a gift by a *bokor*, or 'sorcerer', in Haiti in the 1990s. She thought at first that she had inadvertently commissioned a piece of art that would make a pretty ornament for her coffee table until she found out it held two zombies. She explains that a zombie is 'a part of the soul that is stolen and made to work'. These are not the shuffling, or lately, sprinting, cannibal corpses beloved of George A. Romero and others, but '*zonbi* [*sic*] *astral*, a dead person's spirit that is magically captured and contained', usually also involving the magically induced premature death of the said person. The victim enters a limbic state – killed 'by the hands of man' but not yet 'by the hand of God' – and in this condition can be made to serve the *bokor*.[354]

---

[352] Mohammad Ishak, '2 Bomoh Capture 9 Djinns', *New Straits Times*, 10 October 2010. *Bomoh* was used in both the singular and plural in the article.

[353] http://www.thehouseofvoodoo.com/item_oddities/zombies/x25/, accessed 2 October 2010.

[354] McAlister, pp. 305–21.

McAlister watched as the *bokor* placed two human skulls on the floor, doused them with rum and set light to them. Blue flame danced over the grinning death's heads. It flickered and died, leaving a spicy perfume in the air. The sorcerer bent over the skulls and shaved a strip of bone from each. He then burnt a US one-dollar bill on the blade of a knife and mixed the ashes with the skull shavings. He tipped these into an empty rum bottle, adding liquor, leaves, perfume and a strange pink powder. The bottle was wrapped in the colours of the Petwo nation spirits – red, white and black – and decorated with pins, magnets, open scissors, four round mirrors, and a woman's earring. McAlister's bottle was a *wanga*, a magical working. As her research took her deeper into voodoo, she would also discover that it was 'a living grave'.[355]

The Haitian *bokor*'s zombie bottle is a descendant of the *nkisi* (*minkisi*, pl.) known amongst the people of the Congo Basin. Usually translated as 'charm' or 'fetish', it is more specifically a spirit container, manufactured and manipulated by a human operator, the *nganga-nkisi*. White clay, to symbolize the land of the dead, or earth from the grave itself, is used to hold the zombie within its new tomb. A variation of the zombie bottle is the *nganga* of the Palo Monte Mayombe religion in Cuba. Originally meaning 'medicine-man', *nganga* is here used for the 'spirit pot', often made of iron and looking not unlike a witch's cauldron. Like supernatural Tamagotchis these bottles and pots also need care and attention, and regular feeding – just remember not to give them salt.[356]

Such dealings with the dead were classified by medieval and later writers as necromancy, from the Greek *nekrós*, 'dead', and *manteia*, 'divination'. It was dangerous magic. The Bohemian poet, Johannes von Tepl (c. 1350–c. 1415) described it in grisly terms: 'with the sacrificial fingers of the dead and sigils (talismans) the formidable spirit is conjured'. It is no surprise that

---

[355] McAlister, pp. 306–7, 312, 314.
[356] McAlister, p. 310–11; Judith Bettelheim, 'Palo Monte Mayombe and its Influence on Cuban Contemporary Art', *African Arts*, 34.2, 2001, pp. 36–49, 94–6.

Hartlieb catalogued it as one of 'the forbidden arts'. The theologians of this period denied that the spirits of the dead were actually raised through necromancy, asserting that their places were instead taken by dissembling demons. This meant that necromancy was in effect to consort with demons and accordingly defined as black magic, or nigromancy from the Latin *niger*, 'black'. Although Hartlieb did not make such a sophisticated argument, he was clear about the Devil's involvement: 'He who wants to practice this art must make various offerings to the Devil [. . .] vow to him and be in league with him'. In the sixteenth century, Agrippa also described this dark art in similar terms:[357]

> *Necromancy* hath its name, because it worketh on the bodies of the dead, and giveth answers by the ghosts and apparitions of the dead, and subterrany spirits, alluring them into the carcasses of the dead, by certain hellish charms, and infernal invocations, and by deadly sacrifices, and wicked oblations.[358]

However, he was more specific than Hartlieb on the mechanisms behind this art. He furnished his description with a plethora of classical and biblical references to Odysseus and Circe, and Saul and the Witch of Endor, amongst others. The dramatic story of Saul, King of Israel, turning to the Witch of Endor to call up the spirit of the Prophet Samuel was an especially popular one amongst occultists and demonologists as both a proof of necromancy and an example of its prohibition. But behind the obvious learning was the primitive theory that 'souls after death do as yet love their body which they left'. From this it followed that those who have not been given a proper burial or who have died a

---

[357] Von Tepl, *Der Ackermann und der Tod*, 1401, trans. Felix Genzmer, Philipp Reclam, 1984; Johannes Hartlieb, *Das Buch der Verbotenen Künste*, trans. Falk Eisermann and Eckhard Graf, Eugen Diedrichs Verlag, 1998 [1456], p. 69, my translation; Richard Kieckhefer, *Magic in the Middle Ages*, Canto, 1989:152–3; Ruickbie, *Faustus*, pp. 40–1.

[358] Heinrich Cornelius Agrippa von Nettesheim, *De occulta philosophia libri tres*, n.p., 1533, trans. John French as *Three Books of Occult Philosophy*, Gregory Moule, 1651, pp. 489–90.

violent death still linger about their corpse or place of death. Such spirits can be 'allured' by the use of things that in life they found dear, but more importantly 'the souls of the dead cannot be called up without blood and a carcasse'. The best places for necromancy were duly considered to be 'burial places and places of execution, and where public slaughters have lately been made, or where the carcasses of the slain, not as yet expiated, nor rightly buried'. The same idea is expressed in the *Secretum Secretorum* document reproduced by Reginald Scot in 1584 with an even more graphic account of 'the maister standing at the head of the grave'. Unlike Hartlieb and the theological view, Agrippa took a classical stance and would seem to have believed that the dead could be made to answer the magician's interrogations. He even extended this necromantic theory to make the argument that the Christian saints listen most attentively to appeals made in the presence of their relics.[359]

Angel Magic

She ignored the voice in her head telling her that her car was going to be stolen. She had been hearing voices all her life and had learnt not to listen to them. It was a summer afternoon in 1995, the woman was in her late thirties pulling into a car park in her open-top convertible. Two men approached her; one was holding a knife, the other a gun. They made a grab for her car keys and her purse when 'one of my angels just said, "Scream"'. That stopped them in their tracks, but they were still armed and dangerous: 'then, God had placed in the parking lot a woman who leaned on the horn of her car'. The noise drew the attention of a crowd leaving a nearby church and her attackers ran off. 'I almost died,' she later said, 'by not listening to my angels.' She claims the experience changed her life and now travels the world telling people about angels.[360]

[359] Agrippa, p. 489; Scot, p. 232.

[360] Ray Hemachandra, 'Angel's Wings and Human Prayer', *New Age Retailer*, 20 July 2005, quoted on http://www.angeltherapy.com/view_article.php?article_id=28, accessed 22 July 2010.

Described on her website as 'a spiritual doctor of psychology and a fourth-generation metaphysician', Doreen Virtue (which she insists is her real name) claims to hold a number of degrees in 'counselling psychology'[361] and has written over twenty books on subjects as diverse as the chakras, health, diet, 'Crystal Children', 'Indigo Children', unicorns, and, of course, angels. Her titles include *Angel Words* (2011), *The Angel Therapy Handbook* (2011), *How to Hear Your Angels* (2007), *Angel Medicine* (2004), *Healing with the Angels* (1999) – there are too many to list them all. She even teaches 'Angel Therapy' courses for would-be practitioners. Over the course of four days Virtue and her staff perform 'short theatrical productions with audience participation' for those paying $1,555 per person. Sales of over 700,000 copies of Virtue's *Messages from Your Angels* card deck were reported in its first year.[362]

According to Virtue, 'angels are real' and everyone has at least two guardian angels in addition to a spirit guide who are ready to 'assist with our careers, health issues, love lives, families and homes'. Some of her angel magic includes asking that guardian angels be stationed at all of your doors and windows to protect you as you sleep, or visualize the archangel Raphael giving you 'a blanket of green healing energy' that you then pull over you. If you do not feel like doing any of this yourself, never fear: 'at night, before I fall asleep', says Virtue, 'I surround the planet with white light' – not forgetting to 'put light into all my products that are in [retailers'] stores'.[363]

---

[361] She claims to hold BA, MA and PhD degrees. Her PhD in counselling psychology is from the California Coast University (CCU), an unaccredited institution at the time of her enrolment and reported to be a 'diploma mill' in the *Dallas Observer*. The CCU was only accredited in 2005 by the US Distance Education and Training Council. Additionally, the psychiatric hospitals at which she claims to have held high positions are both now closed, and a journalist investigating her story was unable to verify these claims. See Jesse Hyde, 'Little Boy Blue', *Dallas Observer*, 9 March 2006.

[362] http://www.angeltherapy.com/about.php, accessed 22 July 2010; www.doreenvirtuellc.com, accessed 22 July 2010; Deirdre Donahue, 'Kits Help Booksellers Reach Nirvana', *USA Today*, 21 July 2003.

[363] Hemachandra; L. A. Justice, 'Heal your spirit with an angel's help', *Sun*, 7 March 2005, quoted on http://www.angeltherapy.com/view_article.

'In June 1994 Margaret Neylon was unemployed, depressed and broke,' according to the biography on her website. 'Then her angel told her "Give a course called 'Talking With Angels'."' 'You don't have to be mad to have an angel,' she says. Aiming squarely at a very particular market segment, her book *Angel Magic* is decorated with sworly text and a cute little 'cherub'.[364]

Cassandra Eason has also written a book called *Angel Magic*. A prolific writer of New Age books for many years – she has over eighty titles to her credit – Eason is perhaps most widely known as the dream analyst on *Big Brother* (series three). She also runs a course on angels. Called 'Touched by Angels' it covers working with guardian angels, archangels, angelology, healing and so on for £75. One can have an angel spell cast by Eason for £30, or an astrological-crystal-angel reading for £50. Also presenting herself as a psychic, she was asked by a UK newspaper in 2006 to predict the winning lottery numbers. As the balls rolled for a record roll-over EuroMillions draw of €126 million, her number did not come up.[365]

The roots of angel magic go deeper, of course. The *Testament of Solomon* is essentially a grimoire of angelic invocation. The surviving Greco-Roman magical papyri from Egypt of the second century BCE to the fifth century CE contain such spells of supplication as that which implores the 'excellent ruling angels' to intercede against the sufferer's fever and another that names Michael, Gabriel, Raphael, and others, as well as charms to drive out possessing demons. Some books on angel magic claimed to have been given by angels themselves, such as the third- or fourth-century CE *Sefer Ha-Razim* supposedly given by the angel Raziel to Noah and the medieval *Sefer Raziel Ha-Malach* supposedly given by Raziel to Adam. The Coptic manuscript known as 'The

php?article_id=28, accessed 22 July 2010.

[364] Margaret Neylon, *Angel Magic: All About Angels and How to Bring their Magic into your Life*, Thorsons, 2001; http://www.margaretneylon.com/about.html, accessed 28 July 2010.

[365] Cassandra Eason, *Angel Magic*, Little, Brown, 2010; Amit Roy, '3 in Europe get lottery lucky', the *Telegraph* [India], 5 February 2006.

Magical Book of Mary and the Angels', dating from the ninth to tenth centuries CE contains such invocatory lines as 'let the angels and the archangels appear to me today'. The Elizabethan polymath and magician John Dee famously developed his Enochian system of magic during communications with supposed angels in the late sixteenth century. A certain Dr Rudd produced *A Treatise on Angel Magic* in the seventeenth century with instructions on how to conjure angels to 'visible appearance'. Even Crowley's *Magick* is a work on angel magic, amongst other things, leading to the highest goal of invoking one's 'Holy Guardian Angel'.[366]

Magic Today

Despite Faustus' example at the beginning of this chapter, invoking the Devil is much out of fashion these days. Most witches and pagans I interviewed for my doctoral research used magic for healing (36.9 per cent), or for either personal (20 per cent) or social (18.5 per cent) development. For comparison, a survey running on the internet for over a year has found that out of 968 replies the largest number (35.8 per cent) wanted to use magic to change their relationships. Health came next (21.1 per cent) with job third (16.3 per cent). Sex (12.6 per cent) came bottom of the list after family (14.2 per cent).[367]

---

[366] Spells catalogued as PGM LXXXVIII. 1–19, PGM XC. 1–13 and PGM IV. 86–7 in Hans Dieter Betz (ed.), *The Greek Magical Papyri in Translation*, vol. I, University of Chicago Press, 1996, pp. 38, 302; Michael A. Morgan, *Sepher Ha-Razim: The Book of Mysteries*, Society of Biblical Literature, 1983; see also the scholarly edition by Bill Rebiger and Peter Schäfer (eds), *Sefer ha-Razim I und II – Das Buch der Geheimnisse I und II*, Mohr Siebeck, 2009; P. Heid Inv. Kopt. 685, Institut für Papyrologie, Ruprecht-Karls-Universität, Heidelberg, published by Marvin Meyer (ed.), *The Magical Book of Mary and the Angels*, Universitätsverlag C. Winter, 1996; quotation p. 13; Rudd, *A Treatise on Angel Magic*, British Library MS. Harley 6482; John Dee, 'Claves Angelicæ', British Library, Sloane 3191, and 'The Book of Enoch', British Library, Sloane 3189 and 2599.

[367] Leo Ruickbie, 'The Re-Enchanters: Theorising Re-Enchantment and Testing for its Presence in Modern Witchcraft', unpublished PhD thesis, King's College, London, 2005; see Leo Ruickbie, *Witchcraft Out of the Shadows*, Robert Hale, 2004, p. 205; 'If you could magickally improve one area of your life, what would it be?' 14 February 2009 to 2 August 2010, http://naturalwicca.

Historically, magic was generally seen as the work of spirits. The complicated repertoire that emerged in the grimoires of circles and talismans was seen as a means of influencing, even commanding, spiritual entities. It was also seen as working with the spirit. The spirit could, according to our examples, be either extracted for personal protection or trapped for nefarious purposes. In folklore it is usually the villain of the piece who hides his soul; in magic it is the practitioner who can both send forth his or her own soul and extract the souls of others. Given the belief in an afterlife, it was thought that the dead could also be manipulated in this way. The principal technique to use someone else's soul relies upon sympathetic magic, according to Frazer. Something of the person, such as a bone shaving, or something having been in contact with the person, such as earth from a footprint, can be used to capture and control the soul whether the person is living or dead. Spirits of the dead could also be simply attracted by the potent symbols of life: blood and flesh. 'Higher' spirits, such as angels, can be both supplicated and commanded, although 'spells' like Virtue's green blanket are rather more imaginative exercises.

In contrast to these historical views, I found that magical practitioners in post-industrial Britain mainly described magic as a form of transformative energy or mental technique, but as we have seen there are practitioners around the world – from Haiti to Malaysia – who are still interpreting and using magic from the perspective of spirits. However they might define this mysterious technique, there are also those still using the old grimoires – especially the *Key of Solomon* – just as the real Faustus might have done in his day, 500 years ago.

---

com/index.php/component/poll/1-life, accessed 8 August 2010. Note that 968 is the number of returns received and may not be an accurate reflection of the number of people who took part. The online survey also used fixed categories that will have influenced the returns made.

7. Spiritualism

Snow was still on the ground and storm clouds threatened more. Dark came early to the door and drafts whistled coldly through the cracks. But that was not the reason the Fox family had taken to sleeping in one room. As night fell, pitch black and silent as the grave, upon their humble house in a lonely hamlet, it started again. Invisible hands hammered wild blows upon the walls and doors as they lay shivering in their beds.

The place was known as the 'Burned Over District', a region that got its name from the wild-fires of religious revival that frequently swept through the lives of its inhabitants. Here, in an isolated settlement called Hydesville in the far north of New York State, in 1848, lived two sisters – Catherine (Kate, Katie or Cathie), aged twelve, and Margaretta (Maggie), aged fifteen – with their parents, John and Margaret, in a 'simple wooden homestead'. From these humble beginnings, the Fox sisters would become an international sensation – and the world would come to believe that the spirits of the dead could communicate with the living.[368]

---

[368] Ann Leah Underhill, *The Missing Link in Modern Spiritualism*, T. R. Knox, 1885, p. 7 – Underhill was one of the married names of Leah Fox and as she explained (note, p. 40) Catherine was called Cathie by her parents, but later Katie by the public; Frank Podmore, *Modern Spiritualism: A History and a Criticism*, Methuen, 1902, pp. 179–80; Thomas Olman Todd, *Hydesville: The Story of the Rochester Knockings*, Keystone Press, 1905, p. 18; Amy Lehman, *Victorian Women and the Theatre of Trance*, McFarland, 2009, p. 79. Also of interest is Emma Hardinge Britten, *Modern American Spiritualism*, self-published, 1870.

In 1848 revolution was in the air. The barricades were up in Paris and a Second Republic was declared. The March Revolution had thrown Germany into turmoil. The Italian states were up in arms against Austria. In Tipperary the Irish rebelled against British rule. In London the Chartists marched on Parliament. Karl Marx and Friedrich Engels published their *Communist Manifesto*. But in this out of the way corner of rural North America, these two young girls were about to start their own revolution.

The Foxes moved into the house in Hydesville in December 1847. Faint nocturnal knocking sounds started to be heard in January of the new year, growing stronger into February and March. Additional phenomena began to be reported: chairs were moved, bedclothes would be whisked off sleepers, Katie said she felt a cold hand upon her face. Eventually, noises could be heard all over the house. As Mr and Mrs Fox stood either side of a door, they could hear knocking on the door between them. 'We heard footsteps in the pantry and walking downstairs,' said Mrs Fox. She thought 'the house must be haunted by some unhappy, restless spirit.' Events reached a crescendo on the night of Friday, 31 March.[369]

As the family huddled in a single bedroom together, the knocks echoed in the darkness. The father, John Fox, tried the doors and windows, looking for the source of the noise, but he knew it was fruitless – he had tried many times before. Then Katie called out, 'Here, Mr Splitfoot, do as I do'. She clapped her hands together a number of times. The mysterious knockings responded with the same number of sounds. Maggie tried next. 'Now do as I do,' she said, 'count one, two, three, four,' clapping whilst she did so. The raps answered in kind, four times. Maggie was too frightened to try the experiment a second time. Katie, however, in what her mother described as 'her childish simplicity', had an explanation: 'O mother, I

---

[369] Signed testimony of Margaret Fox dated 11 April 1848, in Underhill, pp. 5–10.

know what it is; tomorrow is April-fool day, and it's somebody trying to fool us'.[370]

Mrs Fox decided to try and test it with a question 'that no one in the place could answer'. She asked it how old her children were. Mrs Fox had had seven children, of which only six were still living. The knocking rapped out the correct ages for six children, paused then gave three more knocks. The seventh child had died at the age of three. Then she asked 'Is this a human being that answers my questions so correctly?' No answer. 'Is it a spirit?' 'Yes' came the knocks in reply.[371]

According to all accounts, Mrs Fox's questioning revealed that the knocks were being made by a thirty-one-year-old pedlar who had been murdered for his money, leaving a widow, now also dead, and five children. His body was buried in the cellar. By now the children were 'clinging to each other and trembling with terror'. The Foxes called in their neighbours, the Redfields, as witnesses. They then called others. Soon the Deuslers, the Hydes and the Jewells were crowding into the bedroom. The questioning continued with William Deusler leading the interrogation. The sum of money involved had been $500. The crime had been perpetrated about five years ago in the east bedroom on a Tuesday at midnight. His throat had been cut with a butcher's knife. Mrs Fox took the children and left the house. Deusler said he left at about midnight. Mr Fox and others stayed the night trying to find out more about the case. On Saturday night the questioning continued.[372]

News spread fast. The next evening Deusler reckoned that there were as many as 300 people in and around the Foxes' house. Deusler noted amongst them Hiram Soverhill, Esq., one

---

[370] Underhill, p. 7; Todd, pp. 27–33; Lehman, p. 80. Todd says that Katie made only movements with her hands, Podmore, p. 180, and Lehman says finger snapping, but Mrs Fox's testimony reprinted in Underhill states 'clapping'.

[371] Underhill, p. 7. Todd, p. 35, gave a different account of the questioning procedure.

[372] Underhill, pp. 7–9; Todd, pp. 35, 37–40. On pp. 37–42 Todd reproduces the signed testimony of Deusler dated 12 April 1848.

of the Republican 'Young Men', sometime school-teacher, constable and 'overseer of the poor', and Volney Brown, a former officer of the 39th Infantry, both evidently citizens of some standing. They, too, asked questions and had their answers sounded out in knocks.[373]

Committees of friends and neighbours were formed and stationed round the house, alert to any attempt at deception. The noises grew quieter as the witching hour approached and some of the crowd began to dissipate. The Foxes' son, David, and some others started digging in the cellar until they hit water at a depth of 3 feet (1m) and had to give up.[374]

By Sunday 500 people had gathered. The small cottage was jam-packed with the curious. They were milling through the rooms. They were peering in through the windows. They were everywhere. When he arrived in the afternoon, Deusler had the house cleared.[375]

With one of the Foxes' sons-in-law, Stephen Smith, and several others, Deusler went into the cellar and asked the spirit if a body had been buried there. For the first time the noises would now be reported as being heard during the hours of daylight. 'The moment I asked the question,' wrote Deusler, 'there was a sound like the falling of a stick [. . .] on the floor in the bedroom over our heads.' He sent Smith up to investigate, but he came promptly back and said the room was empty. It is not clear where the Fox family were at this point. Deusler tried to recreate the sound by dropping objects on the floor, but was unable to do so. He reported that there was only one floor between the bedroom and the cellar, allowing no hiding place for anything that might have been used to make the noise. He

---

[373] Underhill, p. 9; Todd, p. 40; 'Young Men of Arcadia', *The Western Argus*, 10 September 1834; George W. Cowles (ed.), *Landmarks of Wayne County, New York*, D. Mason & Co., 1895, pp. 358, 364; L. H. Clark, *Military History of Wayne County, N.Y.; The County in the Civil War*, Clark, Hulett & Gaylord, 1883, pp. 178, 184.

[374] Testimony of David S. Fox, dated 11 April 1848, in Underhill, pp. 18–19.

[375] Dr Campell's account reproduced in Britten, p. 34; Todd, pp. 40, 43.

repeated the questions on Monday night and got the same
response. He finished his account by saying that he had never
believed in haunted houses before, but that this was 'a mystery
to me which I am unable to solve'.[376]

On Monday, David Fox led others in digging up the cellar
again, bailing out the water as it rushed in. Again they had to
abandon work. He came back on Tuesday with a pump, but not
even pumping and hand-bailing the water could lower the level.
There was little more they could do until the year brought hot
weather and a dry season.[377]

On 11 April, both John and Margaret Fox made signed
statements of all that had transpired. Margaret was clearly
much put out by events. 'I am very sorry,' she wrote, 'that there
has been so much excitement about it. It has been a great deal
of trouble to us.' John expressed similar feelings: 'It has caused
a great deal of trouble and anxiety. Hundreds have visited the
house, so that it is impossible for us to attend to our daily
occupations.' Margaret remained agnostic, at a loss to account
for the noises. She was not, as she wrote, 'a believer in haunted
houses or supernatural appearances'. John, however, had 'no
doubt but that it is of supernatural origin'. David, too,
confessed 'I cannot account for this noise as being produced
by any human agency'.[378]

At the same time, Lucretia Pulver, who had been a maid to
the last family occupying the house, also gave her testimony.
She claimed to have lived and worked there for about three
months one winter, during which time she, too, had heard the
mysterious rapping sounds and footsteps from downstairs.
The dog, she said, would lie under the bed and howl all night
long. She claimed that before the sounds were heard a 'foot-
pedlar' had called at the house and then strangely was never
seen again. She said that she saw her mistress altering coats

---

[376] Todd, pp. 41–2.
[377] Underhill, p. 19.
[378] Underhill, pp. 9–10, 19.

that were too large for her husband. She said she found evidence of strange diggings in the cellar that were explained away as rat-holes.[379]

Anna Pulver also remembered the former mistress of the house complaining of hearing strange footsteps in the night. Former residents Mr and Mrs Weekman came forward to add their testimony, throwing fuel on the fire with more stories of terrified children and unusual noises. Jane C. Lape even claimed to have seen the ghost of the pedlar. The well near the house, when the water smelt so foul in the summer of 1844, was mentioned as something suspicious. A lot of question marks were now beginning to form an accusing finger.[380]

The Foxes abandoned the house, going to live with their son David. People still visited and still claimed to hear rapping noises. The phenomena also transferred themselves to David's house, some two miles distant. At night they would hear the ghastly re-enactment of the murder: 'gurgling, strangling, sawing, planing, and boring'. By the end of July, David and a group of friends returned to resume the digging. The ground had dried out and there was the chance that they might now make some progress. His wife, Elizabeth, laid on a feast of puddings, pies, cakes and sweet-meats, and work began.[381]

On the first day they dug down to a depth of between 4 and 5 feet (1.2 to 1.5 m), finding charcoal and lime, then some hair, then some teeth. Darkness brought a halt to the digging and they returned the next day, but so did the crowds. Cartloads of rowdies with 'shouts of ribaldry and roars of laughter' arrived for the entertainment. The women formed a picket-line round the house, whilst the men rolled up their sleeves and continued digging. This time they unearthed some bones 'which doctors pronounced to be human bones' from the ankle, hands and skull. Meanwhile the crowd outside broke through, crowding

---

[379] Testimony of Lucretia Pulver, dated 11 April 1848, in Underhill, pp. 13–15.
[380] Testimony of Anna Pulver, dated 11 April 1848, in Underhill, p. 16; Underhill, pp. 16–18.
[381] Underhill, pp. 20–2, 32.

into the cellar, spitting and throwing sticks and stones. But the digging went on.[382]

Shovelling out layers of sand and gravel, they hit what appeared to be a board and tried to bore through it. Over their heads the floorboards were creaking with the weight of people trampling through the house. The cellar was mobbed. There were shouts of 'Drag the women out!' and 'Drag the men out!' They were called crazy. Overflowing excitement and barely repressed violence jostled shoulder-to-shoulder. Luckily, perhaps, daylight was fading fast and brought work to a halt once more.[383]

Leah, another of the Foxes' daughters, arrived on the scene. Following the death of her husband, Mr Fish, she had built up a successful business as a music teacher in Rochester. The family decided that Katie should return with Leah. Interestingly, Leah later wrote, 'we hoped, by separating the two children (Maggie and Katie), that we could put a stop to the disturbance'. Mrs Fox had noticed that the noises seemed to occur round Katie in particular.[384]

The mysterious rapping followed them on the canal boat back to Rochester and settled in to its new home on Mechanics' Square, showing every intention of playing merry havoc with their lives. That first night, Leah's daughter Lizzie was reduced to a screaming fit after she felt a cold hand on her face in the darkness. Leah struck a light and read out from a bible, but the girls continued to feel hands upon them. Eventually they were able to put out the light and try sleeping once more. Leah tucked the bible under her pillow, but before she could even put her head down, it shot out from underneath. The box of matches shook in front of her face and 'such a variety of performances ensued that we gave up in despair to our fate, whatever it may be'.[385]

The next night at about midnight, they were rudely awoken

[382] Underhill, pp. 22–5.
[383] Underhill, p. 25.
[384] Underhill, p. 32.
[385] Underhill, pp. 33–4.

by the sound of all the tables and chairs being moved about downstairs. Footsteps then clattered on the stairs up to the room next to their bedroom. It sounded as though someone wearing clogs danced a jig to the applause of a sizeable audience. They then all trooped back downstairs, slamming the doors noisily behind them. Similar disturbances followed over the next weeks, until Leah resolved to move – thinking it was the house that was haunted – and took another property on Prospect Street backing onto an old cemetery called 'the Buffalo Burying-ground'. Finally, they spent an uneventful night. The mother, Margaret Fox, arrived with Maggie the next day and Leah excitedly told them that they had escaped the noises.[386]

At midnight the spirits were back. Footsteps were heard creeping up the stairs. 'We could hear them,' Leah wrote, 'shuffling, giggling, and whispering'. Repeatedly, they came into the bedroom to 'give our bed a tremendous shaking, lifting it (and us) entirely from the floor, almost to the ceiling, and let us down with a bang; then pat us with hands'. The whole panoply of poltergeist phenomena manifested itself: objects were lifted, objects were thrown, furniture was moved about, people were slapped and touched, they were pricked with pins, a ghostly figure was seen, the piano played by itself, and a varied range of noises were heard. Katie fell into a trance, describing 'the terrible occurrence at the Hydesville house', sobbing uncontrollably and repeating many verses of poetry.[387]

They had tried to ignore the disturbances, believing them to be caused by evil spirits, but the disturbances would not be ignored. Finally, in the late summer of 1848, they turned to the method first employed by David in Hydesville of calling out the letters of the alphabet and noting which one received a rap in response and in this way were able to receive communications from the source of the noises, whatever it was. The first message read:

---

[386] Underhill, pp. 35–6.
[387] Underhill, pp. 37–41, 45, 48.

Dear friends, you must proclaim these truths to the world. This is the dawning of a new era; and you must not try to conceal it any longer. When you do your duty, God will protect you; and good spirits will watch over you.[388]

They dubbed the system 'God's Telegraph'. As Leah put it, 'We were truly converted [. . .] we had something to live for'. They arranged a signal with the spirits, that they should rap five times when they wanted to communicate. But still they resisted taking the next step until their dead grandfather used the 'telegraph':[389]

My Dear Children:– The time will come when you will understand and appreciate this great dispensation. You must permit your good friends to meet with you and hold communion with their friends in heaven.[390]

They shared the message with their friends and from there it spread. A committee was formed to deal with the wave of enquiries and the 'rushing crowd of curiosity seekers' who wished to hear the 'Rochester Rappings'. People did not just wish to chat with deceased relatives, but wanted to know how to make a fortune, what the secrets of their rivals were, how to resolve their domestic problems, what the winning lottery numbers would be, and what stocks and shares to invest in. Leah recorded that answers were given, but that none ever led to success. She thought that the spirits seemed to delight in deceiving those who asked such questions. It did not stop the crowds. They called at all hours of the day and night. The family scarcely had time to keep the house in order, and Leah lost all of her music pupils.[391]

As Leah told the story, the spirits compelled them to hold a

---

[388] Underhill, pp. 48–9.

[389] Underhill, pp. 49, 51.

[390] Underhill, p. 51.

[391] Underhill, pp. 52–3, 55, 59; Britten, p. 43.

public performance. The Corinthian Hall was hired for the evening of 14 November 1848, and Leah and Maggie displayed 'the manifestations' before a large audience. They also announced that a Committee of Investigation would be formed to search for fraud in their activities. A local paper, the *Rochester Democrat*, scented blood and published a long editorial, denouncing 'the rapping humbug'.[392]

The curtain was up, but it was not humbug. The committee found nothing to suggest deception and as they delivered their report before an audience at a second night at the Corinthian many greeted it with surprise. A second committee was formed and reported on the next evening before an even larger audience: 'there was no kind of probability or possibility of [the sounds] being made by ventriloquism, as some had supposed; and they could not have been made by machinery'. The outcry was even greater than before. A third committee was formed – the 'Infidel Committee' – including, in particular, all of those most vocal in their belief that it was an unmitigated fraud. One would 'forfeit a new hat', another would 'throw myself over Genesee Falls', if they could not prove it to be humbug.[393]

They met in the rooms of Dr Gates in the Rochester House. In a private room beforehand, Leah and Maggie were undressed by three specially appointed women and given clothes provided by the committee. They were brought into the main room and seated at a large table. Leah and Maggie waited. The committee waited. No sounds were heard. They waited all morning, but without any of the usual manifestations. Lunch was served and the committee thought it good sport to tease Leah and Maggie as they ate. Tears streaked Maggie's cheeks. Leah pushed her food around, unable to taste it. The sceptics were in good cheer.[394]

---

[392] Underhill, pp. 63–4.
[393] Underhill, pp. 65–8.
[394] Underhill, pp. 68–9.

As they all sat around the table it suddenly began to shake. One end slowly lifted into the air, then the other. With much creaking in protest, the table rose above their heads. Everyone, except Leah and Maggie, looked on in horror. The waiters ran from the room. The three women comforted the two sisters and the Infidel Committee declared their defeat: 'Girls, you have gained a victory. We will stand by you to the last'.[395]

They still had to make their report public at the Corinthian Hall, however. Warning was sent to the committee that if they gave a favourable report, they would be attacked. The friends of Leah and Maggie thought there would be a riot and urged them not to go. Everyone feared for their own safety. Maggie thought they would surely be lynched. After all, it was 1848.[396]

All the same, they went: Leah and Maggie, and the Infidel Committee. Each member of the committee took centre stage and made his report in turn, explaining the experiment, the precautions taken and the observations made. But the 'rowdy element' would have none of it and worked themselves up into a 'howling mob'. They had warmed a barrel of tar and hidden it near the door to use on Leah, Maggie and the Committee as they left. The police were called. Squibs were set off, violence threatened. But the Chief of Police had cordoned off the stage with policemen and another had brought 'fifty good men' of his own. The rabble dissipated. 'We had,' said Leah, 'passed the fiery ordeal.'[397]

Spiritualism did not begin with the Fox sisters – Leah called what they did 'modern Spiritualism' – but it did now find itself propelled to the centre of the public imagination. Poltergeist phenomena had been recorded long before, of course, and a seventeenth-century Jewish sect had even used 'table-turning' as a centrepiece magico-religious rite. Spirit communication also had an ancient pedigree – attempts to talk to the dead were

---

[395] Underhill, pp. 69–70.
[396] Underhill, p. 71.
[397] Underhill, pp. 71–3, 100.

considered necromancy. Sometimes the dead were believed to try and communicate with the living, as we saw with regard to purposeful ghosts.[398]

Spirit-rapping, said Sir Arthur Conan Doyle, had been heard before. Best known as the creator of Sherlock Holmes, Doyle was also an ardent Spiritualist and had written a two-volume study of the subject, identifying several prior cases of spirit-rapping – in 1520 at Oppenheim in Germany; in 1661 at the house of Mr Mompesson in Tedworth: the famous Drummer of Tedworth; and in 1716 at the vicarage of Epworth.[399]

There were even earlier cases to be found. *The Spiritual Magazine* for March 1861 quoted from the Roman Catholic missionary Évariste Régis Huc's (1813–60) recent account of Christianity in the Orient involving the travels of William of Rubruck (Willem van Ruysbroek), the French ambassador to the Khan of Tartary in the thirteenth century:

When they (the soothsayers to the Tartar Emperor) were interrogated, they evoked their demons (spirits) by the sound of the tambourine, shaking it furiously; then falling into an ecstasy, they feigned to receive answers from their familiar spirits, and proclaimed them as oracles. It is rather curious, too, that table-rapping and table-turning were in use in the thirteenth century among these Mongols in the wilds of Tartary. Rubru[c]k himself witnessed an instance of the kind. On the eve of the Ascension, when the mother of Mangou [was] feeling very ill, the first soothsayer was summoned for consultation, he 'performed some magic by rapping on a table'.[400]

---

[398] Brian Inglis, *Natural and Supernatural: A History of the Paranormal*, Prism/Unity, 1992, p. 206.

[399] Sir Arthur Conan Doyle, *The History of Spiritualism*, 2 vols, Cassell, 1926, vol. 1, p. 58.

[400] 'Glimpses of Spiritualism in the East', *The Spiritual Magazine*, 1 March 1861, p. 118, quoting Évariste Régis Huc, *Christianity in China, Tartary and Thibet*, 2 vols, Sadlier & Co., 1857, vol. I, p. 199. The same account is

This account reveals its biases, but those aside, it is an interesting case. *The Spiritual Magazine* had delved deep into the past to find this precedent for Spiritualism. In the process it had established a connection with shamanism, which was as yet to receive serious anthropological study.

Nearer the Foxes' own time, Emmanuel Swedenborg's discourses with the disincarnate had given rise to a thriving sect after his death in 1772. Franz Anton Mesmer's spectacular results with 'animal magnetism' led some to suggest that the spirits were involved. The term séance, for example, was used in the context of Mesmerism before it became applied to Spiritualism.[401] Spectacular cases of spontaneous mediumship had been reported in the early years of the nineteenth century: Friederike Hauffe, 'The Seeress of Prevorst', who would talk to the spirits every evening; the maid Mary Jane who could talk to the fairies after being mesmerized by her employer in Massachusetts; Andrew Jackson Davis, 'The Poughkeepsie Seer', uneducated, but able to transcribe learned discourses on philosophy and science, as well as see through walls, whilst in trance.[402]

By 1850 the Fox sisters were holding séances in New York. The business-minded Leah managed Katie and Maggie, steering them to success. They became household names, but they were no longer alone. By 1851 every town and city in New York State had its medium giving public trance lectures or private sittings. Competition was growing on every side and not just from the developing professional and semi-professional medium class. Practical handbooks were being published, telling readers how to hold their own séances. According to Uriah Clarke in his

---

strangely absent from William of Rubruck, *The Journey of William of Rubruck to the Eastern Parts of the World 1253–55*, trans. William W. Rockhill, Hakluyt Society, 1900.

[401] *The Athenæum*, 1845, pp. 268, 334, reference to a 'mesmeric séance'.

[402] Lehman, p. 82; Inglis, pp. 199–203. See Justinus Kerner, *Die Seherin von Prevorst*, 1829; Justinus Kerner, *The Seeress of Prevorst*, trans. Catherine Crowe, Partridge & Brittan, 1855; and Andrew Jackson Davis, *The Principle of Nature, Her Divine Revelation, and a Voice to Mankind*, 1847.

1863 book *Plain Guide to Spiritualism*, for example, the ideal number of sitters ranged from three to twenty with a balanced number of men and women. The participants were instructed to 'put yourselves in sympathy' with whatever it was they believed they were trying to communicate with and 'become an instrument for the manifestations of the spirits'.[403]

SPIRITUAL MISSION.—Three mediums on a spiritual mission to this city for a few days, now stopping at Hungerford's Hotel, in Duane-street, near Hudson-street. They will examine diseases, and prescribe for the same. Price $2; for spiritual investigations $1. – *Tribune*, 8 February 1853

SPIRITUAL MANIFESTATIONS.—Mrs A. L. Coan, declared to be the best medium, for rapping and writing by the influence of departed spirits, in Boston, will receive company for sittings every day in the week, from nine o'clock A.M. till ten P.M. Rooms No. 8 Howard-street, opposite the Athenaeum. Sittings fifty cents each. – *Boston Herald*, 15 February 1853

It was, as Milton said, that 'Millions of spiritual creatures walk the earth / Unseen, both when we wake and when we sleep', but, now, not unheard. Spiritualism was all the rage. It had its own periodicals, such as *The Spirit Messenger*, *The Shekinah*, and *The Spiritual Magazine*. Sir David Brewster, the inventor of the kaleidoscope, wrote that 'there are *thousands* of tables turning every night in London, so general is the excitement'. Even Queen Victoria and Prince Albert sat down to a séance. By the end of the century there were an estimated three million people in the USA who believed in the powers of the 10,000 or so trance mediums who were then practising.

---

[403] Inglis, pp. 206, 209; Uriah Clarke, *Plain Guide to Spiritualism*, W. White & Co., 1863, p. 172.

Amongst them were many remarkable characters. Marietta Davis went into a trance for nine days. When she came round again she said that she had been in heaven, talking to old friends and meeting Jesus. The teenage Cora Scott was drawing huge crowds with her elevated trance communication and stunning good looks. Perhaps the most startling was Daniel Dunglas Home (1833–86) who flew in and out of windows for an encore.[404]

Born in Currie near Edinburgh, Home claimed to be the illegitimate son of Alexander, tenth Earl of Home. He claimed that his cradle had been rocked by invisible hands and that the supernatural disturbances that attended him led to his eventually being turned out of his home. Active in America from 1851, by 1852 he was holding up to seven sittings a day. From 1855 to 1862 he was touring Europe. But where others hired halls and performed for the masses, Home only appeared before select private audiences. Initially he enjoyed great success amongst the upper classes, was lavished with expensive gifts and made a socially advantageous marriage to the daughter of a Russian general. However, when his wife died in 1862 her relatives seized her assets and Home was cheated out of any inheritance. Travelling to Rome he found himself expelled in 1864 by order of the Vatican for being a 'sorcerer'. Back in London he was cruelly satirized as Robert Browning's 'Mr Sludge the Medium' (1864): 'I cheated when I could, / Rapped with my toe-joints, set sham hands to work [. . .]' He became involved with the wealthy widow Jane Lyon and, initially, his fortunes dramatically improved, especially when the late Mr Lyon told his wife

---

[404] The first edition of *The Spirit Messenger* was published in Springfield, USA, 10 August 1850, edited by Apollos Munn and R. P. Ambler. *The Spiritual Magazine* was first published in London, January 1860; another *Spiritual Magazine*, also known as *The American Spiritual Magazine*, was edited by Samuel Watson, first published in 1875; John Milton, *Paradise Lost*, Bk IV, ll 677–8; Cora Linn Victoria Scott [Richmond/Tappan], *The Discourses Through the Mediumship of Mrs Cora L.V. Tappan*, J. Burns, 1875; Brewster quoted in Inglis, p. 214; Gordon Stein (ed.), *The Encyclopedia of the Paranormal*, Prometheus Books, 1996, p. 154.

to treat Home like a son and present him with several large cash gifts. But when Lyon later changed heart in 1868, she took him to court to recover the money. The court found in her favour: Home had exercised 'improper influence'. He was ordered to return £60,000 – remarkably he was able to do so, but the case brought much adverse publicity. Association with Viscount Adare, who privately published *Experiences in Spiritualism with Mr D. D. Home* in 1869, revived his reputation. He married a second time in 1871 to Julie de Goumeline and her wealth allowed him to retire from Spiritualism.[405]

Home's repertoire included levitation, bodily elongation, immunity to fire, manifestation of spirit-hands ('pseudopods'), spirit music and table-tipping. He had enjoyed the admiration of the great names of his day: Edward Bulwer-Lytton, John Ruskin, William Makepeace Thackeray and Henry Wadsworth Longfellow. Ralph Waldo Emerson thought him a 'prodigious genius'. Investigated by the scientist Sir William Crookes in 1871, he was pronounced genuine. Society for Psychical Research members William Fletcher Barrett and Frederic W. H. Myers came to the same conclusion in 1889, discounting some of the claims of fraud as hearsay. It is frequently said of him that he was never publicly proven to be a charlatan, but research by the noted sceptic the late Dr Gordon Stein has since uncovered several instances in which he was privately caught in the act of deceiving his audience, although this too has been contested.[406]

---

[405] Joseph McCabe, *Spiritualism: A Popular History from 1847*, Unwin, 1920, pp. 94–5; *Enc. Para.*, pp. 325–9.

[406] William Fletcher Barrett and Frederic W. H. Myers, *Journal of the Society of Psychical Research*, July 1889, pp. 104–5; *Enc. Para.*, pp. 325–9; Stuart Gordon, *The Paranormal: An Illustrated Encyclopedia*, Headline, 1992, p. 313. See Gordon Stein, *The Sorcerer of Kings: The Case of Daniel Dunglas Home and William Crookes*, Prometheus Books, 1993, and the review in *Journal of the Society of Psychical Research*, 60, July 1994, pp. 45ff. Peter Lamont was equivocal in *The First Psychic*, Abacus, 2006, p. 267.

Influential Mediums

Name	Lived	Notability
Andrew Jackson Davis, 'The Poughkeepsie Seer'	1826–1910	voluminous trance-writer
Helene Petrovna Blavatsky	1831–91	founded the Theosophical Society in 1875
Daniel Dunglas Home	1833–86	supposedly never caught cheating
Fox Sisters		started the 'table-rapping' phenomenon leading to the
Margaretta	1833–93	development of Spiritualism
Catherine	1837–92	
William Stainton Moses	1839– 92	one of the founders of the Society for Psychical Research
Davenport Brothers		
Ira Erastus	1839–1911	world-touring spirit cabinet séances
William Henry	1841–77	
Eusapia Palladino	1854–1918	the most famous physical medium
Leonora Piper, 'Mrs Piper'	1859–1950	the most famous direct voice medium
Edgar Cayce, 'The Sleeping Prophet'	1877–1945	psychic diagnoses of illness
Marthe Beraud, aka Eva Carrière	1886 – ?	first produced what was called 'ectoplasm'
Helen Duncan	1897–1956	convicted in 1944 under the Witchcraft Act of 1735
Doris Stokes	1920–87	first medium to play the London Palladium
Jane Roberts	1929–84	channelled the 'Seth Material'
J[udy] Z[ebra] Knight	1946 –	channel of the Lemurian 'Ramtha'

The Davenport Brothers, Ira Erastus Davenport (1839–1911) and William Henry Davenport (1841–77), claimed an earlier pedigree than the Fox sisters. Apparently the spirits had made their presence known in 1846 with a midnight cacophony of 'raps, thumps, loud noises, snaps, crackling noises'. Together with their younger sister Elizabeth they experimented in table-rapping, getting immediate results. Ira developed the gift of automatic writing. Soon all three were levitating and 'hundreds of respectable citizens of Buffalo are reported to have seen these occurrences'. At breakfast the cutlery and dishes would dance a jig. A lead pencil appeared to write with no human hand guiding it. Musical instruments floated in the air, playing themselves.[407]

Their professional career began in 1854, specializing in a 'spirit cabinet' style of séance. Securely tied up, they would be placed in a closed cabinet and spiritual wonders would ensue. One witness said 'hands were seen appearing at a small aperture [. . .] not only seen, but were felt'. When the cabinet was re-opened they would be seen to still be bound as securely as before. Several Harvard professors tested them in 1857, truss-ing the boys up in 500 feet of rope, sealing the knots with linen thread and seating a certain Professor Pierce between them before closing them all in the cabinet. Materializations were observed outside the cabinet. When it was re-opened some of the rope had wrapped itself around the hapless professor's neck. Dumbfounded, the professors decided not to publish their intended report.[408]

The brothers toured Europe in the mid-1860s, visiting first England then France with their 'Spiritualistic Manifestations'. After their first private performance at the Regent Street, London, residence of the then famous actor and playwright Dion Boucicault, a journalist for the *Morning Post* reported that

---

[407] Conan Doyle, vol. 1, pp. 218–19.

[408] Edward Dicey, 'The Davenport Brothers', *Macmillan's Magazine*, XI, November 1864 – April 1864, pp. 35–40; T. L. Nichols, *A Biography of the Brothers Davenport*, Saunder, Otley and Co., 1864, pp. 87–8; Inglis, p. 241.

there could be no 'presumption of fraud'. They were met with great fanfare in France. For their opening night they filled every seat at the Salle Herz in Paris at 25 francs a head for a two-part show of the 'Cabinet' and the 'Dark Séance'. But there was such a great hue and cry that after only forty-five minutes the police were called to clear the hall. The French magician Jean-Eugène Robert-Houdin thought them 'mere performers of juggling tricks', although he did not travel up to the capital to witness the debacle in person. They continued a zig-zag itinerary to Ireland, Germany, Belgium, Russia, Poland and Sweden before coming back to London and finally returning to America. William later died in Melbourne during their Australian tour in the 1870s. Sir Arthur Conan Doyle thought them 'the greatest mediums of their kind that the world has ever seen'. However, in his final years, Ira wrote cryptically to the escapologist Harry Houdini, saying 'We never *in public* affirmed our belief in Spiritualism'.[409]

[409] Conan Doyle, vol. 1, pp. 224, 230–2, 234; Jean-Eugène Robert-Houdin, *The Secrets of Stage Conjuring*, trans. Professor Hoffmann, Routledge, 1881, pp. 160–2, 168–70. Conan Doyle, vol. 1, pp. 234–5, questions the veracity of the statements Houdini reproduces as being from Ira Davenport.

Key Terms in Spiritualism

Apports
'Objects are brought from many miles distant, and tossed on the table. These are technically termed *apports*.' (Andrew Lang, 1894)

Control
'Used of the intelligence which purports to communicate messages which are written or uttered by the [. . .] medium.' (F. W. H. Myers, 1896)

Ectoplasm
'A supposedly psychic substance or materialisation which exudes from the medium's body.' (*Pears Cyclopaedia*, 1897)

Involuntary Utterance (later 'xenoglossy')
'Of which the speaker is himself incapable, is not the least noteworthy of the modes and evidences of spirit-intercourse.' (*The Spiritual Magazine*, 1860)

Luminous Phenomena
'Usually described as very brilliant, sometimes they appear as stars, or as balls of fire, at other times they shoot meteor-like through the apartment, or gleam over the walls; or appear as luminous currents circling round a particular centre.' (*The Spiritual Magazine*, 1860)

Medium
'A person through whom communication is deemed to be carried on between living men and spirits of the departed.' (F. W. H. Myers, 1896)

Pseudopods
'Psychic projections from the medium's body.' (E. E. Fournier D'Albe in Schrenck-Notzing, 1920)

Rapping
'A rap, clear, distinct, and free, as if made on, or within the table, by a piece of watch-spring.' (*Blackwood's Edinburgh Magazine*, 1853)
'Sounds, like raps or detonations, are heard on the table, the chairs, the walls, or the floor, often varying in power and tone.' (*The Spiritual Magazine*, 1860)

Without apparent theology or dogma, only the séance or trance as its central rite, Spiritualism could take myriad forms as its followers chose. A religion to some, scientific inquiry to others, a vehicle for social justice or home entertainment for the rest.[410] Most, if not all, of its adherents couched what they did in Christian terms, even if they had 'Red Indian' spirit guides. The Spiritualists often described that what they did as a spiritual revolution, but it was simply a novel way to express the sentiments of Christianity. After all, Christianity taught that there was an afterlife, and the Bible made famous the necromancy of the Witch of Endor, demonstrating to the believer that our spirits lived on and could be called back to earth and communicated with. It did, however, take Protestantism one step further. If every man should be his own priest, then he could also be his own prophet, speaking to God without intermediaries and bringing back pearls of wisdom.

This was where the revolution lay. This was where the barricades went up, but it was not, ultimately, where the battle was fought – that would be between the mediums and the investigators, many of them distinguished men of science.

Making his report before the Congregational Association of New York and Brooklyn in 1853, Revd Charles Beecher saw two explanations for the phenomena of Spiritualism: the 'Pneumatic Theory' that the human spirit survived death, maintained its identity and could 'continue to act through some imponderable element'; and the 'Apneumatic Hypothesis' that the observed effects were psychological in nature, mediums being '*automatons*, moved by some power inherent in their own brains'. Author Samuel Byron Brittan commended Beecher for not taking the easy route of dismissing Spiritualism out of hand, which he characterized as typical of the clergy. Indeed, Beecher was forced to the conclusion that spirits of the deceased must be involved, but his early consideration of the psychological is notable and shows the sophistication of some of the researchers,

---

[410] Lehman, pp. 81–4, 88.

at least, at that time. In over 150 years, the debate has not advanced much beyond this impasse.[411]

A certain Monsieur Mannet, a French Bachelor of Letters, proposed to the *Scientific Review* that the marvellous phenomena of the séance were produced by the serving of tea spiked with a 'decoction of hemp-resin or haschish [*sic*]'. The editor of the *Scientific Review* said that he had tried it, in the interests of science of course, and could confirm its properties. *The Gentleman's Magazine*, however, pointed out that beverages were not always served at séances.[412]

The mystery of 'spirit-rapping' was claimed to have been solved almost as soon as it appeared. In 1854 a young German girl was holding a séance in Frankfurt am Main. Spirit-rappings were produced, a '*tap, tap,* by which questions were answered'. Dr Schiff sat forward in his seat: how did she make these noises? She sat apart, 'perfectly isolated', and made no perceptible movements. It seemed the usual mystery. Going home afterwards, an idea hit the doctor 'that the noise might be occasioned by straining the tendons and muscles'. We are all familiar with the sound of cracking knuckles, but this usually involves overt manipulation of the joint. Schiff experimented with several methods to find one that could produce the right sound whilst still being virtually undetectable. And he did:

> By simply displacing the *peronæus longus* which passes behind the ankle up the leg; such displacing being effected by a scarcely perceptible change in the position of the foot, and being accompanied by a loudish snap.[413]

---

[411] Samuel Byron Brittan, A Review of Revd Charles Beecher's *Report Concerning the Spiritual*, Partridge and Brittan,1853, pp. 9–10; Charles Beecher, *A Review of the Spiritual Manifestations*, G. P. Putnam & Co., 1853.

[412] 'Notes and Incidents', *The Gentleman's Magazine*, June–November, 1868, p. 259.

[413] *Notes and Queries*, 10.244, 1 July 1854, p. 5, footnote.

Schiff practised the technique 'until he got to be a first-rate "medium"'. He presented a paper on his findings to the Académie des Sciences in Paris, 12 June 1854, to their 'gratification and amusement', and it was widely reported in medical journals at the time. Some years later Jobert de Lamballe made similar observations in the diagnosis of a patient with spontaneously occurring 'rapping' sounds. The parents of the patient, a fourteen-year-old girl, were convinced that the origin was supernatural, but Lamballe demonstrated that the sounds were made by involuntary spasms of the peronæus brevis. From this he applied his findings to 'spirit-rapping', declaring it to be a naturally produced phenomenon. Oddly, it had passed almost unnoticed that three medical doctors from the University of Buffalo had reached the same conclusions even earlier, in 1851, and after examining the Fox sisters themselves.[414]

Professor Austin Flint and his colleagues Drs C. B. Coventry and Charles A. Lee visited the sisters, apparently paying a dollar each. At first they were 'surprised and puzzled by the loudness of the sounds, the apparent evidences of non-instrumentality [. . .] and the different directions from which they seemed to emanate'. But as they watched the performance – with Leah 'conducting' and Maggie apparently the source – they became convinced that Maggie was making the sounds herself. They just could not figure out how. They knew, as we all do, that joints could make snapping noises. One of the doctors had once been consulted by a patient with loud popping sounds coming from a joint as he walked. Another accidentally met a man who said his wife could produce such mysterious sounds. She had kept him ignorant of the cause, 'in jest', but on the doctors' asking she revealed that it was her knee-joint. The possibility that something similar was the cause of the 'spirit-rapping' was therefore evident.[415]

---

[414] *Notes and Queries*, 10.244, 1 July 1854, p. 5, footnote; *The Dublin Hospital Gazette*, 15 August 1854, p. 224; 'Audible Knockings of the Muscles', *American Medical Gazette*, 10.10, October 1859, pp. 747–9.

[415] Austin Flint, 'On the Discovery of the Source of the "Rochester Knockings" and

They wrote to the *Commercial Advertiser* on 17 February 1851, exposing the sisters as charlatans. Their evidence: that noisy knee-joint. The sisters saw the letter and wrote back, somewhat indignantly. They were not 'willing to rest under the imputation of being imposters' and offered themselves to a 'proper and decent examination'. A challenge had been made. It was accepted.[416]

It was not a duel to be fought on the heath at dawn. The two parties met in the evening in a comfortably furnished room in Buffalo; the doctors and the sisters with some selected supporters. The sisters sat on a sofa together and, after a pause, the rappings were heard, loud and rapid. The doctors asked the 'spirits' if they would consent to the examination. They rapped in the affirmative. The sisters were removed from the sofa and arranged on chairs, legs extended, feet separated, heels resting on cushions and their toes 'elevated'. The doctors had predetermined that this posture should prevent any knee-joint clicking. They sat back in a semicircle round the sisters and waited. They waited for more than thirty minutes: 'but the "spirits", generally so noisy, were now dumb'. They re-arranged the sisters, putting them back on the sofa, Leah sitting normally at one end, Maggie with her legs stretched out. The doctors asked the 'spirits' to make their presence known. Still nothing was heard. They let Maggie sit normally on the sofa. Rapping was heard. When the doctors held the sisters' knees, no sounds were heard. They concluded that the sounds were coming from the knee-joint of Maggie. And they told the sisters as much, at which point

on Sounds Produced by the Movements of Joints and Tendons', *The Quarterly Journal of Psychological Medicine and Medical Jurisprudence*, 3.3, July 1869, pp. 417–46, which also reprints the original articles by Flint et al.: 'Discovery of the Source of the Rochester Knockings', *Buffalo Medical Journal*, 6, March 1851; 'Rochester Knockings', *Buffalo Medical Journal*, 6 April 1851; and 'Spirit-Rappings in the French Academy of Sciences', *Buffalo Medical Journal*, 10, September 1854. The fact that so many women were 'spirit-rappers' they attributed to the wearing of skirts, which inadvertently concealed the slight movements made.

[416] Flint, pp. 423–6.

Maggie began to 'weep hysterically' and the investigation was brought to a close.[417]

These revelations, however, had little immediate impact on the careers of the Fox sisters, or on anybody else, it seems. Indeed, Flint had recourse to write to the Académie des Sciences in 1854 after reading about Dr Schiff's discoveries, asserting his claim to have got there first, and then to the *Quarterly Journal of Psychology* in 1869, reminding its readers that he had already investigated and resolved the matter.

The keen-eyed Revd Hiram Mattison had seen a report of the investigation and published it in his 1853 book *Spirit Rapping Unveiled!* He could add more to the list: the Revd H. O. Sheldon had discovered the trick and could rap with the best of them on his toe-joint; and the testimony of witnesses at the trial of the teenage medium Almira Bezely for the murder of her brother stated that she had made the rapping with her foot. In 1854 John Netten Radcliffe published the confession of a Mrs Norman Culvers who claimed to have been taught how to crack her toe-joints by Maggie Fox herself. But again these disclosures barely had an effect on the movement's popularity.[418]

Readers of the *New York Herald* opened their papers on 24 September 1888 to read in bold letters: 'God has not ordered it. A celebrated medium says the spirits never return.' It was an announcement by Maggie Fox. 'I am going to expose the very root of corruption in this spiritualist ulcer,' she declared. It was not just simple fraud, but in some cases a cover for 'shameless goings on that vie with the secret Saturnalia of the Romans'.[419]

A few weeks later Rueben Davenport, correspondent for the *New York Herald*, published a complete account in his *The Death-Blow to Spiritualism* with the full blessing and signed statement to that effect of the Fox sisters themselves. Maggie

---

[417] Flint, pp. 426–8, 431.

[418] John Netten Radcliffe, *Fiends, Ghosts and Sprites: Including an Account of the Origin and Nature of Belief in the Supernatural*, R. Bentley, 1854, p. 139.

[419] Quoted in Rueben Briggs Davenport, *The Death-Blow to Spiritualism*, G. W. Dillingham Co., 1888, p. 51.

had already written to the *Herald* on 14 May 1888 denouncing Spiritualism: 'I call it a curse, for it is made use of as a covering for heartless persons like the Diss De Barrs, and the vilest miscreants make use of it to cloak their evil doings [. . .] and a snare to all who meddle with it'. She sailed from Britain to America, intending to reveal all about Spiritualism. A *Herald* journalist was granted an interview ahead of her planned lecture. He described her as 'a small magnetic woman of middle age, whose face bears the traces of much sorrow and of a world-wide experience', adding that she 'was the most famous of the celebrated trio of witches'.[420]

Maggie blamed her older sister Leah. It was she, she said, who had 'made me take up with it'. She blamed her drinking on Spiritualism, saying 'I would drown my remorse in wine'. And she blamed the decline of her career on herself: 'I was too honest to remain a "medium"'.[421]

Before Maggie made her exposure, the *Herald* sought out the opinions of other Spiritualists. From one anonymous medium, the paper printed her opinion that 'I don't believe she [Maggie] can expose any fraud'. She added that 'I have heard that the Fox sisters are dreadfully addicted to drink. I don't know how far it is true, but I wouldn't believe anything she might say in way of exposure.' She finished by hinting at some sort of blackmail: 'May be [*sic*] she's out of money and thinks the spiritualists ought to do something for her.' Henry J. Newton, President of the First Spiritualist Society in New York, called them 'silly pretended revelations'. He had been present at séances given by the Fox sisters themselves and was thoroughly convinced that they were genuine, in spite of what the sisters themselves might say.[422]

Katie, now Mrs Catherine Fox Jencken, arrived on 9 October from London on the steamship SS *Persian Monarch*, apparently

---

[420] Published 27 May 1888, reproduced in Davenport, pp. 30–1, and 32–3.
[421] Davenport, p. 35–6.
[422] Davenport, pp. 45–7.

unexpectedly and immediately declared her intention to stand beside her sister. She, too, blamed Leah.[423]

The Academy of Music in New York was booked for 21 October 1888. It was an ugly Neo-Classical blockhouse that had declined from the grand opera produced in its heyday to a venue for vaudeville. But its 4,000 seats were packed to hear 'The Curse of Spiritualism'. Katie sat in a box near the stage. Spiritualists in the audience heckled. Maggie stood in the glow of the footlights 'trembling with intense feeling'. The audience waited with bated breath as she began: [424]

> That I have been chiefly instrumental in perpetrating the fraud of Spiritualism upon a too confiding public, most of you doubtless know. The greatest sorrow of my life has been that this is true, and though it has come late in my day, I am now prepared to tell the truth, the whole truth and nothing but the truth – so help me God![425]

It sounded like she was on trial. She was. But the real court was her conscience. A four-legged wooden stool was placed in front of her. She removed her shoe and placed her right foot upon it. 'The entire house became breathlessly still,' reported the *New York World*. Several 'little short, sharp raps' rang out. Mr Splitfoot had arrived. Three medical doctors were called up to the stage from the audience. Maggie still had her foot on the stool. More rappings were heard. The doctors bent over her foot and examined it. They 'unhesitatingly agreed that the sounds were made by the action of the first joint of her large toe'.[426]

The *Herald* asked Katie about the earlier manifestations and the finding of bones in the cellar of their old house in Hydesville. 'All humbuggery;' she said, 'every bit of it.' And she denounced

---

[423] Davenport, pp. 54–5.

[424] Davenport, pp. 55, 75.

[425] Davenport, p. 75.

[426] Davenport, p. 77.

her sister Leah's published retelling of the story as 'nothing but falsehood'.[427]

Hydesville was named after Dr Hyde, not Mr, but here there was still something like a split personality at work: two 'innocent' girls and their Mr Splitfoot. Back in that humble cottage in Hydesville in 1848, right at the beginning, before any great fuss had been made about the 'rappings', little Katie had already explained the whole phenomenon: an April Fool's joke. But no one had paid much attention to her words. Forty years later Maggie confessed that it had all been a fraud with Katie looking on, silent. Flint et al., Schiff and Lamballe were all vindicated. The great procession of spirits had indeed been a mere popping of tendons and joints, or had it?

The confession should have been the end of Spiritualism, but it was not. The Fox sisters could only speak for themselves and a year after making it, Maggie retracted her confession and returned to the séance room. Dr Isaac Funk, co-founder of the publishing house Funk & Wagnalls, said of her at the time that 'for five dollars she would have denied her mother'. Within the next four years all three sisters – Leah, Maggie and Katie – would be dead.[428]

In 1904 it was reported in the *Boston Journal* that the skeleton of a man had been found in the 'Spook House' as the Foxes' former home had come to be known. Now in the possession of William H. Hyde, the house had already been thoroughly searched, but 'an almost entire human skeleton' was said to have been found by schoolchildren 'between the earth and crumbling cellar walls'. In 1905 Dr Mellen told her story to the Medico Legal Society of New York. She had treated Maggie in her last bedridden days in a tenement on Ninth Street. Mellen was clear that Maggie could not move hand nor foot at the time, there was neither a hiding place for an accomplice, and yet she had heard

[427] Davenport, pp. 57–8.
[428] Isaac K. Funk, *The Widow's Mite and Other Psychic Phenomena*, Funk & Wagnalls, 1904, p. 241; Lewis Spence, *Encyclopedia of Occultism and Parapsychology*, 2 vols, Kessinger, 2003, vol. 1, p. 349.

the knockings – on the wall, on the ceiling, on the floor. Not only were they heard, but they answered in response to questions, just as they had all those years ago in Hydesville. Dr Mellen told the society 'she was as incapable of cracking her toe-joints at this time as I was'. These proofs, if they were proofs, came too late for the Fox sisters.[429]

What was the truth: the confession or the retraction? The psychology of the mediums is complicated, as Derren Brown's famous television experiment 'Séance' showed. With a group of students he recreated all of the classic phenomena of Spiritualism without the participants' conscious knowledge of what they were doing. The fraud, if it is one, seems in some cases to be perpetrated on us by our unconscious. The so-called evidence has only raised many more questions, and the possible answers seem a long way from the more comforting thought that the human personality can survive death.[430]

With the religious manifestation of Spiritualism in steep decline after the 1920s – although the Spiritualist paper *Psychic News* lingered on until 2010 – it found itself reinvented. For the New Age it became 'channelling'. There was nothing new about it. Helene Petrovna Blavatsky had 'channelled' the Mahatmas and written about it at length in the two volumes of *The Secret Doctrine* published in 1888. John Ballou Newbrough (1828–91) had 'channelled' the angels for his automatic typing marathon called *Oahspe*.

With the manifestation of phenomena so closely studied, tested and often exposed as fraudulent, the mediums reduced their repertoire, falling back on the less evidential and therefore less testable form of indirect communication. Derek Acorah (1950–), amongst others, has taken this new stripped down mediumship onto television, most notably with Yvette Fielding's *Most Haunted* series, introducing a new generation to supposed spirit communication.

---

[429] *Boston Journal*, 23 November 1904, reproduced in Todd, pp. 59–60 from 'Truth Crushed to Earth will Rise Again', *Banner of Light*, 3 December 1904; Spence, p. 349.

[430] 'Derren Brown: Séance', first broadcast on Channel 4, 31 May 2004.

Unlike revealed religion, such as Christianity, the claims of Spiritualism could be directly tested. Given that its claims were so tremendous in their implications – proof of the afterlife would overturn the developing materialistic worldview of science – the tests it would be put under would be strenuous. The *ad hoc* committees that had investigated the Fox sisters became more organized. Psychical research, as it was called, developed as a new scientific discipline, even if science did not want to acknowledge it until it wore the more respectable academic robes of parapsychology.

It would not be the last time that it would be claimed that the spirits were knocking on the door to the world of the living. When she was in her early teens, Sophie Harris claimed to have communicated with the dead just like the Fox sisters, only more than 150 years later. Around the year 2007 whilst staying overnight at her grandmother's house – reputedly over a hundred years old – she had the feeling of being watched when she went upstairs to bed. The door would swing open and whoever, or whatever, it was would stand there watching her, or so she thought. An aunt and great-aunt began to feel the presence, too. About a year later, once more in the house, she heard a series of knocking sounds. When she spoke, the rhythm changed. She asked it to knock once for 'yes', twice for 'no'. Her first question was 'Is there someone there?' One knock – yes. 'Can you talk to me without knocking?' Two knocks. 'Do you mean me any harm?' One knock.[431]

[431] 'Experiences', *Paranormal*, 56, February 2011, p. 70.

8. Science

The messenger burst into the palace. The empire of Astyages, last king of Media, had fallen. Cyrus the Persian was on the warpath. In his marble hall, Croesus, King of Lydia (modern Turkey) pondered his next move. Astyages had been the husband of his sister in a marriage to cement their alliance. Now he had been deposed and there was no one standing between Cyrus and Lydia. He saw that he must act now, before Cyrus' power grew greater, but should he offer treaty or war? The oracles would know, but which among them could really see beyond the sight of man?[432]

He sent messengers to all the great centres of divination in the sixth century BCE: the oracles of Apollo at Delphi, of Abae in Phocia, of Dodona, of Amphiaraus, of Trophonius, of Branchidae in Milesia, and of Ammon in Libya. His messengers were instructed to keep an accurate reckoning of the time and to consult the oracles on the hundredth day, asking them to describe what Croesus, back in his capital of Sardis, was doing at that moment. The messengers returned, having carefully written down the answers they had received. In order to test them, Croesus had devised an unlikely activity. He had cut up a lamb and a tortoise and cooked them in a bronze pot covered by a bronze lid. Croesus examined the bundle of reports. At Delphi the Pythian priestess had replied:

---

[432] Herodotus, *The Histories*, Bk 1, Ch. 46–53, trans. A. D. Godley, Harvard University Press, 1920.

I know the number of the grains of sand and the extent of the sea,
And understand the mute and hear the voiceless.
The smell has come to my senses of a strong-shelled tortoise
Boiling in a cauldron together with a lamb's flesh,
Under which is bronze and over which is bronze[433]

He had found his oracle. He offered up sacrifices of animals, gold and other riches 'to win the favour of the Delphian god'. When asked what he should do about Cyrus, the oracle answered that 'if he should send an army against the Persians he would destroy a great empire'. Cyrus led his soldiers into battle. In a typically Greek twist, it was Croesus' own empire that he destroyed. Being captured, Cyrus burnt him to death and conquered Lydia.[434]

Croesus, known now for his legendary wealth, might also be regarded as the first to have tested the abilities of self-professed psychics. Like the oracles of the ancient world, the claims being made by the mediums of the industrial age were so extraordinary, so potentially revolutionary, that they demanded investigation. That the initial investigations of the Fox sisters – as recounted by the less than detached Leah – were positive was a major factor in their success. What seems inexplicable is that when they were exposed as frauds, and even after they had confessed as much, people still believed that they, and the other mediums using the same techniques, were genuine. This desire, this demand, to believe, even in the face of the evidence, was and still is cruelly abused. But the chance that there could be a germ of truth in all this chaff has strained the abilities of many extremely able individuals. Mesmerism and Spiritualism created psychical research. Psychical research, in turn, led to the

---

[433] Herodotus, Bk 1, Ch. 47.

[434] Herodotus, Bk 1, Ch. 86. In Ch. 87–8 Herodotus said that Apollo was believed to have extinguished the flames and that Cyrus afterwards made him an adviser, but historically it seems more likely that he was executed. See Stephanie West, 'Croesus' Second Reprieve and Other Tales of the Persian Court', *Classical Quarterly*, 53, 2003, pp. 416–37.

development of parapsychology as a scientific discipline. It was, as Nietzsche said, the magicians who created this hunger for forbidden powers.

Mesmerism

His patients had already arrived and were waiting. He could hear the pianist playing quietly in a side room. He liked the effect. The gentle background music made a nice counterpoint to the sometimes dramatic demonstrations. He pushed open the door into a dimly lit room; a few trimmed wicks flickered and reflected in the mirrors arranged round the walls. Exotic perfumes hung in the air like invisible genies. His patients were standing around the apparatus, a large covered wooden tub with long articulated rods hanging down from the top like spiders' legs. He had more patients than he could treat individually, hence the 'Magnetic Basin', Baquet or Paropothus, as he variously called it. They turned as one as he came in. His purple robe swirled about him as he flourished his magnetic wand; brown eyes, black and glittering in the lamplight. There were gasps of anticipation. 'Magnetized' water loaded with iron filings and ground glass swished against the sides of the oak tub, hidden in the darkness.[435]

'There is only one illness,' he told them, 'and only one cure.'[436] To many, Franz Anton Mesmer was not a scientist. He was a magician. To others he was their saviour.

Mesmer undoubtedly thought of himself as a scientist – after all, he had had scientific training. Born in the village of Iznang on the shores of Lake Constance, Swabia, in 1734, he went on to study medicine at the University of Vienna. In 1766 he argued

---

[435] Mesmer's theatrical style of treatment is well attested. See for example, *Enc. Para.*, p. 337. Other details from the Paris police 'Aufenthalts Karte' reproduced in 'Some Researches of Dr Justinus Kerner', *The Spiritual Magazine*, vol. VI, no. 10, 1 October 1865, p. 434, and p. 449; Lehman, p. 32. Description of the tub based on the sole surviving example now in the Musée d'Histoire de la Médecine et de la Pharmacie, Lyon, France, other varieties of construction can be found in illustrations and descriptions from the period.

[436] Quotation in Waterfield, p. 71, from Mesmer, *Memoir*, 1779, p. 79.

in his doctoral thesis 'On the Influence of the Planets on the Human Body' that a 'subtle fluid [. . .] pervades the universe, and associates all things together in mutual intercourse and harmony'. It was by no means a radical proposition for the times, nor original, much of it being lifted from the work of Richard Mead, but it sufficed to see him through his *viva*. With a doctorate under his belt, he began practising medicine in Vienna from about 1768. Shortly afterwards he married a wealthy widow, Maria Anna von Posch, in St Stephen's Cathedral with the Archbishop of Vienna, no less, presiding. He set up practice at 261 Landstrasse in the most fashionable quarter of town and became a patron of the arts – Wolfgang Amadeus Mozart premiered his first opera, *Bastien und Bastienne*, at Mesmer's home.[437]

Mesmer could have continued in such style, doling out the inefficacious treatments of his time to the wealthy of Vienna, but the ideas fired in his doctoral work drove him to search the subject deeper. His meeting with the Hungarian Jesuit Maximilian Hell in the early to mid 1770s was to prove the turning point. Hell was famous for curing the sick by placing magnetized steel plates on their bodies. Mesmer abandoned the bleeding, blistering and opiates of regular medicine. Using and further developing Hell's technique Mesmer effected many cures, theorizing on the existence of 'animal magnetism', that is, a magnetic force of biological, as opposed to non-organic, origin. When Mesmer said 'There is only one illness', he was referring to the disruption of the flow of the magnetic fluid; 'and only one cure' was, of course, what would later be called Mesmerism.[438]

---

[437] 'Fridericus Antonius Mesmer', 'De planetarum influxu in corpus humanum', Vindibonae, 1766; quoted in Inglis, p. 141; 'Some Researches . . .', *The Spiritual Magazine*, p. 438; Robin Waterfield, *Hidden Depths: The Story of Hypnosis*, Routledge, 2003, pp. 66–7; Judith Pintar and Steven J. Lynn, *Hypnosis: A Brief History*, Wiley-Blackwell, 2008, p. 13.

[438] *Enc. Para.*, pp. 336–7, gives 1774 for the meeting with Hell; 'Some Researches . . .', *The Spiritual Magazine*, p. 438, gives 1772; Waterfield, pp. 66–7; Pintar and Lynn, p. 14.

He made a tour of Hungary, Switzerland and southern Germany to promote his new ideas. In Bavaria in 1775 he was asked to investigate Father Johann Joseph Gassner (1727–79), a country priest and exorcist extraordinaire. Like Mesmer, Gassner was producing near miraculous cures of the sick, but his theoretical underpinning was theology rather than medicine, possession rather than magnetism. The sick in their thousands, and not a few who were simply curious, were flocking to Gassner and asking him to cast out their demons. Gassner's technique was deceptively simple. He had dispensed with the rigmarole of the official rite of exorcism and laid hands on patients as any faith healer might today. He would begin by identifying the nature of the disease by asking, in Latin: 'If there be anything preternatural about this disease, I order in the name of Jesus that it manifest itself immediately'. If convulsions or other symptoms followed, then Gassner took this as a sign that demons were behind the illness. He would then command the demon to demonstrate the illness in various parts of the sufferer's body. He could also produce emotions as diverse as grief, anger and even silliness. Now having the demon perform at his command, he would drive the spirit out through a toe or finger.[439]

Not surprisingly, Mesmer's conclusion was that Gassner was unconsciously using animal magnetism to produce his cures. But for Mesmer, who had taken over Hell's magnetized plates, here was a demonstration that the same cures could be produced without the plates at all. Mesmer's report to the Bavarian Prince-Elector Maximilian III upheld the Enlightenment in the face of this outbreak of the supernatural, supplanting the old spirits with new forms of energy. It was a triumph for Mesmer: he was elected a member of the Bavarian Academy of Sciences. For Gassner it was defeat. Both the Bavarian government and the

---

[439] Pintar and Lynn, p. 15; Waterfield, p. 73; Podmore, p. 27. For a detailed study see H. C. Erik Midelfort, *Exorcism and Enlightenment: Johann Joseph Gassner and the Demons of Eighteenth Century Germany*, Yale University Press, 2005.

Church banned his activities and his books. He died in obscurity four years later.[440]

Despite these early successes, controversy would hound Mesmer out of Vienna. The Royal Academy in Berlin rejected his therapy as 'destitute of foundation and unworthy [of] the slightest attention'.[441] A setback, but that was not the reason he had to leave. The young musician Maria Theresia von Paradis – the protégé of the Empress Maria Theresa, after whom she was named – sought out Mesmer to treat her illness in the mid to late 1770s. Blind from infancy, she believed that the Swabian wonder-worker would be able to cure her. She was then about eighteen years old and her swollen and disfigured eye-sockets already bore witness to more brutal and less successful treatments. With her parents' blessing, she even moved in to Mesmer's house. It is reported that Mesmer was able to alleviate her condition. However, in consequence her musical abilities suffered and the pension from the empress (settled on her because of her blindness) was under threat. When her father came to remove her, she refused. There was a scene. Her father drew his sword. Her mother knocked the girl's head against a wall. She was, at last, dragged off. Rumour-mongers whispered that she had been receiving more than medical treatment. She suffered a relapse and Mesmer's enemies condemned his treatment as a fraud. Mesmer fell into a deep depression. Deciding to abandon his medical practice, his grand estate and his wife, he packed his equipment and left for Paris.[442]

It was as if Paris had been waiting for him. Alchemy, phrenology, and other occult sciences, were all the rage. As Henriette Louise von Waldner, Baroness d'Oberkirch, observed: 'It is

---

[440] Pintar and Lynn, p. 16; Waterfield, p. 74; Alan Gauld, *A History of Hypnotism*, Cambridge University Press, 1995, p. 3.

[441] Benjamin Franklin, *Animal Magnetism: Report of Dr Franklin and Other Commissioners, Charged by the King of France with the Examination of the Animal Magnetism as Practised at Paris*, H. Perkins, 1837, p. 47.

[442] Lehman, p. 33; Pintar and Lynn, pp. 17–18. Variations of Paradis' name include Marie-Thérèse, Paradies and Paradise.

certain that Rosicrucians, adepts, prophets and all that goes with them, were never so numerous or so much listened to'. This had been the Paris of the Comte de Saint-Germain and would yet be the Paris of Cagliostro, as much as it was of the Encyclopedists. Mesmer expected a ready audience. He moved into the Hôtel Bouret on the Place Louis-le-grand, today the Place Vendôme where one will find the Ritz Paris. The Baroness d'Oberkirch visited him there, reporting that 'his apartments were crowded from morning to night'. He had a letter of introduction to the Austrian ambassador, Count Florimund Merci-Argenteau. He made overtures to the Académie Royale des Sciences and the Société Royale de Médecine. Both of them snubbed him. Not everyone in Paris was ready to embrace his new ideas. Perhaps they did not like his German accent or Viennese connections.[443]

Mesmer retreated to the outlying village of Créteil and concentrated on building up a practice. His treatments became more theatrical. His patient list grew. As many as 200 people a day were seeking his help. He invented the 'baquet' in order to cope with them all. He moved back to Paris, taking a large property on the rue Coq Héron. Something like mass hysteria seemed to be sweeping the French capital. The Baroness d'Oberkirch noted that 'Magnetism became quite the fashion'. The novelist Stefan Zweig later called it Mesmeromania. A rumour that a tree in the Bois de Boulogne had been 'magnetized' caused Parisians in their hundreds to crowd round it, trying to get close enough to hug it and be cured. He found eager and in many cases influential students, such as Charles d'Eslon, a Doctor Regent of the Faculty of Paris and physician to the King's brother, the Comte d'Artois, and the wealthy

---

[443] Henrietta Louisa von Waldner, Baronne d'Oberkirch, *Memoirs of the Baroness d'Oberkirch*, 3 vols, Colburn and Co., 1852, vol. 2, p. 280; *Enc. Para.*, p. 337; Pintar and Lynn, pp. 18, 20; Waterfield, pp. 78–80; Frank Podmore, *Mesmerism and Christian Science: A Short History of Mental Healing*, George W. Jacobs & Co., 1909, pp. 4–5, 7; Gauld, p. 4. See also Mesmer, *Mémoire sur la Découverte du Magnétisme Animal*, 1779.

landowner the Marquis de Puységur. He won the sympathy of Queen Marie Antoinette and through her would even be offered a generous pension, which he ungraciously rebuffed. He formed a semi-Masonic secret society called the 'Society of Universal Harmony' to regulate the teaching and dissemination of his therapeutic method. By the mid 1780s there were an estimated 6,000 unsanctioned mesmerists operating in the Paris area. Between them Mesmer and d'Eslon were thought to have already treated some 8,000 patients. The Académie Royale des Sciences began to take notice.[444]

In 1784 a royal commission was established to investigate Mesmerism. It included the leading lights of the Académie Royale des Sciences and the University of Paris' Faculty of Medicine, such as the famous chemist Antoine-Laurent Lavoisier, Joseph Ignace Guillotin, eponymous inventor of the guillotine, and the American ambassador Benjamin Franklin. However, instead of Mesmer himself, they chose to observe his student d'Elson at work. They were not concerned whether or not Mesmerism worked, but specifically set out to determine whether or not the practice proved that there was a universal fluid as Mesmer claimed.

Franklin and the others watched d'Eslon arrange his patients round the baquet so that the articulated rods could be applied to the affected parts of their bodies. They could also be roped together; sometimes holding hands was sufficient. As well as the physician, a number of assistants brandished iron rods, about 10 to 12 inches in length, supposedly conductors of the magnetic force. The commission observed that some patients remained calm, others coughed or spat, complaining of mild pain, whilst a third group underwent violent and prolonged convulsions. 'Nothing can be more astonishing than these convulsions': they appeared to be contagious, could last up to three hours and put the victim entirely under the power of the mesmerist. It was

---

[444] D'Oberkirch, ibid.; Christopher Turner, 'Mesmeromania, or, the Tale of the Tub', *Cabinet*, 21, Spring 2006, n.p.; Waterfield, pp. 84, 86.

Mesmer's practice to make a separate, padded *Salle des Crises* available to receive the more violent convulsives. The commission described several cases in the report:[445]

Dame P—
'[. . .] the patient began to feel a nervous shuddering; she had then successively a pain in the back of her head, in her arms, a creeping in her hands, that was her expression, she grew stiff, struck her hands violently together, rose from the seat, stamped with her feet [. . .]'[446]

Mademoiselle B—
'[. . .] she felt a sensation of dejection and suffocation; to these succeeded an interrupted hiccup, a chattering of the teeth, a contraction of the throat, she complained of a pain in the loins; now and then she struck her foot with extreme quickness on the floor; afterwards she stretched her arms behind her, twisting them extremely [. . .]'[447]

The commission had brought an 'electrometer' and a 'needle of iron'. They found that the baquet had neither an electrical current nor a magnetic field. They could not see it, smell it nor feel it as d'Eslon said they would be able. None of the commission who underwent the treatment felt any better after it; if anything, some reported feeling worse. They decided 'to make experiments upon persons really diseased' and chose seven 'out of the lower class'. Again most felt nothing, but three experienced something, although what exactly the committee failed to discover. There was no 'physical agent', they said, capable of producing the supposed effects of Mesmerism. Furthermore, magnetism was least noted in those 'who have submitted to it with any degree of incredulity' and apparent only in those with 'an imagination more easily excited'.[448]

[445] Franklin, pp. 10–24.
[446] Franklin, p. 29.
[447] Franklin, p. 34.
[448] Franklin, pp. 10–24.

They concluded that universal magnetic fluid was 'absolutely destitute of proof' and 'that the imagination is the true cause of the effects attributed to the magnetism'. They were right. Mesmer himself had almost reached the same conclusion. 'It cannot be demonstrated,' he told the commission, 'that either the physician or the medicine causes the recovery of the patient.' D'Eslon had come closer: animal magnetism, he told the commission as it gathered in Franklin's house, 'might be no other than the imagination itself, whose power is as extensive as it is little known'.[449]

Despite the credentials of the commission, it was not very scientific. They went about their investigation in an *ad hoc* manner. They readily explained away observed effects and relied for a great part of their evidence upon the experiments of Dr Jumelin, a practising doctor but an untrained mesmerist with a connection to the university. They went so far as to declare Mesmerism dangerous, although they had no proof to that effect. It would not pass muster today, but the commission's report destroyed Mesmer. Within weeks of publication, 20,000 copies had been sold. The Public Ministry were a hair's breadth from outlawing magnetism. The Académie had every practitioner struck off the register, the well-connected d'Eslon included. Criticism and ridicule came from every corner: from the popular stage as much as from academia. He was savagely satirized in the plays of Pierre-Yves Barré and Jean-Baptiste Radet. To compound matters, von Paradis was in town and Mesmer unwisely attended the concert. It was clear to everyone that she was as blind as ever. A French cartoon, *Le Magnétisme dévoilé* of 1784, showed a scene like a Witches' Sabbath: Franklin brandishing his report as Mesmer escapes on a broomstick, leaving a young woman – von Paradis? – blindfold and *déshabillé*, in a state of partial undress.[450]

---

[449] Franklin, pp. 33, 41, 43 – Franklin notes that d'Eslon had made a similar remark as early as 1780; Pintar and Lynn, p. 21; Inglis, p. 143.
[450] Franklin, p. 42; Waterfield, pp. 92–3; Turner, n.p.

Mesmer disappeared. He left Paris without telling even his closest disciples his plans. For the next twenty years some few hints of his existence are scattered across Europe. He died of a stroke in 1815 in a village not far from Iznang.[451]

Away from the scandal and intrigue of the capital, sequestered at his large estate in Buzancy, near Soissons, Armand-Marie-Jacques de Chastenet, Marquis de Puységur, was on leave from the army and finding himself at a loose end he decided to try out Mesmerism on his tenants. It was early 1784 and Mesmer had yet to fall. His brothers had talked him into joining the Society of Universal Harmony and for his 100 louis d'or subscription he had been given some lessons in the new therapy.[452]

Victor Race, a twenty-three-year-old shepherd confined to bed with fever and inflammation of the lungs (*fluxion de poitrine*), was one of his first subjects. Puységur made the mesmeric passes, but instead of becoming violently convulsed, Race appeared to fall asleep. Strangely, even asleep he could still answer his master's questions. He could get up and walk about. He even appeared to have a different personality. Gone was the dull shepherd; in his place was someone of intelligence who spoke about the other self in the third person. Puységur thought it was the 'perfect crisis', but adjusting his terminology he called the state 'mesmeric somnabulism' or 'magnetic sleep'. He was later able to get the mesmerized Race to do things simply by silently willing them. Even more surprisingly, Race could diagnose his own illness and prescribe treatments for it, and not just for his own illness. Others performed similarly. They even developed more paranormal powers of clairvoyance (in both its original French sense of seeing clearly and its later supernatural sense) and prophecy.[453]

---

[451] Pintar and Lynn, p. 22; Waterfield, p. 100.

[452] Pintar and Lynn, p. 23, give 1784; Waterfield, p. 105, gives 1783; Podmore, p. 71, gives 1784. See A. M. J. Chastenet de Puységur, *Mémoires pour Servir a l'Histoire et a l'Etablissement du Magnétisme Animal*, n.p., 1784, and *Du Magnétisme Animal, Consideré dans ces Rapports avec Diverses Branches de la Physique Générale*, Desenne, 1807.

[453] Pintar and Lynn, pp. 23–4; Waterfield, pp. 105–8, 112; Podmore, pp. 72–4;

The Revolution put an end to further experiments. The mesmeric societies that had spread throughout France were disbanded. Puységur had set up his own society to teach his technique and by 1789 had over 200 members. This, too, was dissolved. Puységur spent some years in prison, but escaped the upheaval with his life and, in time, would return to Mesmerism. Many of those who had sat on the commission would not be so lucky.[454]

Ultimately, what was the difference between Gassner and Mesmer, except one of terminology? Exorcism and magnetism, spirits and 'subtle fluids' were simply names for unknown quantities. Mesmer had vanquished exorcism with his 'science', but science had ultimately claimed him, too. Competing interpretations of the paranormal had been trounced by the sceptics. His therapy had brought relief to hundreds of sufferers of diverse disorders, but the grey eminences had swept all that aside in defence of their ivory towers. Mesmer had laid the foundation for his disciple Puységur's discovery of 'magnetic somnambulism' and what Scotsman James Braid would later call 'hypnotism', a technique so powerful that patients might go under the knife with no more than words for an anaesthetic. He had opened a door on inexplicable extra-sensory perceptions, but, like the poet Shelley's Ozymandias, whose shattered statue lies half-buried in the desert sands, only a fragment of Mesmer's reputation remains: one sole surviving 'baquet' in the Musée d'Histoire de la Médecine et de la Pharmacie, Lyon, France.[455]

Sean O'Donnell, 'Science and Psi: A Largely Temporal Phenomenon?', *Paranormal Review*, 33, January 2005, p. 29.

[454] Pintar and Lynn, p. 27; Waterfield, p. 119; Podmore, p. 85.

[455] For further reading see Adam Crabtree, *Animal Magnetism, Early Hypnotism, and Psychical Research, 1766 to 1926: An Annotated Bibliography*, Kraus International Publications, 1988. 'Mesmerism' was also used successfully in place of anaesthetic, for example, by the Scottish surgeon James Esdaile from 1845, see Pintar and Lynn, p. 41, or Gauld, p. 221.

Psychical Research

> A human Skull! I bought it passing cheap,
> No doubt 'twas dearer to its first employer!
> I thought mortality did well to keep
> Some mute memento of the Old Destroyer.
> – Frederick Locker, *London Lyrics*, 1881

It was a London winter, wet and mild under leaden skies. Jaundiced and grey winter fogs crawled along the Thames. In Finchley, far from the polluted miasma, a balding professor with a neatly clipped beard was walking down Hendon Lane to the Villa Rosa, home of a well-known journalist. The professor, William Fletcher Barrett (1844–1925), lectured on physics at the new Royal College of Science for Ireland in Dublin and would later be knighted. The journalist, Edmund Dawson Rogers (1823–1910), had the look of a country parson about him: thin hair brushed back and left to grow over the collar; a long, straggling beard, square-cut, hung down like a napkin across his neck, a bright light shone in his eyes behind the polished glass of small oval spectacles. He had founded the National Press Agency and was then still managing it. He had a reputation for 'blunt frankness' but offset it with an engaging good humour. The professor would later be characterized as 'vain and querulous'; he was undoubtedly ambitious. But the two did not meet to discuss physics, the end of the First Boer War, or the rise of the Muslim extremist known as the Mahdi in Sudan. They met to talk about Death and his imminent redundancy.[456]

In flickering candlelight, Rogers had seen Daniel Dunglas Home give a séance in London with raps, table levitations and

---

[456] Edmund Dawson Rogers, *The Life and Experiences of Edmund Dawson Rogers, Spiritualist and Journalist*, Office of 'Light', 1911, pp. 5, 43; Fraser Nicol, 'The Founders of the SPR', *Proceedings of the Society of Psychical Research*, 55, March 1972, pp. 341–2. On the fog: Max Schlesinger, *Saunterings In and About London*, N. Cooke, 1853, p. 84. See Alan Gauld, *The Founders of Psychical Research*, Schocken, 1968.

disembodied accordion playing. Across the country people were falling into mesmeric trances and exhibiting clairvoyance, talking to the dead in séances, or hunting real ghosts down to their lairs for fun. Mesmerism had reached Britain by the 1830s. It was widely spread when Spiritualism joined the scene in the 1850s. The publication of Catherine Crowe's *Night-Side of Nature* in 1848 had kindled a popular interest in apparitions and related subjects. Cambridge University had its 'Ghost Society' (1851) and Oxford its 'Phasmatological Society' (1879); and The Ghost Club was founded in London in 1862, tracing its beginnings to Trinity College, Cambridge, in the 1850s. Although Sir William Crookes had abandoned psychical research in the face of scandal and the hostility of his peers, there was still a desire to investigate these phenomena more exactly.[457]

Barrett and Rogers sat up late into the night as the professor recounted his paranormal experiences. Since reading a paper on thought-transference to the British Association at Glasgow in 1876, Barrett had been pushing for the establishment of a committee to examine the field in more depth. It was, claimed Rogers, he who suggested that a society be set up 'to attract some of the best minds' to the subject.[458]

Scientists and Spiritualists came together on 6 January 1882 to discuss what could be done. Rogers had invited them to the headquarters of the British National Association of Spiritualists at 38 Great Russell Street, opposite the British Museum, and Barrett presided. The scene of ghost-haunted séances since 1875, it is now a fish and chip shop. Joining them were Frederic W. H. Myers

---

[457] Gordon Stein (ed.), *The Encyclopedia of the Paranormal*, Prometheus Books, 1996, p. 707, incorrectly gives 'Phantasmological'; Rogers, pp. 35–6; Sir Charles Oman, 'The Old Oxford Phasmatological Society', *Journal of the Society of Psychical Research*, 33, March–April 1946, pp. 208–12; Alan Murdie, 'A Very Brief History of the Ghost Club', www.ghostclub.org.uk, 2009, accessed 16 December 2010. The Cambridge group is also sometimes referred to as the Cambridge Ghost Club, as by Nandor Fodor, *Encyclopedia of Psychic Science*, Arthurs Press, 1934.
[458] Rogers, p. 46.

(1843–1901), MA, a former Fellow of Trinity College, Cambridge, Edmund Gurney (1847–88), MA, another former Fellow of Trinity, and the sceptical but vigorous researcher Frank Podmore (1856–1910), a civil servant. They decided to form the Society for Psychical Research (SPR) and persuaded Henry Sidgwick (1838–1900) to be their first president. Sidgwick was another Trinity man, a former member of the Cambridge Ghost Society and shortly to become professor of moral philosophy at Cambridge University. The SPR was formally constituted on 20 February 1882. The society's stated goal was 'to investigate that large body of debatable phenomena designated by such terms as mesmeric, psychical and spiritualistic', expressly 'without prejudice or prepossession of any kind'. By the end of the year they had 150 members who shared these aims.[459]

They took rooms at 14 Dean's Yard, around the corner from Westminster Abbey in London, then the home of SPR member Dr William H. Stone, Fellow of the Royal College of Surgeons and physician to the Clergy Mutual Assurance Society. Sidgwick donated 150 books on psychical research to begin their library, with the other founding members adding more. A special dark room and powerful electro-magnet were installed for experiments. Their accounts to the year end showed a then handsome figure of £216 and 15 shillings.[460]

Its membership never exceeding a 1,000 in the Victorian period, it nonetheless became something of a national institution. Serving Prime Minister William Gladstone, Alfred, Lord Tennyson, John Ruskin, the future Prime Minister (1902–5) Arthur Balfour, Lord Rayleigh and others, all lent their support; the Revd Charles Lutwidge Dodgson, better known by his

---

[459] *Enc. Para.*, p. 708; 'Objects of the Society', *Proceedings of the Society for Psychical Research*, 1, 1882, pp. 3–6; Janet Oppenheim, *The Other World: Spiritualism and Psychical Research in England, 1850–1914*, Cambridge University Press, 1988, p. 57; Roger Luckhurst, *The Invention of Telepathy, 1870–1901*, Oxford University Press, 2002, p. 51; Peter Hallson, 'The Birth of the SPR', *Paranormal Review*, July 2002, pp. 3–5; Nicol, p. 344.

[460] 'Anniversary Meeting', *Proceedings of the Society for Psychical Research*, 1, 1883, pp. 158–60; *Debrett's Peerage*, Dean & Son, 1876, p. 16.

pen-name Lewis Carroll was a member, as was Robert Louis Stevenson. Barrett travelled to the USA and instituted an American Society for Psychical Research, founded in Boston in January 1885, with the astronomer Simon Newcomb as its first president and the famous psychologist William James (1842–1910) as its most notable member. Even with such august members and supporters, the SPR still met with as much sceptical hostility from other scientists, medical doctors and academicians as anyone studying the field today.[461]

The formation of the SPR would, nevertheless, herald a 'golden age' of psychical research. There was a Committee on Thought-Reading, a Committee on Haunted Houses, a Committee on Mesmerism, a Committee on Spontaneous Experiences, a Committee on Physical Phenomena, a Literary Committee, and the Reichenbach Committee on the perception of 'self-luminous' substances as described by the Baron Karl von Reichenbach.[462] Despite the professors on the council and the great and the good among its supporters, most of the spade work would be done by amateurs, albeit Victorian amateurs in the best tradition deserving of that name. From its beginning up until the turn of the century, the society's efforts took three main directions: telepathy, then called thought-reading or 'thought-transference' until Myers coined the new term; what they termed 'hallucinations'; and mediums. The sea-faring nation that had become the world-straddling British Empire was now also a soul-faring one, taking that empire further than anyone had before, beyond the prison of the body, beyond the veil of death.[463]

The first committee to make its report was that on thought-reading. An article published in *Nature* the year before had already dismissed the whole subject as 'so puerile a hypothesis'. On 17 July the society gathered in Willis's Rooms, otherwise

---

[461] *Enc. Para.*, pp. 582, 708; 'First Report on Thought-Reading', *Proceedings of the Society for Psychical Research*, 1, 1882, p. 13, and 1883, pp. 322, 326; Nicol, p. 350.

[462] See *Proceedings of the Society for Psychical Research*, 1, 1882–3.

[463] *Enc. Para.*, pp. 708–9; Nicol, p. 350.

known as Almack's – a suite of assembly rooms on King Street, St James's, that had been famous for its grand balls and concerts – to hear the case for the opposition.[464]

A Revd A. M. Creery of Buxton, Derbyshire, described as 'clergyman of unblemished character', had discovered that four of his five children, all girls, had the apparent ability to read thoughts. Barrett, Gurney and Myers duly arrived on the scene. Over six days in April 1882 they made 382 trials of guessing objects, cards, numbers and fictitious names with three of the children: Alice, Maud and Mary. They took precautions against such things as 'involuntary actions', unconscious lip movement and so on, by having the child wait outside the room when the item was chosen and having her look to the floor when she came in. They ruled out deception and collusion, since they were obviously not cheating themselves. Only chance remained. They calculated that the average number of successes by an 'ordinary guesser' would be 7.33. The children got 127 right on the first guess. Sometimes they were allowed subsequent guesses, bringing the number of 'hits' to 202. Calculating the odds on making eight consecutive successful guesses with the cards, they reckoned they were over 142 million to one. The odds for eight consecutive successful guesses with names they thought were 'something incalculably greater'. They felt they were safe to rule out coincidence.[465]

It seemed like real proof, but the girls' ability began to decline and Gurney, in later tests, caught them cheating by signalling to each other. The reverend, then a Corresponding Member of the SPR, wrote to the society expressing his 'intense pain' at the

---

[464] William Fletcher Barrett, Edmund Gurney and Frederic W. H. Myers, 'First Report of the Committee on Thought-Reading', *Proceedings of the Society for Psychical Research*, 1, 1882, p. 34; George Romanes, 'Thought-Reading', *Nature*, 23 June 1881; Peter Cunningham, *Hand-Book of London*, 2nd ed., John Murray, 1850, p. 10.

[465] Barrett, Gurney and Myers, pp. 20–7. An earlier series of trials had been made, see Balfour Stewart, 'Note on Thought-Reading', *Proceedings of the Society for Psychical Research*, 1, 1882, pp. 35–42, and A. M. Creery, 'Note on Thought-Reading', in the same issue, pp. 43–6.

revelations and assured them that he did not believe that such subterfuges had been used in the earlier experiments. It made no difference: the evidence was tainted; the proof had vanished like morning mist.[466]

The work on hallucinations began by collecting first-hand accounts from those who had experienced, whilst awake, sober, sane and not suffering from fever, a hallucination – a 'phantasm' as they also called it – of a living thing (human or animal), sounds produced by it, or an emotional awareness of it. Naturally, some of these experiences were simply hallucinations, but they found a number of cases that appeared to be something more. These they called 'veridical'. Such cases included 'crisis apparitions' when someone experiences something uniquely related to a person (appearance, voice) they know at a time when that person undergoes a crisis, very often death; 'collective percipience' (mass hallucination) when more than one person experiences the same phenomenon; and accounts of what we would generally term hauntings, the experience repeated amongst different people at different times of encountering the same thing at the same place.

In 1886 Gurney, Myers and Podmore published the results of their labours in the two-volume, 1,400-page *Phantasms of the Living*. It made *The Times* on the day it was published, 30 October. In all, 701 cases were discussed, of which 352 'phantasmal' experiences were classified as high-quality evidence. Building on their work on 'thought-transference', Gurney theorized that crisis apparitions were mental projections produced by the percipient after becoming telepathically aware of the crisis being experienced by the other. Work continued after

---

[466] The cheating was first brought to notice in an editorial note, *Journal of the Society of Psychical Research*, 3, October 1887, p. 164. A. M. Creery, letter to the Editor, *Journal of the Society of Psychical Research*, 3, November 1887, pp. 175–6. Edmund Gurney, 'Note Relating to Some of the Published Experiments in Thought-Transference', *Proceedings of the Society for Psychical Research*, 5, 1888, pp. 269–70. See the discussion of this case in Matthew Colborn, 'The Decline Effect in Spontaneous and Experimental Psychical Research', *Journal of the Society of Psychical Research*, 71, 2007, p. 2.

Gurney's untimely death two years later, culminating in the monumental 'Census of Hallucinations'. Completed in 1894, the census had surveyed 17,000 people on their experiences of hallucinations, including 'phantasms of the dead'. With all this evidence to work with, Sidgwick and the others determined that crisis apparitions could not be explained away: 'Between deaths and apparitions of the dying-person a connexion exists which is not due to chance alone. This we hold as a proved fact'.[467]

With most of the mediums it was the, by now, old familiar story: lies, deceit and disappointment. The 'physical mediums' – those claiming to be able to produce materializations from the spirit world – were the worst. The 'mental' mediums – those claiming to be in contact with the spirits – were less often detected in fraud. Among them, Leonora Piper is thought to have presented the best evidence for the spirit world; Helena Petrovna Blavatsky and William Eglington, the worst.[468]

Discovered by William James in America in 1885, Leonora Evelina Piper, née Simonds (1859–1950), was investigated on and off for the better part of thirty years. She was born in Nashua, New Hampshire, in 1859. At 22 she married a Boston clerk, William J. Piper. Some time in her mid-twenties, whilst visiting the blind medium J. E. Cocke, she spontaneously went into a trance and a supposed spirit, an Indian girl with the bizarre name of Chlorine, began speaking through her. In time Martin Luther, Commodore Cornelius Vanderbilt, Longfellow, George Washington, Abraham Lincoln, Johann Sebastian Bach, Julius Caesar, even Richard Hodgson and Myers after their deaths, and others, would all be claimed to have spoken through her.[469]

She became a professional medium performing as 'Mrs Piper'. Consequently, the American Society was obliged to

---

[467] *Enc. Para.*, p. 709; Henry Sidgwick, et al., 'Report on the Census of Hallucinations', *Proceedings of the Society for Psychical Research*, 10, 1894, p. 394; Nicol, pp. 353–5.

[468] *Enc. Para.*, p. 709.

[469] *Enc. Para.*, p. 535; Nicol, p. 362.

hand over $10 a sitting: she appears as the very thinly veiled 'Mrs P' in their records. William James learnt of her through the glowing recommendation of his mother-in-law. He and his wife Alice began attending séances in 1885. Alice immediately fell under her spell. James, too, would later pronounce:[470]

> Taking everything that I know of Mrs P into account, the result is to make me feel as absolutely certain as I am of any personal fact in the world that she knows things in her trances which she cannot possibly have heard in her waking state.

For all his reputation, William James' approach was lackadaisical, as he was compelled to concede. He took no notes. He made no tests. He just sat there. His opinion is just that: unverifiable hearsay. Piper was, however, keenly scrutinized by the British. Whilst still in America, Hodgson had her followed by private investigators. When she arrived in Britain in 1889, Oliver Lodge 'overhauled the whole of her luggage' and, with Myers, inspected her letters, but only with her permission did they read them. She was also lodged in members' houses or other chosen locations during her stay in order to provide better opportunities for surveillance and control. The first séance took place on 30 November 1889 at Myers' house in Cambridge. Myers sat behind a curtain to take notes whilst Lodge watched Piper's performance:[471]

> Mrs Piper sat still, leaning forward in her chair, and holding my hands. For some time she could not go off, but at last she said, 'Oh, I am going,' the clock happened to strike one (for a half hour) and she twitched convulsively, ejaculated 'don't,'

[470] William James, 'Certain Phenomena of Trance: (5) Part III', *Proceedings of the Society for Psychical Research*, 6, 1890, p. 651.

[471] Nicol, p. 351; James, p. 651; Frederic W. H. Myers, Introduction to 'A Record of Observations of Certain Phenomena of Trance', *Proceedings of the Society for Psychical Research*, 6, 1890, pp. 438–9; Oliver Lodge, 'Account of Sittings with Mrs. Piper. Formal Report', *Proceedings of the Society for Psychical Research*, 6, 1890, pp. 446–7.

and went into apparent epilepsy [. . .] Gradually she became
quiet, and still holding my right hand, cleared her throat in a
male voice, and with distinctly altered and hardened features,
eyes closed and unused the whole time.[472]

After his detectives failed to find evidence of fraud, Hodgson
allowed himself to believe in the sincerity of her mediumship.
Lodge made the cautious assessment that 'much of the information she possesses in the trance state is not acquired by
ordinary commonplace methods', but was certain that she was
'utterly beyond and above suspicion'. Nonetheless, he attributed the source, not to spirits, but to secondary consciousnesses
and trance personalities receiving information telepathically. He
glibly disposed of muscle-reading and 'unconscious-indication'.
Myers did not like 'trance-utterances' and for a good reason,
'since real and pretended trance-utterances have notoriously
been the vehicle of much conscious and unconscious fraud'.
But even Myers had to admit that Piper's 'utterances show that
knowledge has been acquired by some intelligence in some
supernormal fashion'. Even so, he was aware that Piper's trance
personality 'Dr Phinuit' frequently fished for information and,
for a spirit who claimed to be a French doctor, knew precious
little of French or medicine.[473]

On 20 October 1901 Piper shocked her followers with a two-
and-a-half page article in the *New York Herald* disavowing her
spiritual powers. Under the headline 'I Am No Telephone to the
Spirit World', Piper announced that she was retiring from mediumship with the bombshell that 'I must truthfully say that I do
not believe that spirits of the dead have spoken through me'.
She did not, in fact, retire. There would be other séances and
other investigations. She lived out her last years in Boston, dying
in 1950 at the age of 91.[474]

[472] Lodge, p. 444.
[473] Lodge, pp. 443, 447–9, 451; Myers, pp. 430, 440; James, p. 655.
[474] *Enc. Para.*, pp. 537–8.

Helene Petrovna Blavatsky (1831–91) – 'Madame Blavatsky' – is still a name to conjure with in occult circles. Her organization, the Theosophical Society, is still going strong. In the nineteenth century her reputation was enormous and she was making bold paranormal claims. The SPR felt duty bound to investigate. In 1884 the council appointed a committee and the committee sent Hodgson off to India after the evidence. It would result in what Fraser Nicol has called 'the most sensational report on physical phenomena ever published by the SPR'. Often called the Hodgson Report, the committee concluded that Blavatsky was not, as she claimed, 'the mouthpiece of hidden seers', but 'one of the most accomplished, ingenious, and interesting imposters in history'. Even before the investigation, she had already confessed earlier indiscretions to Alexander Aksakof (1832–1903). Much of what she later passed off as messages from Koot Hoomi and other discarnate 'Mahatmas' was plagiarized from other works – something that was noticed by at least one author himself – and the rest was what Dr Theodore Besterman (1904–76), investigating officer for the SPR from 1927 to 1935, would memorably call 'muddled rubbish'.[475]

In 1886 the most famous medium in the world was William Eglington (1857–1933). He had produced apports out of thin air, manifested physically solid spirits, even levitated himself to the ceiling, but he was particularly famed for his slate-writing in broad daylight. He was investigated by Sidgwick's wife Eleanor Mildred, an able researcher in her own right and Principal of Newnham College. In her report for the SPR she concluded that she had 'no hesitation in attributing the performances to clever conjuring'. Eglington countered by publishing forty-four pages of favourable testimony in *Light* and called on Spiritualist supporters in the SPR to resign. Only Stainton Moses and five others saw fit to obey the call. Worse, one of Eglington's previously most impressed clients, S. John Davey, agreed to take part

---

[475] Nicol, pp. 358–9.

in a series of experiments with Hodgson. Playing the role of medium in a fake slate-writing séance, it became painfully clear to Davey how unreliable the sitters' observations were. They saw things that did not take place, generally misinterpreted what did happen and forgot much more besides. Disappointing for the Spiritualists, it was nonetheless a landmark study in the deficiencies of eye-witness testimony that is still relevant today.[476]

Rogers himself resigned soon after the SPR's founding. Like Stainton Moses and the others, he objected to the direction the society was taking. In the hands of Sidgwick, Gurney and Myers it was holding true to science and they felt that Spiritualism, in consequence, was suffering. About two-thirds of the original council had been Spiritualists, but by 1887 that had fallen to a quarter. The SPR's decision to hold no prejudices or prepossessions suited unbiased research but not the faith of the believers. Rogers would instead put his energies into the London Spiritualist Alliance, which he founded with Moses, and into editing its periodical *Light*.[477]

For Rogers, in the oft-quoted words of Philip James Bailey, 'Death is another life [. . .] Larger than this we leave and lovelier'. These were sentiments the scientists would not have disagreed with. For Myers, death as an absolute finality made life pointless. Although he had discredited the Creery children and unmasked a score of cheating mediums, Gurney later remarked that he 'felt the world *without* survival [of the spirit] hopelessly meaningless and largely positively evil'. The sceptics wanted to believe, but, unlike the Spiritualists, that belief had to have a firm basis in fact, for a world based on toe-joints and trickery was worse than meaningless.[478]

---

[476] Nicol, pp. 356–8; Eleanor Mildred Sidgwick, Mr. Eglington, *Journal of the Society of Psychical Research*, June 1886, pp. 282–7.

[477] Nicol, p. 344.

[478] Nicol, p. 347; Rogers, p. 65; Philip James Bailey, *Festus: A Poem*, W. Pickering, 2nd ed., 1845, p. 259.

Parapsychology

On 7 May 1915 the heavy fog that had shrouded the Irish Sea was starting to lift. Kapitänleutnant Walther Schweiger ordered Kaiserliche Marine submarine U-20 to surface. They had been patrolling off the southern coast of Ireland as part of the German U-boat blockade of Britain since 30 April. Oil was running low and there were only two torpedoes left, and not their best ones. Standing in the conning tower, Schweiger swept his binoculars across the sea. At 14:20 (13:20 GMT) Schweiger spotted smoke stacks on the horizon. 'I saw it was a great steamer,' he said afterwards. He ordered diving stations to periscope depth and closed at high speed to 2,296 feet. He launched a single torpedo.[479]

On lookout Able Seaman Leslie Morton saw the telltale wake of the onrushing danger: 'Torpedo coming on starboard side!' It struck 9½ feet below the waterline, punching through to the boiler room before exploding. Almost immediately there was another, much larger explosion. The ship was going down rapidly. Passengers surged on deck.[480]

Among them was Ramon. Around him, people were panicking, frightened, trying to struggle into life-jackets, shouting and screaming in English, a language foreign to him. Ramon had fled Havana under an assumed name for political reasons. That may or may not have been how he got the scar over his left eyebrow. He tore a sheet from his pocket book and scrawled a hurried message. There was the sound of another explosion. He put the message in a bottle, corked it and threw it into the waves. Perhaps the wife and children he had left behind would someday read it. RMS *Lusitania* sank in eighteen minutes, taking with it 1,198 souls. But the story of Ramon would not be known until several years later.[481]

Extra-Sensory Perception (ESP) began in Mexico with a German doctor and a patient with insomnia. Dr Gustav

---

[479] Lowell Thomas, *Raiders of the Deep*, Periscope Publishing, 2002 [1928], pp. 94–5.
[480] Thomas, pp. 94–5; 'Lusitania', *Boy's Life*, May 1964, pp. 22–3.
[481] Thomas, pp. 94–7, 102.

Pagenstecher (1855–1942) was practising medicine in Mexico City in 1919 when an educated and well-to-do lady, Senora Maria Reyes de Z. – later identified as Zierold – came to see him about her sleeping problem. He proceeded to hypnotize her and assessing the depth of her trance state found that she had lost the use of all five senses, although, as she said, 'I can hear nothing except the voice of my hypnotist'. He must have been rather alarmed to have produced such a catatonic condition, but he discovered that if an object were placed in her hand she would automatically grasp it and give information about it – the technique known as psychometry. He tried various things out: a shoe, a tropical plant seed, stone fragments from ancient monuments and so on. When he gave her a piece of marble, Zierold described an open space where 'it seems they are building a town' with something like a church in the background. Pagenstecher did not know anything about the marble, but afterwards found out that it had come from the Forum Romanum. At second and third sittings, Zierold was able to supply more details and made a post-hypnotic sketch: 'it is clear that she had visualized the Forum, as it exists today, with great clearness'.[482]

Despite the apparent loss of her senses, Pagenstecher discovered that she would react as if a light had been shone into her eyes, not when one was actually shone into her eyes, but when Pagenstecher shone it into his own. All of her senses seemed to have been transferred to Pagenstecher. 'I can taste

---

[482] 'Dr Pagenstecher's Experiments in Psychometry', *Journal of the Society of Psychical Research*, 21, February 1924, pp. 216–19. See also Walter Franklin Prince, 'Psychometrical Experiments with Senora Maria Reyes de Z.', *Proceedings of the Society for Psychical Research*, 15, 1921, pp. 189–312, Journal of the American Society of Psychical Research, 16, 1922, 5–40, and Gustav Pagenstecher, 'Past Events Seership: A Study in Psychometry', *Proceedings of the American Society of Psychical Research*, 16, 1922, 1–136. Z. quoted in W. H. C Tenhaeff, *Aussergewöhnliche Heilkrafte*, Walter-Verlag, 1957, translation in *Journal of the Society of Psychical Research*, 39, March 1958, p. 200. Identification of Z. made incidentally in Alejandro Parra and Juan Carlos Argibay, 'Comparing a Free-Response Psychometry Test with a Free-Response Visual Imagery Test for a Non-Psychic Sample', *Journal of the Society of Psychical Research*, 71, April 2001, p. 92.

[. . .] sugar or salt when these substances are placed on Dr P.'s tongue. I can hear the ticking of a clock held to his ear'. For some reason Pagenstecher also weighed himself and his patient before and after the experiments. Bizarrely, he found that both of them lost weight, although this returned to normal within about half an hour.[483]

A friend of Pagenstecher's, then living in Japan, sent an envelope to a lawyer in Mexico City. Inside the envelope was a letter to Pagenstecher and two sealed envelopes. The letter explained that one of the envelopes contained a note written under conditions of great distress; the other a description of the note's writer. The letter asked Pagenstecher to give the envelope with the note to Zierold to 'read' in her particular way; neither envelope should be opened until the close of the experiment. Dr Walter Franklin Prince, research officer of the ASPR, made a journey in 1921 to see Zierold for himself and was present when Pagenstecher put one of the sealed envelopes into her hand.

Zierold described a ship, frightened people on deck; they were speaking English and trying to put on life belts. A man with a scar over his left eyebrow tore a page out of a notebook and wrote on it. There was an explosion and he threw the note, now sealed in a bottle, into the sea.

Pagenstecher and Prince broke the seals on the envelopes and took out a slip of paper from one. It was torn down one edge. In hastily written Spanish it read:

> The ship is sinking. Farewell my Luisa; see that my children do not forget me. Your Ramon. Havana. May God care for you and me also. Farewell.[484]

From the second envelope they took a short explanation of the circumstances of the note. It had been taken from a bottle that had been found off the coast of the Azores. Enquiries had been

---

[483] 'Dr Pagenstecher's . . .', pp. 216–19.
[484] 'Dr Pagenstecher's . . .', p. 218.

made at Havana. Someone using the name of Ramon P., physically remarkable for the scar over his left eyebrow, had disappeared in the 1910s. A wife, Luisa, and children were tracked down. His handwriting resembled that in the note. Luisa said that he had left for Europe and feared that he had perished with the *Lusitania*.[485]

Pagenstecher made his case to the Mexican Medical Society, which appointed an investigatory commission. They reported favourably, as did Prince for the ASPR. In 1922 Pagenstecher joined the SPR. In writing up his records of Zierold in 1924, he coined the term 'extra-sensory perception'.[486]

Parapsychology (*Parapsychologie*) began in Germany. The psychologist Dr Max Dessoir coined the term in 1889, but it did not gain wider currency until the 1920s. It first appeared in English in 1923, yet it was Baron Albert von Schrenck-Notzing's renaming of Alexander Aksakof's periodical *Psychische Studien* as the *Zeitschrift für Parapsychologie* ('Journal for Parapsychology') in 1926 that established the word and its connotations. In 1928 an Institut für Parapsychologie was established in Berlin. Finally, the publication of Hans Driesch's influential book *Parapsychologie* in 1932 brought the term into common usage.[487]

---

[485] There are a number of discrepancies in the account given: when describing the events around the note, Zierold said that it was night-time; Ramon P. was said to have disappeared in 1916 – it was an afternoon in 1915 when the *Lusitania* sank. For a critical interpretation see Wilhelm Gubisch, *Hellseher, Scharlatane, Demagogen? Kritik an der Parapsychologie*, E. Reinhard, 1961.

[486] Gustav Pagenstecher, *Aussersinnliche Wahrnehmung*, C. Marhold, 1924. For some later experiments see Gustav Pagenstecher, 'Experimentalberichte', *Zeitschrift für Parapsychologie*, in three parts from issue 4–6, April–June 1928.

[487] Max Dessoir, 'Die Parapsychologie', *Sphinx*, 7, 1889, pp. 341–4; still in its German form in T. Konstantin Oesterreich, *Occultism and Modern Science*, 2nd ed., English translation, Methuen, 1923, reviewed by Eric J. Dingwall, *Journal of the Society of Psychical Research*, 21, April 1923, pp. 78–80; Eberhard W. Bauer, 'Periods of Historical Development of Parapsychology in Germany', in D. Delanoy (ed.), *Proceedings of Presented Papers, The Parapsychological Association 34th Annual Convention*, 1991, pp. 18–34 – my thanks to Mr Bauer for sending this and other materials. The *Zeitschrift für Parapsychologie* was established in 1874 by Alexander Aksakof as *Psychische Studien* and was published under the new name from 1926, see the 1st ed., 1926, p. 1, online at http://www.

Up until then people had called what they were doing 'psychical research'. However, this was more than a change of name; it was also a change of emphasis. It put the research next to psychology, implying that the phenomena were a product of the mind, and it brought the research into the laboratory. Whilst the SPR could convert one of their offices into a dark room or séance room as required, it was done on an *ad hoc* basis, and much research was still being conducted under less than satisfactory conditions. With the advent of parapsychology came properly controlled experimental facilities. The era of the gifted amateur was giving way to the era of the professional scientist. Joseph Banks Rhine and William MacDougall, head of the Psychology Department at Duke University, specifically used 'parapsychology' to make the distinction between the old psychical research approach and the new experimental one.[488]

There had been earlier work in Germany, but as in the UK, it had concentrated on mediumship and was organizationally informal. The astrophysicist Friedrich Zöllner (1834–82), for example, had held a series of experimental séances in Leipzig from 1877–8 on the basis of which he argued – controversially – that space was four-dimensional. Max Dessoir had established the Berliner Gesellschaft für Experimental-Psychologie and investigated the medium Henry Slade in 1886. He had followed up on Dr W. Preyer's work on muscle reading and found that he, too, could produce apparently telepathic effects using Preyer's explanation of the method. In 1887 he was voted a corresponding member of the SPR. Schrenck-Notzing already had a well-equipped laboratory in Munich and from 1926 until his sudden death in 1929 he took a leading role in the recently renamed *Zeitschrift für Parapsychologie*.[489]

---

ub.uni-freiburg.de/index.php?id=zs_parapsychologie. Heather Wolffram, *The Stepchildren of Science*, Rodopi, 2009, p. 26.

[488] *Enc. Para.*, p. 496.

[489] Bauer, pp. 18–34; Max Dessoir, 'Experiments in Muscle-Reading and Thought-Transference', *Proceedings of the Society for Psychical Research*, 4, 1886, p. 111; *Journal of the Society of Psychical Research*, 3, October 1887, p. 1.

'Psychical research' continued in the UK, but, as in Germany, it was becoming more scientifically organized. A major step was Harry Price's National Laboratory of Psychical Research in London. Before the ghosts of Borley Rectory, Price had spent his time with the mediums. Elected a member of the SPR in 1920, he was in some ways carrying on the work of its founders in the séance room, but his relationship with the SPR would never be an easy one. He investigated the mediums William Hope and Willi Schneider in 1922, and Stella Cranshaw and Jean Guzik in 1923. He would also hold séances with Helen Duncan in 1931. In March 1925 he held the inaugural meeting of the National Laboratory of Psychical Research (NLPR) at the Royal Societies Club in London. In January 1926 it opened its doors at 16 Queensbury Place in South Kensington – premises shared with the London Spiritualist Alliance. It was a suite of six rooms on the top floor laid out as a laboratory, séance room, 'baffle chamber', dark room, office and a fully equipped workshop, all with enamelled name plates on the doors. Price boasted that the NLPR had 'the finest installation in the world for experimental research work in the field of psychic science'. Whether it was or not, it was certainly well-equipped. Price had stereoscopic cameras, an 'Optiscope', a dictaphone system, a flawless quartz crystal sphere, a specially designed 'transmitting thermograph', radioactive sulphide of zinc for making luminous paint, an electroscope, a galvanometer, and much more besides, all valued at £3,000. Price claimed that it was the first laboratory of its kind in Britain, a country, furthermore, without a 'permanent body of psychical research workers'. Eric Dingwall, the SPR's research officer, called these 'somewhat surprising remarks'. One of the first subjects to be studied there was Eleonore Zugun, the so-called 'poltergeist girl'.[490]

---

[490] Paul G. Adams, 'Harry Price Timeline – 1925–1929', http://www.harrypricewebsite.co.uk/Timeline/1925–1929.htm, 2004–2005, accessed 2 December 2010; Harry Price, 'A Model Psychic Laboratory', *British Journal of Psychical Research*, 1.1, May–June 1926, pp. 11–19; Eric J. Dingwall, 'Notes on Periodicals', *Journal of the Society of Psychical Research*, 23, June 1926,

Price approached both the French Institut Métapsychique International (in 1929) and the SPR (in 1930) with proposals of a merger, only to be rebuffed by both. However, his overtures to the University of London in 1933 to equip a Department of Psychical Research met with more success. A London University Council for Psychical Research was established, although, ultimately, the department was never realized. It would be Bonn University that would seize the opportunity, offering Price his wished-for department in 1937. But war was on the horizon. The failure of Price's plans and the suppression of research in Nazi Germany allowed the torch of parapsychology to pass across the Atlantic.[491]

Telepathy

The odds against it were a hundred billion to one. He shuffled a pack of Zenner Cards – circle, cross (or plus sign), square, star, wavy lines – and took one out, holding it face down. A twenty-six-year-old theology student called Hubert Pearce, a plumber's son from Clarendon, an insignificant dot in the backwoods of Arkansas, was about to become the shining star of parapsychological research. He made his first guess. Dr Joseph Banks Rhine turned over the card: 'Right'. He had turned up one day at one of Rhine's lectures because he was scared that he might be telepathic. Rhine asked him to guess again. 'Right.' He got ten right in a straight run. Rhine paused. Could Pearce do it again? Rhine pulled another ten cards. Pearce called another ten right answers. This was parapsychology's royal flush, twice in a row. Pearce's worst fears were confirmed.[492]

---

p. 96; Eric. J. Dingwall, 'Notes on Periodicals', *Journal of the Society of Psychical Research*, 24, June 1928, p. 299. Dr Hans Rosenbusch would claim in 1927 to have exposed Zugun not soon after, see 'The Poltergeist Girl – Unmasked in Munich', *Daily News*, 21 February 1927.

[491] Adams; Sofie Lachapelle, 'Attempting Science: The Creation and Early Development of the Institut Métapsychique International in Paris, 1919–1931', *Journal of the History of the Behavioral Sciences*, 41.1, Winter 2005, pp. 1–24.

[492] Odds given by Peter Hallson, 'Some Thoughts on the Decline Effect', *Paranormal Review*, January 1999, p. 15.

The astonishing odds would be chalked up during the first series of ESP tests conducted at Duke University in 1933. Over the next two years Pearce would be repeatedly tested, but he was not the only subject. When Rhine published the results in 1934 in his landmark book *Extra-Sensory Perception*, he and his colleagues had conducted 90,000 trials in the prior three-year period.[493]

Rhine was a botanist by training and had once intended on a career as a minister, but he and his wife, Dr Louisa Rhine, also a botanist, had listened to Sir Arthur Conan Doyle lecturing persuasively on the survival of the spirit and joined the ASPR. They began looking for answers. On 1 July 1926 their quest found them mounting the stairs of 10 Lime Street in Boston, Massachusetts, the home of the then famous medium Mina Crandon (1888–1941), known as 'Margery'. During her exhibitionist séances, at which sitters were served champagne, her thin dressing gown would invariably fall open, revealing that the silk stockings on her legs were the only things she was wearing underneath. Margery was a sensation. Harry Houdini had already imprisoned her in a wooden box to test her powers – inconclusively – and the ASPR were championing her mediumship as solid proof of survival after death. Despite the diversions, the Rhines could see that fraud was involved. The publication of their exposé in 1927 ended their relationship with the ASPR and 'Margery' would ultimately split the ASPR.[494]

In 1928, disappointed with 'Margery', the Rhines moved on

---

[493] J. B. Rhine, *Extra-Sensory Perception*, Boston Society for Psychic Research, 1934, excerpted in Robert Schoch and Logan Yonavjak, *The Parapsychological Revolution*, Tarcher/Penguin, 2008, p. 132.

[494] J. B. Rhine and Louisa E. Rhine, 'One Evening's Observation on the Margery Mediumship', *Journal of Abnormal and Social Psychology*, 24.2, January 1927; Brian Mackenzie, 'The Place of J. B. Rhine in the History of Parapsychology', *Journal of Parapsychology*, 45, March 1981, pp. 75–6; Stacy Horn, *Unbelievable*, HarperCollins, 2009, pp. 17–24; *Enc. Para.*, pp. 393–9. Not everyone at the ASPR had fallen for her charms: with extraordinary dedication E. E. Dudley had discovered that the thumbprint supposedly left by a spirit, Mina's dead brother Walter, was in fact that of her dentist, see *Enc. Para.*, p. 397.

to Lady, 'the telepathic horse', seeking to rule out the problem of human deviousness. Lady would touch her nose to blocks with numbers or letters of the alphabet on them in response to questions put both verbally and mentally. She apparently scored well above chance. The Rhines were aware of Oskar Pfunst's earlier work with a similar beast called 'Clever Hans', and so tried to control for 'unconscious guidance' from the humans around her, although unsuccessfully. By not fully grasping that the cues were entirely involuntary they concluded, incorrectly, that Lady was indeed telepathic. Rhine scouted around for other 'infra-human telepathic subjects', as he put it, but finding none, decided to turn to humans once again.[495]

In 1930 he was having 'guessing contests' with groups of children. Then he moved on to college students. For a time he also tried hypnosis as a means of accessing ESP, but found the process slow and the results insignificant. Trying experiments using ordinary playing cards, Rhine discovered that people had particular preferences for a suit or card. His colleague, the psychologist Dr Karl Zenner (1903–64), devised the famous set of cards around 1930–1 to overcome this problem. A set of five distinctive symbols were used in a deck of twenty-five cards, giving a chance expectation of 5 right in every run. The more trials they conducted the more they found that their modest results began to mount up. His first notable success was with Adam J. Linzmayer. Rhine believed that he was on the brink of proving the possibility of 'the transfer of thought from one mind to another without the intermediation of the sense' – telepathy.[496]

The SPR had early concluded that telepathy was a reality after the Creery case – a finding they would later be forced to reject. After a series of experiments in 1890, Baron Albert von

---

[495] J. B. Rhine and Louisa E. Rhine, 'An Investigation of a "Mind-Reading" Horse', *Journal of Abnormal and Social Psychology*, 23, 1929, pp. 287–92; Rhine, *Extra-Sensory*, p. 132; Mackenzie, pp. 77–8; Oskar Pfungst, *Clever Hans (The Horse of Mr von Osten): A Contribution to Experimental Animal and Human Psychology*, trans. C. L. Rahn, Henry Holt, 1911 [1907].

[496] Rhine, *Extra-Sensory*, pp. 7–10, 132; Mackenzie, p. 80; Horn, p. 31.

Schrenck-Notzing had already argued that there was 'evidence in favour of the reality of true psychical transference'. Some of the pictures he used in his tests were even reminiscent of Zenner's symbols. But the sheer weight of Rhine's evidence, collated through thousands of man-hours of dedicated work, and reduced to clean, compelling statistics would prove more decisive than a series of informal sessions with cheating teenagers or aristocrats. The most important development was the move away from the study of professional 'psychics' and apparently gifted amateurs to the study of (almost) randomly selected 'ordinary' subjects. Some of the psychics could fool some of the scientists some of the time – as Margery did – but with randomized selection the inevitable base temptation of gulling the credulous for money (or anything else) was removed. As Charles Fort (1874–1932) – the man who gave us the word Fortean – once said, 'There is not a physicist in the world who can perceive when a parlor magician palms off playing-cards', but now the parapsychologists were no longer studying 'parlour magicians'.[497]

Clairvoyance

In the late summer of 1933 Pearce called on Rhine's assistant Gaither Pratt, in his research room on the top floor of the Social Science Building, Duke West Campus, as arranged. They synchronized watches and Pearce left. Pratt watched from his window and after a few moments he saw Pearce cross the quadrangle to the library. He waited a few moments more until he was sure Pearce was at his appointed seat at the back of the library. They were ready to begin. Pratt shuffled the Zenner cards and placed the deck on the table in front of him. He checked the time, then took the first card off the top of the deck and put it face down in the centre of the table without looking at it. He waited for one minute, then, putting the card to one side, repeated the action

[497] Albert von Schrenck-Notzing, 'Experimental Studies in Thought-Transference', *Proceedings of the Society for Psychical Research*, 7, 1891–1892, p. 6; Charles Hoy Fort, *New Lands: More Unexplained Occurrences*, Forgotten Books, 2008 [1925], p. 56.

with the next card and so on until he had gone through the whole deck. Sitting in the library a hundred yards away, Pearce wrote down his predictions, one every minute. When Pratt finished he turned over the cards and noted their order. Five minutes later he would shuffle the cards again and they would repeat the test. At the end of the experiment they put their records into envelopes and sealed them. They then personally delivered them to Rhine. They discovered that Hubert Pearce was not just telepathic, he was also clairvoyant.[498]

Rhine had decided to test to see if distance had any effect on Hubert's abilities. He also wanted to devise an experiment where collusion (even involuntary) between subject and scientist could be automatically ruled out without having to rely on the participants' good character. With the distance tests, he thought that nobody could ever accuse them of cheating. In a final group of tests, Rhine observed Pratt during the procedure, just to make sure. Also this was not just mind-reading any more. Clairvoyance was, as Rhine defined it, 'the extrasensory perception of objects or objective events, as distinguished from the mental states or thoughts of another person'. Pratt had not looked at the cards. He did not know what they were. Pearce would have to be able to read the cards for himself, despite the fact they were face down on a table a hundred yards away.[499]

At first Pearce's results were not impressive. He was even scoring below chance, but as they continued, he got better. From August 1933 to March 1934 they would conduct 1,850 distance trials in total with distances ranging from 100 to 250 yards. After statistical analysis the results were staggering. As the British mathematician and psychical researcher S. G. Soal

---

[498] J. B. Rhine, 'Some Selected Experiments in Extra-Sensory Perception', *Journal of Abnormal and Social Psychology*, 31, 1936, pp. 216–28; J. B. Rhine and J. G. Pratt, 'A Review of the Pearce–Pratt Distance Series of ESP Tests', *Journal of Parapsychology*, 18, 1954, pp. 165–78; Horn, pp. 38–9.

[499] See C. E. M. Hansel, 'A Critical Analysis of the Pearce–Pratt Experiment', *Journal of Parapsychology*, 25, 1961, pp. 87ff, for his views on the inability of this methodology to automatically exclude fraud; Rhine, *Extra-Sensory*, pp. 7–10.

once said, 'a million persons might go on guessing for years without producing such a series'. Rhine himself gave the odds of this happening due to chance as 10^{-22}. Rhine was convinced that these results 'allow no other interpretation except that they were due to extrasensory perception'.[500]

Then after two years of incredible results, Pearce lost his apparent abilities. The reason, it seems, was a broken heart. Pearce's girlfriend left him shortly after the distance experiments and he never reached the level of his earlier performances. He graduated the next year and went back to Arkansas. His involvement in parapsychology almost cost him the career as a minister he had been striving for. As it was, he was given a rundown country church in the mountains. He would find love again, but those astonishing powers were gone for good.[501]

Despite the setback, it was enough to justify Duke University's decision to create a Parapsychology Laboratory in September 1933 and make Rhine its director. Even with this new recognition, not to mention such apparently black and white experimental results, the scientific establishment was not ready to accept that ESP could be possible. The science writer and sceptic Martin Gardner wrote to Pearce bluntly asking him to confess to having cheated. Mark Hansel spent considerable time thinking of ways, however improbable, that Pearce might have cheated, even suggesting that Pearce had crawled through the ceiling space in order to be able to spy upon Pratt as he turned over the cards. Gardner himself would later come to recognize that 'there is obviously an enormous, irrational prejudice on the part of most American psychologists [. . .] against even the possibility of extra-sensory mental powers'.[502]

[500] S. G. Soal, Reviews, *Proceedings of the Society for Psychical Research*, 45, 1938, p. 93; Rhine and Pratt, pp. 171, 174; Horn, p. 39.
[501] Horn, pp. 39–40, 232.
[502] Horn, pp. 51, 78, 155, 228.

Psychokinesis

The idea had come from a young amateur gambler who had visited the lab to tell them he could influence dice rolls with his force of will. Rhine and the gambler got down on the floor of his office and started rolling dice. Rhine was not impressed. 'The gambler went on his way,' wrote Gaither Pratt, 'but he left this beautifully simple idea behind.' They now had what they thought was the perfect way to test for psychokinesis (PK), the power of the mind over matter.[503]

Rhine and Pratt began rolling dice. They got students at the university to roll dice. They even got Rhine's children and their friends to roll dice. They began throwing the dice from cupped hands, then against a wall, next down a chute, and finally they built a machine to do it for them. They gave prizes to the children, making it a party game. They tried drinking coffee and alcohol, and taking the narcotic sodium amytal to see if that made a difference. And they rolled the dice again and again over nine years.[504]

The Rhines' first report excitedly declared that 'the experiments on PK show first that the mind has a force, real kinetic force, and that it can also operate outside of the body'. But were the results due to PK or precognition? Rhine thought he could rule out precognition by agreeing on a 'rigid order of target face' or allowing the subject to choose it for themselves during a trial. But it was the same problem in his ESP experiments, only reversed. What was needed some direct physical effect that could not involve precognition.[505]

---

[503] Louisa E. Rhine and J. B. Rhine, 'The Psychokinetic Effect, I: The First Experiment', *Journal of Parapsychology*, 20, 1943, 20–43; Harvey J. Irwin, *An Introduction to Parapsychology*, 4th ed., McFarland & Company, 2004, p. 107; Pratt quoted in Horn, p. 74.

[504] Horn, pp. 74–5.

[505] Quoted in Horn, p. 74; Rhine and Rhine, 'Psychokinetic', pp. 20–43. For other confirmatory experiments see L. A. Dale, 'The Psychokinetic Effect: The First A.S.P.R. Experiment', *Journal of the American Society of Psychical Research*, 40, 1946, pp. 123–51; Robert A. McConnell, et al., 'Wishing with Dice', *Journal of Experimental Psychology*, 50, 1955, pp. 269–75; J. G. Pratt and H. Forwald, 'Confirmation of the PK Placement Effect', *Journal of Parapsychology*,

The answer, if it was an answer, lay halfway across the world. A six-year-old boy in Tel Aviv, Israel, in the 1950s, stared fascinated as the hands of his watch bent before his eyes. He next tried cutlery, then nails, all bent by the power of his mind. Being abducted by aliens had given him new and amazing powers. At least that is the story that Uri Geller has given of himself. He later retracted the aliens. What is indisputable is that, after being discharged from the Israeli Army in the 1960s, Geller developed a magic routine with Shimson 'Shipi' Shtrang and together they worked nightclubs and private parties performing an act they billed as ESP. They were discovered by American parapsychologist Dr Andrija Puharich and Geller was promoted in the US as the genuine article. To some it looked like the physical evidence was finally available.[506]

After a radio broadcast in Texas in the early 1970s, a number of people claimed that after listening to Geller, metal objects in their homes had bent spontaneously. He used this when appearing on BBC Radio 2's 'The Jimmy Young Show' in the UK on 3 November 1973, asking listeners who believed that they might be able to bend metal to bring some object close to their radio sets so that he could 'trigger' their latent psychokinetic powers. This distance macro-PK experiment apparently worked and for a while was known as 'The Geller Effect'. He was not just proficient in PK, but ESP as well. A study by two scientists at the Stanford Research Institute, California, concluded that 'we can safely say that it is evident that Geller does have paranormal perceptual abilities'. Rhine himself was 'impressed by the number of serious competent people who have seen his demonstrations of physical effects under circumstances which, as reported, would not allow any kind of known sleight of hand or trickery'. He then went on to say that Geller's

22, 1958, pp. 1–19.
[506] Uri Geller, *Uri Geller: My Story*, Holt and Co., 1975, p. 102; Andrija Puharich, *Uri: A Journal of the Mystery of Uri Geller*, Anchor Press/Doubleday, 1974; *Enc. Para.*, pp. 613–14.

effects were 'genuinely parapsychic', although he reserved final judgement.[507]

A number of other spoon-benders soon appeared on the scene: Jean-Pierre Girard in France; Stephen North in the UK; Steve Shaw and Mike Edwards in the USA; Masuaki Kiyota and Merac in Japan. It seemed like a wave of psychic powers had been released, although no one else mentioned aliens. Parapsychology had a new category: PKMB – psychokinetic metal bending.[508]

Rhine was right to remain cautious. According to the then president of the Israel Parapsychology Society, Dr Heinz Berendt, a former girlfriend claimed to have acted as a stooge in Geller's early stage show routine and a former impresario, Dany Pelz, also said that Geller covertly observed his audience before coming onstage and displaying apparent ESP in identifying someone's favourite brand of cigarettes and so on. Berendt reasoned that there was nothing paranormal about Geller's feats because of 'Geller's own admission that he uses tricks' and noted that Geller had ignored their repeated requests to study him. James Randi, former magician turned debunker, would later publish a still taken from Geller's appearance on an American TV programme, Barbara Walter's 'Not for Women Only', that seemed to show that one of the spoons used had been pre-fatigued. Journalist C. Eugene Emery, Jr, claimed to have personally caught Geller cheating in *ad hoc* ESP and PK tests.[509]

---

[507] Russell Targ and Harold Puthoff, 'ESP Experiments with Uri Geller', in J. D. Morris, et al. (eds), *Research In Parapsychology*, Scarecrow Press, 1973, p. 60; and Russel Targ and Harold Puthoff, 'PK Experiments with Uri Geller and Ingo Swann', in Morris, *Parapsychology*, pp. 125–8; Rhine quoted in Heinz C. Berendt, 'Uri Geller – Pro and Con', *Journal of the Society of Psychical Research*, 47, December 1974, pp. 481, 483; *Enc. Para.*, p. 614. Targ and Puthoff also published their findings on Geller in 'Information Transmission Under Conditions of Sensory Shielding', *Nature*, 251, 18 October, pp. 602–7.

[508] *Enc. Para.*, p. 614.

[509] Berendt, p. 477; James Randi, *The Truth About Uri Geller*, Prometheus Books, 1982, p. 179; C. Eugene Emery, 'Psychic or Charlatan: Uri Geller Reverses his Disappearing Act', *Providence Sunday Journal*, 12 April 1987, pp. A21ff, and C. Eugene Emery, 'Catching Geller in the Act', *Skeptical Inquirer*, 12.1, 1987,

At the height of his fame, a 1974 poll by the *Daily Mail* revealed that 95 per cent of its readers believed Geller could produce paranormal phenomena. Now, as SPR member John Randall observed, there is no research into metal-bending being conducted, as far as he is aware, and the subject has been largely (perhaps conveniently) forgotten by parapsychology.[510]

Spoon-bending might be the most well-known example of supposed psychokinesis, but it is surely also the most banal and least convincing. We have already seen how the physical mediums were displaying dramatic phenomena from sound to spirit manifestations and materializations. Parapsychologists now refer to this class of phenomena as macro-PK. Poltergeists, too, are seen by some as an example of macro-PK, or more particularly following Professor William Roll's coinage as 'recurrent spontaneous psychokinesis' (RSPK). Macro-PK applies to any form of PK that is immediately apparent, but there is also a range of weaker effects – micro-PK – that are often only observable through statistical analysis of experimental results. Rhine's dice-rolling experiments were classic studies of micro-PK. Of course, there are also areas, such as psychic healing, that can seemingly involve both macro- and micro-PK effects.[511]

Precognition

In 1952 Rhine called back one of the students he had been testing for ESP, not because Lois Duncan was the next Hubert Pearce, but because, as she put it, 'I had broken a record for incorrect responses'. She would drop out of Duke University, but become a best-selling novelist. The 1997 film adaptation of one of her earlier books, *I Know What You Did Last Summer*

pp. 75–80; *Enc. Para.*, p. 614. Stated using 'tricks' in Calev Ben-David, 'A Life of the Mind', *The Jerusalem Report*, 8 September 1994, p. 46.

[510] John Randall, 'The Near-Death Experience: A Reliable Paranormal Phenomenon?', *Journal of the Society of Psychical Research*, 74, October 2010, p. 254.

[511] *Enc. Para.*, pp. 604–5; J. G. Pratt and W. G. Roll, 'The Seaford Disturbances', *Journal of Parapsychology*, 22.2, June 1958, p. 79.

(1973), would take over $125 million at the box office. In 1989, when our story begins, she had completed her thirty-eighth book, but the celebrations would be cut short when the plot of *Don't Look Behind You* became real life. Afterwards, Duncan would come to believe that she had just written a 289-page premonition.[512]

Don't Look Behind You told the story of an FBI agent's daughter called April. April is caught up in her father's violent world when the family is forced into hiding under the US Federal Witness Security Program. Missing her friends, April runs away and returns to the former family home. A hitman discovers her whereabouts and pursues her across Florida.

April was based on Duncan's own daughter Kaitlyn (also Kait) Arquette. Duncan presented her with the bound galleys, inscribed 'For my own special April', adding 'Always be sure to look behind you, Honey!' One month later Kaitlyn was shot twice in the head. She died twenty hours later.[513]

In the novel, April is chased by a hitman driving a Chevrolet Camaro. Kaitlyn was also chased by a Camaro. In the novel the hitman is called Mike Vamp. After Kaitlyn's murder, police indicted a man called Mike who was known by the nickname 'Vamp'. Just as April's family went into hiding under the Federal Witness Security Program, so Duncan and her husband were forced into hiding in 1990 after receiving death threats from the relatives of two suspects in Kaitlyn's murder case.

The police thought Kaitlyn's murder was a random drive-by shooting. Her sister Robin had concerns about Kaitlyn's Vietnamese boyfriend, Dung Nguyen. They were apparently about to break up and Kaitlyn was scared of his friends. There

[512] Lois Duncan, *Who Killed My Daughter? The True Story of a Mother's Search for Her Daughter's Murderer* Delacorte Press, 1992; reviewed by William Roll in *Journal of Parapsychology*, 57, 1993, pp. 305–7. See also Lois Duncan and William Roll, *Psychic Connections: A Journey into the Mysterious World of Psi*, Delacorte Press, 1995.
[513] Reported in *The Albuquerque Journal*, 18 July 1989; and *The Albuquerque Tribune*, 18 July 1989.

were rumours of what Duncan called 'a car-wreck scam' – staging rental car crashes to make fraudulent insurance claims. Trying to find out more, Robin went to psychic Betty Muench (1933–2010). Using automatic writing Muench made claims of drug-dealing politicians and gang involvement. Desperate for some progress in a case the police seemed to have abandoned, Duncan would later consult another three psychics – Noreen Renier, Nancy Czetli and Greta Alexander.[514]

These three already had reputations as 'psychic detectives'. Greta Alexander (1932–98) claimed being hit by lightning in 1961 had given her psychic powers. She was a 'cult figure' with a waiting list of seven months to a year. Her clients included the MGM contract actress Debbie Reynolds, who starred in the 1952 film *Singin' in the Rain*, and actress Ruth Warrick, who appeared in Orson Welles' 1941 film *Citizen Kane*. She claimed to have two guardian angels called Raoul and Isaiah – 'her boys', as she called them. Alexander had most famously been involved in the Mary Cousett murder case in 1983 and according to newspaper reports had found missing person Rex Carpenter in 1991.[515]

Nancy Czetli (also known by the surnames Anderson, Myer-Czetli and Myer, her maiden name) took an MA in 'Writing Popular Fiction' before turning to psychic detection. According to her website she has 'assisted in the investigations of over 765 homicides' and claims to have given 'new, accurate information about the case that helps in the search for a resolution' 90 per cent of the time. One of her more famous successes was supposedly finding the body of Sylvester Tonet in 1988, although police detective Will Greenaway, who had worked on the case, had been 'unimpressed' with the information she provided. At the time of writing, she charges $200 an hour.[516]

---

[514] Duncan, ch. 3.

[515] Ward Lucas, 'A Product of the Media: Greta Alexander', in Joe Nickell (ed.), *Psychic Sleuths: ESP and Sensational Cases*, Prometheus Books, 1994, pp. 130–55; 'Psychic Greta Alexander', *Chicago Sun-Times*, 19 July 1998.

[516] http://www.nancymyer-psychicdetective.com/aboutuspagehtml.html,

Noreen Renier (c. 1937–) was said to have predicted the assassination attempt on Ronald Reagan and the successful assassination of Egypt's President Anwar Sadat. At one time or another, she has been billed as 'the only psychic to ever work with the FBI'. Renier had volunteered for a parapsychological study undertaken at Duke University, although details are sketchy. Anthropologist David E. Jones at the University of Central Florida also investigated her supposed psychic abilities and those of three others in the 1970s. He argued that 'a positive conclusion is unavoidable. There are individuals who have abilities which we now refer to as paranormal or psychic'. However, fellow anthropologist Kenneth L. Feder would be less than complimentary about how he came to that conclusion. Renier's fee in the 1990s was around $400 a case.[517]

'My speciality is homicide work,' Renier told Duncan after she contacted her. She went on to explain that 'I've worked with police from all over the United States and as far away as Japan'. Her technique was psychometry: 'If I'm sent an object that was on the body of the victim, I can usually describe the victim and recreate the murder scene'. She said that she would go into a trance and 'get impressions', which she could not remember afterwards. She talked of 'channelling' the spirit of the dead victim.[518]

Duncan sent Renier some of Kaitlyn's personal belongings and arranged a telephone conference to take part in the psychic investigation. 'I feel a knife so strongly,' said Renier. 'Why do I feel a knife?' 'She wasn't killed with a knife,' replied Duncan.

accessed 6 December 2010; Joe Nickell, 'Psychic Sleuthing: The Myth-Making Process', *Skeptical Inquirer*, 26 September 2005.
[517] Gary P. Posner, 'The Media's Rising Star Psychic Sleuth: Noreen Renier', in Nickell, pp. 60–85; David E. Jones, *Visions of Time: Experiments in Psychic Archaeology*, Theosophical Publishing House, 1979, p. 16; Kenneth L. Feder, 'Psychic Archaeology: The Anatomy of Irrationalist Prehistoric Studies', *Skeptical Inquirer*, Summer 1980, pp. 32–43; William G. Roll, Review of Noreen Renier, *A Mind for Murder*, Berkley Books, 2005, *Journal of Scientific Exploration*, 20, 2006, p. 140; Duncan, p. 290.
[518] Duncan, pp. 248, 290.

'She was shot.' A moment later Renier stated, 'I wasn't shot. I don't *think* I was shot . . .' 'She was shot while she was driving,' said Duncan. 'Oh, then she was driving?' said Renier. 'Good! I felt so sure of that.'[519]

Like Muench, Czetli also talked about someone involved in politics, and like Muench, Renier also said there was a gang connection. All three would say that Kaitlyn had witnessed a drug transaction. An investigation by an Albuquerque newspaper would later find evidence of a connection between Kaitlyn's murder and a Vietnamese gang, and an anonymous call to Duncan would claim that drugs had been involved. However, it was Renier who would make what is presented as one of the most astonishing revelations.[520]

The police artist Mike Deal sketched from Renier's description of the killer: tight wiry hair, close-set eyes, big ears, long nose, possibly broken at some point, square chin – a boxer's face, or any mobster extra from *The Godfather*. When Duncan saw it she telephoned Renier immediately. 'Something crazy happened with one of the pictures,' she said. 'Your artist drew a character from one of my books. [. . .] Your artist drew my hitman.' The picture had only been used on the cover of the British edition of *Don't Look Behind You* and not the US edition. Few people in the USA were thought to have seen it. Kaitlyn was one of those. She had seen the picture before she died and Renier interpreted it as a message that 'a hitman was hired to kill her because she was going to expose illegal activities'.[521]

It was not the first time that one of her books had seemingly predicted the future. In *Ransom*, her first suspense novel written in 1966 when Duncan was living in Livermore, California, a group of teenagers are kidnapped by the driver of their school bus. Not long after the book was published, school children in Livermore, California, were kidnapped and held to ransom by

---

[519] Duncan, p. 254.
[520] Ken Dornstein, *Accidentally, on Purpose: The Making of a Personal Injury Underworld in America*, Palgrave Macmillan, 1998, p. 328; Duncan, p. 293.
[521] Duncan, p. 258.

their bus driver. One of the children's parents demanded that Duncan be arrested as an accessory because she seemed to know too much about the case.

This was not the first time that an author had apparently predicted the future, either. 'Precognition is quite well established,' William Roll, then Director of the Psychical Research Foundation, told Duncan, 'and creative individuals seem to have more of this ability than others.' He used the *Titanic* as an example. W. T. Stead's 'How the Mail Steamer Went Down in Mid-Atlantic' (1886) and 'From the Old World to the New' (1892), and Morgan Robertson's *Futility, or The Wreck of the Titan* (1898) all seemed to predict the sinking of RMS *Titanic* in 1912. In all three stories an ocean liner goes down after colliding with an iceberg, but there were more parallels than that.[522]

In 'From the Old World to the New' the name of the captain was E. J. Smith, also the name of the captain of the *Titanic*. The fate of Stead himself was curiously linked to that of the ship. In 1892 the chiromancer Teresina told him he would die aged sixty-three. Another palmist, W. de Kerlor, had dreams and visions of a large, dark ship and a watery grave. Stead lost his life on the *Titanic*, aged sixty-three. Robertson also produced other remarkable parallels: the names of the ships were almost identical, both left port in April, both struck icebergs around midnight, both were travelling at a similar speed, both had sixteen watertight compartments and both could carry around 3,000 passengers.[523]

In 1915 Boston businessman Edward Bowen had an important meeting in London and booked passage on the next

---

[522] Duncan, p. 241; W. T. Stead, 'How the Mail Steamer Went Down in Mid-Atlantic', *Pall Mall Gazette*, 22 March 1886, and 'From the Old World to the New', *The Review of Reviews*, Christmas edition, December 1892. See Martin Gardner (ed.), *The Wreck of the Titanic Foretold*, Prometheus Books, 1985, for these and other examples.

[523] Guy Lyon Playfair, Review of Bertrand Méheust, *Histoires Paranormales du Titanic*, J'ai lu, 2006, *Journal of the Society of Psychical Research*, 70, 2006, pp. 241–2; Bob Brier, Review of Martin Gardner (ed.), *The Wreck of the Titanic Foretold?*, Prometheus Books, 1986, *Journal of Parapsychology*, 50, 1986, p. 288.

available transatlantic steamer from New York to Liverpool, despite the German U-boat blockade. It was a luxury liner, the pride of the Cunard Line and the fastest on the seas, more than able to outrun any German submarine. 'It's the best joke I've heard in many days, this talk of torpedoing', said Captain W. T. Turner as the ship prepared to cast off. Nevertheless, 'A feeling grew upon me that something was going to happen,' said Bowen. He talked it over with his wife and cancelled his tickets. The meeting could wait. The theatrical manager, Arthur 'Al' Woods, had taken a stateroom next to the famous playwright Charles Klein – in 1912 they had both cancelled their passage on the *Titanic*. On the morning of sailing, fear overcame him and he gave it up; but not Klein. On the evening before sailing, the ship's mascot, a black cat called Dowie, made an escape down one of the large hawsers. The firemen and stokers saw in it a terrible omen. The ship was the RMS *Lusitania*. As we saw earlier, the *Lusitania* was sunk by a U-boat, going down with huge loss of life.[524]

From the 1880s to the 1950s, Eleanor Sidgwick, Herbert Saltmarsh and Louisa Rhine between them collected a massive number of case reports of precognition. They found that most of them occurred during dreaming as realistic representations of the event. In 1933 J. B. Rhine had tried precognition experiments with Pearce attempting to guess the order of cards before they were dealt. The American parapsychologist W. E. Cox found that days with train crashes had a relatively lower level of passenger traffic. He theorized that people were subconsciously precognisant of the accidents and so avoided travelling on those days. But this only scratches the surface of the amount of work that has been done, and continues to be done, on this subject.[525]

[524] Adolph A. Hoehling and Mary Hoehling, *The Last Voyage of the Lusitania*, Holt, 1956, pp. 31–2; Frederick Ellis, *The Tragedy of the Lusitania*, National Publishing Co., 1915, pp. 168, 172, 174–5.

[525] E. M. Sidgwick, 'On the Evidence for Premonitions', *Proceedings of the Society for Psychical Research*, 5, 1888, pp. 288–354; H. F. Saltmarsh, 'Report on Cases of Apparent Precognition', *Proceedings of the Society for Psychical*

After the Aberfan disaster in 1966 in which a colliery slagheap landslide caused considerable loss of life, Dr J. C. Barker, then a consultant psychiatrist at Sheldon Hospital in Shrewsbury, appealed through the media for anyone who had had a presentiment of what had happened. He received numerous replies, thirty-five of which were sufficiently detailed to warrant attention. Barker set up the British Premonitions Bureau (BPB) in 1967 to collect people's experiences. It was his hope that the BPB, based at Grove House in London, might act as a psychic early-warning system to prevent similar disasters in the future. By the early 1970s the BPB had received over 3,000 reports. Sadly, it is no longer operational. A number of other such bureaux were set up around the world. In 1968 a Central Premonitions Registry was established in New York under Robert Nelson and there have been similar efforts in Canada. John L. Peterson's Arlington Institute in Arlington, Virginia, continues to try and predict the future with a specially selected group of 'precognisant dreamers'.[526]

One of the many problems for precognition research has always been 'retro-fitting' or postdiction. Given enough time, the cryptic pronouncements of Nostradamus, for example, can be made to fit actual events from the rise of Hitler to the terrorist attack on the World Trade Center, New York. Likewise, a prolific writer such as Duncan is likely to describe things that eventually happen. The supposed novelistic predictions of the sinking of the *Titanic* were published fourteen to twenty-six years before the event. Some of the information provided by Renier seemed hopelessly off-target – a knife instead of a gun.

Research, 42, 1934, pp. 49–103; Louisa E. Rhine, 'Frequency of Types of Experience in Spontaneous Precognition', *Journal of Parapsychology*, 18, 1954, pp. 93–123; Irwin, pp. 95–7; J. B. Rhine, 'Experiments Bearing on the Precognition Hypothesis: I. Pre-Shuffling Card Calling', *Journal of Parapsychology*, 2, 1938, pp. 38–54; W. E. Cox, 'Precognition: An analysis II', *Journal of the American Society for Psychical Research*, 30, 1956, pp. 99–109.

[526] John C. Barker, 'Premonitions of the Aberfan Disaster', *Journal of the Society of Psychical Research* 44, 1967, pp. 169–81; Andrew MacKenzie, *Riddle of the Future: A Modern Study of Precognition*, Arthur Baker, 1974; Dossey, n.p.

Even Renier's best hit – the supposed match between her mugshot and the cover illustration showing the killer – stretches the imagination. Renier's sketch looked like an Italian, the face on the cover like a cousin of Roger Moore. Despite some of the flawed evidence, precognition cannot be explained away. For example, controlled experiments in the laboratory have uncovered strange effects such as changes in skin conductivity occurring prior to emotional stimuli in randomized tests that seem suspiciously similar to precognition. After analyzing almost two million precognition trials involving more than 50,000 subjects in 309 separate studies conducted between 1935 and 1987, researchers Charles Honorton, then director of Princeton's Psychophysical Research Laboratories, and Diane Ferrari found that 30 per cent had produced significant results in favour.[527]

Rhine had wanted to establish a centre for research that would outlive him. It looked as though he had. The Parapsychology Laboratory had produced excellent work. His long-time research assistant and valued colleague Gaither Pratt was expected to succeed him as director. The university had other plans. They wanted to subsume the lab into a new Center for the Study of the Nature of Man that would include anthropology, psychology, physics, even electronics, and much else besides. Rhine feared that the lab would disappear in this untidy heap. But after confidential discussions with Karl Zener and other senior figures at Duke, the university dropped the whole idea and with it any sort of future for the laboratory. Pratt was left dangling. Rhine would retire with full benefits. Pratt, then in his fifties, had sacrificed his career and had nothing in return.

---

[527] Dean Radin, 'Experiments Testing Models of Mind-Matter Interaction', *Journal of Scientific Exploration*, 20.3, 2006, pp. 375–401. For a critical perspective see Richard Wiseman, 'Dreaming the Future?', *Fortean Times*, 273, April 2011, pp. 36–9. For a fuller analysis see Charles Honorton and Diane C. Ferrari, '"Future Telling": A Meta-Analysis of Forced-Choice Precognition Experiments, 1935–1987', *Journal of Parapsychology*, 53, 1989, pp. 281–308.

The two men parted acrimoniously, although they would be reconciled some years later.[528]

When Rhine officially retired in 1962, the Parapsychology Laboratory at Duke University was no more. Rhine established the independent Foundation for Research on the Nature of Man (FRNM) – renamed the Rhine Research Center in 1995 – and the Institute for Parapsychology to continue his work. Rhine had earlier proposed that a Parapsychological Association be created as a professional organization for scientists working in parapsychology. It was formally established on 19 June 1957 in Durham, North Carolina, with the physicist Dr Robert A. McConnell (1914–2006) as its first president. In 1969 the Parapsychological Association was voted a member of the prestigious American Association for the Advancement of Science – it was a landmark development. Today it has a total membership of 271.[529]

There had been many stumbling blocks along the way, but parapsychology is now an established discipline, albeit still an embattled one. The SPR is still going strong, more than a hundred years later, and across the world many similar endeavours have emerged – more than can be mentioned here. France's Institut Métapsychique International, founded in 1919, also continues to this day. Hans Bender established the Institut für Grenzgebiete der Psychologie und Psychohygiene (Institute for Border Areas of Psychology and Psychohygiene) in Freiburg, Germany, in 1950, and a chair of border psychology was established at Freiburg University in 1954. In 1985 the Koestler Chair of Parapsychology was established at Edinburgh University, funded by a bequest made by the writer Arthur Koestler and his wife Cynthia. Under the first incumbent, Robert L. Morris, a Koestler Parapsychology Unit was also set

---

[528] Horn, pp. 229–30.
[529] Horn, pp. 229–30, 233; J. Gordon Melton (ed.), *Encyclopedia of Occultism and Parapsychology*, 2 vols, 5th ed., Gale, 2001, vol. 2, p. 1185; 'History of the Parapsychological Association', Parapsychological Association, http://www.parapsych.org/history_of_pa.html, accessed 28 December 2010.

up. An indirect outcome of this was the formation of the Parapsychology Research Group at Liverpool Hope University in the early 2000s. The Princeton Engineering Anomalies Research (PEAR) programme lasted from 1979 to 2007, coming to an end when, after twenty-eight years of research, it was felt that it had proven that the human mind could exert a non-physical influence on 'engineering devices and information-processing systems'.[530]

Within the English-speaking world, parapsychology as an academic discipline has followed the lead of the SPR. It tends not to investigate the whole range of what is popularly known as 'paranormal', but instead concentrates on telepathy, clairvoyance, precognition (premonition) and psychokinesis – the category of things covered by the term 'psi'. Rhine reduced everything to ESP and PK, although he still had to admit the other aspects as sub-categories. Research has broadened today with investigations into reincarnation, and out-of-body and near-death experiences, encompassing magnetic field and ultrasound effects, as well as theorizing based on the models of quantum physics, but still baulks at the full range of phenomena considered supernatural or paranormal.[531]

Unlike Croesus, what the original members of the SPR, Rhine and many others were really concerned about was not whether one would defeat the Persian army, or succeed in any other future endeavour for that matter, but whether the mind could operate independently of the body, which is to say,

---

[530] GEEPP website, http://geepp.free.fr/index1024.htm, accessed 31 December 2010; IGPP, http://www.igpp.de/english/welcome.htm, accessed 31 December 2010; Koestler Research Unit, http://www.koestler-parapsychology.psy.ed.ac.uk/index.html, accessed 31 December 2010; Parapsychology Research Unit, http://hopelive.hope.ac.uk/psychology/para/Index.html, accessed 31 December 2010; 'Princeton's PEAR Laboratory to Close', PEAR Press Release, 10 February 2007; Dr Carl Williams, personal communication, 4 January 2011.
[531] Rhine, p. 7–10; Horn, p. 240; 'Parapsychology FAQ', Parapsychological Association, http://www.parapsych.org/faq_file1.html#4, accessed 28 December 2010.

whether consciousness could survive death. This survival hypothesis ultimately lies behind all the guessing games and spoon-bending. If the answer is yes, then many of these researchers will already know it, but for the rest of us the doubt, and with it the dread, remains. Death, not space, has always been the final frontier.

9. Conclusion:
Explaining the Inexplicable

The American hypnotherapist Dr Steven Heller (1939–97) once told the story of a professor of psychology, his patient, and the rather cruel trick he played on her in the interests of science. The professor had found the perfect hypnotic subject and wanted to test whether she would re-enter the hypnotic state when carrying out a post-hypnotic suggestion. The ideal place to test this, thought the professor, was not under carefully controlled laboratory conditions, but at the faculty party that evening. While hypnotized he planted the suggestion that when the clock struck 10 p.m. she should take off one of her shoes, set it on the dining room table and place some roses in it. As a further twist he told her that she would have no memory of this suggestion, but would instead believe it to be her own idea and would feel a strong compulsion to finish the task.[532]

As the clock struck 10 that evening the woman duly slipped off one of her shoes, put it on the table and started arranging roses in it. One can see the smirk on the professor's face as he asked, in all feigned innocence, what she was doing. She explained that her husband had given her a crystal vase in the shape of a shoe. She had not known what to do with it until the idea had suddenly come to her now of how to arrange flowers in the vase. Not wanting to forget, she had taken off her own shoe, which looked very much like the vase, and was trying out the idea she had had.

---

[532] Steven Heller, *Monsters and Magical Sticks*, Falcon, 1987, pp. 39–40.

Testing the suggestion further, the professor told her how absurd her story was and tried to talk her out of it. She was convinced that what she was saying was true and as the professor pushed further she became more and more defensive, and finally almost hysterical. The professor, at last, terminated the experiment.

The point is, we do not always know what we think we know. People are suggesting things to us all of the time. We are even suggesting things to ourselves all of the time. We invent personally convincing explanations for why anything we believe in is the gospel truth. As William James once said on the subject of survival after death, the evidence is sufficient to convince the believers but is never enough for the sceptics. It is the case with much of what we have examined in this book. It seems, then, that the explanation may not lie with the evidence, but with the human being who interprets it. History is always psychology and that, I would argue, is the point of sociology. So why do some people believe whilst others are sceptical?

A huge amount of research has been conducted on this subject. Most of it tends to find that the reason people develop or adopt 'paranormal beliefs' (variously defined) is due to some sort of mental or social abnormality, such as deficiencies in reality-testing, or a background of childhood abuse. In their book *Paranormal America*, Christopher Bader, F. Carson Mencken and Joseph Baker argued that rather than being deviant, it is actually relatively mainstream to believe in at least one area they defined as paranormal – astrology, the prophecies of Nostradamus, ghosts, monsters (cryptozoology), UFOs, and the New Age. Just over two-thirds (68 per cent) of people in the USA believe in at least one of these areas. The major difference lay in 'conventionality', with more conventional people holding fewer paranormal beliefs or claiming fewer experiences than the less conventional.[533]

---

[533] See, for example, Erich Goode, *Paranormal Beliefs: A Sociological Introduction*, Waveland Press, 2000; Harvey J. Irwin, 'Reality Testing and the Formation of Paranormal Beliefs', *Journal of the Society for Psychical Research*, 68, July 2004, pp. 143–52; S. L. Perkins and R. Allen, 'Childhood Physical Abuse and Differential Development of Paranormal Belief Systems', *Journal of Nervous*

There are certainly some problems in the way the research data are interpreted. For example, Bader, Mencken and Baker stated that 'belief in paranormal topics is at its lowest among people who believe the Bible is the literal word of God'.[534] This is certainly the case according to their definition of 'paranormal topics', which excludes religious belief. However, historical research has shown that the Bible is the work of multiple authors over a considerable span of time. How would we view such claims today, that a certain individual was the son of God, performed various miracles and returned from the dead? What is viewed as relatively normal within society – Christianity, for example – is excluded from what is seen as relatively *ab*normal, or paranormal – such as UFOs.

Contrary to what actually seems to be the case, we do not directly experience reality, we experience an interpretation of reality. Now for most of us, fortunately, our interpretations are fairly similar, but under certain situations that interpretation can be subject to gross distortion. People can speak to teapots and hear their answers as clearly as you are reading this now. We call them psychotics and give them drugs. People can speak to ghosts and hear their answers. We call them psychics and give them money. People can speak to gods and receive their message. We call them prophets and give them our souls. The social definition of who is speaking is more important than the message and until we know what 'normal' is how can we even grasp what is 'paranormal'? As Ralph Noyes, former Honorary Secretary of the Society for Psychical Research, once pertinently remarked, 'it is the "magical imagination" far more than fraud which clutters our field', which is another way of saying TRONDANT. But then how do we know that we are not all arranging roses in a shoe?[535]

---

and Mental Disease, May 2006, 194.5, pp. 349–55. Christopher Bader, et al., *Paranormal America: Ghost Encounters, UFO Sightings, Bigfoot Hunts, and Other Curiosities in Religion and Culture*, New York University, 2010, pp. 197–200, for the breakdown of 'paranormal beliefs' see Table A.6, p. 212.

[534] Bader, et al., p. 196.

[535] 'Backchat', *Paranormal Review*, 1997, p. 70.

If paranormal beliefs are only held by those with a history of childhood abuse or by those who are considered unconventional, then it pushes the paranormal to the fringes where it is little threat to the mainstream. However, Bader, Mencken and Baker, and all of the other surveys we have drawn on in this book, have repeatedly shown that a large proportion, often the majority, of people hold views that could be termed paranormal beliefs. Does this mean that the 68 per cent who believe in the paranormal in the USA are all unconventional? If so, this surely requires a new definition of conventional.[536]

I have never seen the Seychelles sheath-tailed bat, one of the world's rarest animals, in the wild. I have never seen an apparition, either. Both have been seen by other people. Both are well documented and described. So what is the difference? Is it the reliability of the witnesses? Is it a question of their psychology? Is it a question of their scientific training? Is it a question of the repeatability of the experiments? In 1997 the then president of the SPR, Professor David Fontana, said that fifteen laboratories across the world had conducted a total of 2,549 psychical experiments 'producing results in favour of paranormal abilities with combined odds against chance (in layman's terms) of a million billion to one'. In 2010 Professor Emeritus Daryl J. Bem of Cornell University, New York State, announced the results of his own experiments involving over 1,000 volunteers that showed the existence of psi with odds against chance of 74 billion to one. Out of them all – believer, sceptic, scientist – who is arranging flowers in a shoe?[537]

---

[536] See Jeremy Northcote, *The Paranormal and the Politics of Truth: A Sociological Account*, Imprint Academic, 2007.

[537] Fontana was referring specifically to autoganzfeld experiments, see *Paranormal Review*, 4, November 1997, p. 17; Daryl J. Bem, 'Feeling the Future: Experimental Evidence for Anomalous Retroactive Influences on Cognition and Affect', *Journal of Personality and Social Psychology*, forthcoming, discussed in David Sutton, 'Precognition and Porn: New Evidence for Psi', *Fortean Times*, 270, November 2010.

The Results

At the beginning of this book I asked you to take part in some experiments to show the problems associated with research into the supernatural/paranormal.

In the first experiment I asked you to think of a simple shape and draw it on a piece of paper. It is an experiment that has been tried before. In 1885 Max Dessoir was at the home of Baron Dr Goeler von Ravensburg, testing the psychic powers of his wife Elizabeth. Dessoir would draw a simple shape and he and the baron would concentrate on it, whilst Elizabeth, sitting at another table would try and reproduce it. After a while she said, 'It is a circle outside, and there is something else inside it'. She paused. 'A triangle.' She then drew a perfect reproduction of Dessoir's sketch. Using my psychic powers, I can now tell you that you also drew these shapes: a triangle inside a circle.[538]

In the second experiment I asked you to try and find out what number I was thinking of. I was, of course, mentally projecting this for you from a secret location in central Europe, which I find invariably helps. The number was between 1 and 50, and to make it easier both digits were odd, but not the same. If you thought of 35 or 39, then you were close, but if you thought of 37, then you were 100 per cent right.

---

[538] Max Dessoir, 'Experiments in Muscle-Reading and Thought-Transference', *Proceedings of the Society for Psychical Research*, 4, 1886, p. 126; see also Edmund Gurney, et al., 'Second Report on Thought-Transference', *Proceedings of the Society for Psychical Research*, 1, 1882, p. 81.

In the third experiment I asked you to find an old wind-up watch that no longer works, to then hold it in your hands for some minutes, concentrating on making it work, as I broadcast my psychic powers to operate on the machinery. You should have held it for at least ten minutes, repeating 'work, mend, work'. It apparently worked for many people after Uri Geller transmitted his 'psychic energy' from the observation deck of New York's World Trade Center in 1982. It worked for my mother-in-law after watching Geller on television in 2008 and following his instructions. I believe that it may also have worked for you.[539]

Did I read your mind or transmit my thoughts? Did I release your latent psychic powers? In some cases, it may not have worked. The picture-sending experiment did not work for Uri Geller when he tried it out with Helen Kruger of *The Village Voice* in 1973, but then he still managed to interest the US Department of Defense in his apparent abilities and convinced the scientists at the Stanford Research Institute in California. According to the research, however, in at least one in three cases I should have been right. According to that same research the answer lies in simple psychology and mechanics.

There are not many simple geometric shapes to think of and between them the circle, triangle and square just about cover the range. Results show that more people think of a triangle in a circle than a square in a circle, for example. Guessing a number from 1 to 50 sounds impressive, but due to the parameters I set, this actually only leaves seven numbers to choose from: 13, 17, 19, 31, 35, 37 and 39. Professor David Marks and Dr Richard Kammann once took a group of 202 people and posed these same questions. They found that over a third chose a triangle in circle and the number 37.[540]

The reason why broken watches may start working again is

---

[539] Geller's 1982 performance described in John Fairley and Simon Welfare, *Arthur C. Clarke's World of Strange Powers*, William Collins Sons & Co., 1984, ch. 4.

[540] David Marks and Richard Kammann, *The Psychology of the Psychic*, Prometheus, 1980, pp. 59–61.

due to the fact that, as watchmakers will confirm, more than half of all watches sent in for repair do not have a broken mechanism, but have stopped due to dust, dirt, or oil. The simple act of picking it up again, moving it and warming it in one's hand, may be sufficient to clear the blockage. The president of the Israel Parapsychology Society, Dr Heinz Berendt, reported being impressed by this demonstration until his watchmaker told him it was quite common.[541]

As these experiments show, one of the major difficulties in investigating the supernatural – beyond the elusiveness of the subject matter itself – lies in designing tests that reliably show that something paranormal has actually happened. What do you think happened? To post your results and interpretations – and to find out how the other readers did – log on to my website at www.ruickbie.com.[542]

---

[541] Marks and Kammann, *Psychology*, pp. 91–2, 108; David Marks and Richard Kammann, 'The Nonpsychic Powers of Uri Geller', *Zetetic*, 1.2, 1977, pp. 9–17; *Journal of the Society of Psychical Research*, 47, December 1974, p. 479.
[542] Kruger, 'Psychic Uri Geller – The Man Who Bends Forks With His Eyes', *The Village Voice*, 19 April 1973; Susan Blackmore, *The Adventures of a Parapsychologist*, Prometheus Books, 1986, p. 220.

Further Reading

Ghosts

Cornell, Tony, *Investigating the Paranormal*, Helix Press, 2002

Davies, Owen, *The Haunted: A Social History of Ghosts*, Palgrave Macmillan, 2009

Guiley, Rosemary Ellen, *The Encyclopedia of Ghosts and Spirits*, 2nd ed., Facts on File, 2000

Houran, James, and Rense Lange, (eds), *Hauntings and Poltergeists: Multidisciplinary Perspectives*, illus. 2nd ed., McFarland & Co., 2008

Karl, Jason, *Twenty-First Century Ghosts*, New Holland, 2007

Roll, William George, *The Poltergeist*, Cosimo, 2004

The Undead

Barber, Paul, *Vampires, Burial and Death: Folklore and Reality*, Yale University Press, 2010 [1990]

Beresford, Matthew, *From Demons to Dracula: The Creation of the Modern Vampire Myth*, Reaktion Books, 2008

Davis, Wade, *The Serpent and the Rainbow: A Harvard Scientist's Astonishing Journey into the Secret Societies of Haitian Voodoo, Zombis, and Magic*, Simon & Schuster, 1985; Pocket Books, 1997

Day, Jasmine, *The Mummy's Curse: Mummymania in the English-Speaking World*, Routledge, 2006

Seabrook, William, *The Magic Island*, George C. Harrap & Co., 1929; Marlowe & Co., 1994

Angels

Clarke, David, *The Angel of Mons: Phantom Soldiers and Ghostly Guardians*, John Wiley & Sons, 2005

Davidson, Gustav, *A Dictionary of Angels, Including the Fallen Angels*, Simon & Schuster, 1994

Heathcote-James, Emma, *Seeing Angels: True Contemporary Accounts of Hundreds of Angelic Experiences*, John Blake Publishing, 2001

Lumpkin, Joseph B., *The Books of Enoch: A Complete Volume*, Fifth Estate, 2009

Demons

Ashley, Leonard R.N., *The Complete Book of Devils and Demons*, Barricade Books, 1996; Skyhorse Publishing, 2011

Kelly, Henry Angsar, *Satan: A Biography*, Cambridge University Press, 2006

Toorn, Karel van der, Bob Becking and Pieter Willem van der Horst (eds), *Dictionary of Deities and Demons in the Bible*, 2nd ed., Brill/Eerdmans, 1999

Zaffis, John, and Rosemary Ellen Guiley, *The Encyclopedia of Demons and Demonology*, Facts on File, 2009

Extraterrestrials and UFOs

Clancy, Susan, *Abducted: How People Come to Believe They were Kidnapped by Aliens*, Harvard University Press, 2005

Clark, Jerome, *The UFO Book: Encyclopedia of the Extraterrestrial*, Visible Ink, 1997

Hynek, J. Allen, *The UFO Experience: A Scientific Inquiry*, Henry Regnery Co., 1972; De Capo Press, 1998

Kean, Leslie, (ed.), *UFOs: Generals, Pilots and Government Officials Go on the Record*, Harmony Books, 2010

Randle, Kevin D., *The Roswell Encyclopedia*, HarperCollins, 2000

Redfern, Nick, *Contactees: A History of Alien-Human Interaction*, Career Press, 2009

Ruppelt, Edward J., *The Report on Unidentified Flying Objects*, Doubleday & Company, 1956; Cosimo Classics, 2011

Magic

Crowley, Aleister, *Magick in Theory and Practice*, privately published, 1929; reprinted by Prober Publishing, 2011

Davies, Owen, *Grimoires: A History of Magic Books*, Oxford University Press, 2009

Frazer, Sir James George, *The Golden Bough: A Study in Magic and Religion*, 2 vols, Macmillan & Co., 1890; reprinted in one vol. by Oxford Paperbacks, 2009

Kieckhefer, Richard, *Magic in the Middle Ages*, Canto, 2000 [1989]

Ruickbie, Leo, *Faustus: The Life and Times of a Renaissance Magician*, The History Press, 2009

Spiritualism

Lamont, Peter, *The First Psychic*, Abacus, 2006

Melechi, Antonio, *Servants of the Supernatural: The Night Side of the Victorian Mind*, Arrow, 2009

Pearsall, Ronald, *Table-Rappers: The Victorians and the Occult*, The History Press, 2004

Weisberg, Barbara, *Talking to the Dead: Kate and Maggie Fox and the Rise of Spiritualism*, HarperOne, 2004

Psychical Research and Parapsychology

Horn, Stacey, *Unbelievable: Investigations into Ghosts, Poltergeists, Telepathy, and Other Unseen Phenomena from the Duke Parapsychological Laboratory*, Ecco, 2009

Irwin, Harvey J., and Caroline A. Watt, *An Introduction to Parapsychology*, McFarland & Co., 2007

Oppenheim, Janet, *The Other World: Spiritualism and Psychical Research in England, 1850-1914*, Cambridge University Press, 1988

Schoch, Robert, and Logan Yonavjak (eds), *The Parapsychological Revolution: A Concise Anthology of Paranormal and Psychical Research*, Tarcher/Penguin, 2008

General

Bader, Christopher, et al., *Paranormal America: Ghost Encounters, UFO Sightings, Bigfoot Hunts, and Other Curiosities in Religion and Culture*, New York University, 2010

Stein, Gordon (ed.), *The Encyclopedia of the Paranormal*, Prometheus Books, 1996

Gordon, Stuart, *The Paranormal: An Illustrated Encyclopedia*, Headline, 1992

Rosney, Mark, Rob Bethell and Jebby Robinson, *A Beginner's Guide to Paranormal Investigation*, Amberley, 2009

Index